Taking the
STRAIN

Families, unemployment and
the transition to adulthood

SUSAN HUTSON AND
RICHARD JENKINS

OPEN UNIVERSITY PRESS
Milton Keynes · Philadelphia

Open University Press
12 Cofferidge Close
Stony Stratford
Milton Keynes MK11 1BY

and
242 Cherry Street
Philadelphia, PA 19106, USA

First Published 1989

British Library Cataloguing in Publication Data

Hutson, Susan
    Taking the strain: families, unemployment and the transition to adulthood.
    1. Great Britain. Young Persons. Unemployment. Social aspects
    I. Title   II. Jenkins, Richard, *1953–*
    331.3′4137941

    ISBN 0-335-09918-1
    ISBN 0-335-09917-3 Pbk

Library of Congress Cataloging in Publication Data

Hutson, Susan.
    Taking the strain: families, unemployment, and the transition to
    adulthood/Susan Hutson and Richard Jenkins.
    p. cm.
    Bibliography: p.
    Includes index.
    ISBN 0-335-09918-1
    ISBN 0-335-09917-3 Pbk
    1. Youth—Employment—Great Britain—Psychological aspects.
    2. Unemployment—Great Britain—Psychological aspects.
    3. Unemployed—Great Britain—Family relationships.
    4. Adulthood—Great Britain—Case studies.
    I. Jenkins, Richard, 1953–
    II. Title.
    HD6276.G7H88 1989
    331.3′4137941—dc19   88-39569   CIP

CoCB 0714 (2) 999. 3.90

Typeset by Burns and Smith, Derby
Printed in Great Britain by the Alden Press, Oxford

CONTENTS

ACKNOWLEDGEMENTS

The research on which this book draws was funded in large part by the Joseph Rowntree Memorial Trust; the pilot phase was funded by the Department of Sociology and Anthropology, University College of Swansea. We are grateful to Robin Guthrie and Bill Williams, respectively, for their encouragement and support. The division of labour for the production of this book was that, Susan Hutson having undertaken the bulk of the fieldwork, Richard Jenkins did the bulk of the writing. Our respective families – John, Holly and James and Pearl, Nick and Niel – were an important source of support (and insight into the management of 'growing up' during this process).

Earlier versions of some of our findings and arguments were presented at the American Educational Research Association meeting 1987, Washington DC; the British Sociological Association annual conference 1986, Loughborough; a research seminar on youth unemployment at the Policy Studies Institute, London, 1986; and the Association of Social Anthropologists annual conference, London, 1988. Other related papers have been delivered at seminars in University College of Swansea, Gregynog, Cambridge University, and Durham University. We are grateful to those who participated on these occasions for their useful comments – and to Nickie Charles and John Parker for their help with particular bits of writing. Sue, in particular, wishes to acknowledge the help and support of Sue Yeandle. Needless to say, however, we remain responsible for the book's shortcomings. Glenda and Carol provided us with secretarial and typing support, making our lives easier and the book possible. There are also a number of necessarily anonymous teachers, careers officers and youth workers whose help we gratefully acknowledge.

Finally, as all researchers must, we offer our heartfelt gratitude to our research subjects, the people of Abbeyview, High Oak and Ty-Gwyn who allowed us into their homes and their lives and without whom this book could not have been written.

Susan Hutson and Richard Jenkins

KEY TO QUOTATIONS FROM THE INTERVIEW MATERIAL

...   pause
...//... material edited out
[ ]   explanatory material inserted

| 1 |

INTRODUCTION

To say that youth unemployment in Britain is a major social problem is, in the late 1980s, not only to state the obvious, it is almost to invite the response: 'so what else is new?' This is understandable. Since the early 1970s there has been a steady stream, sometimes assuming the proportions of a torrent (and to some eyes, perhaps, a bore), of books, articles and research reports dealing with the transition from school to work, youth unemployment, education and training and the 'problem of youth' more generally. Even those with an interest in the topic might be forgiven for thinking that there is little more that can usefully be said.

Clearly, as the authors of this study, we do not agree. As with most things, situations change, society moves on, new patterns of social life develop, established ones may be subject to shifts of emphasis and the responses of groups and individuals to altered circumstances are refreshingly unpredictable. In the context of young people and unemployment, what are these altered circumstances?

In the first place, one now has to be cautious in talking about *mass* youth unemployment. To all intents and purposes the introduction of the Youth Training Scheme (YTS) in 1983, and its subsequent extension to two years, has meant that long periods of formal unemployment are a thing of the past for most 16 and 17 year olds. Increasingly, YTS has ceased to be an option. The use of financial penalties has made it, in effect, compulsory (Byrne and Pond 1987–8; Roll 1988). Whether or not YTS is, as a consequence, merely disguised unemployment or a genuine and constructive alternative is an important question.

Regardless of how one might answer that question, however, the fact is that, according to the Department of Employment, in July 1987 there were 'only' 31,206 officially unemployed 16 year olds and 80,879 unemployed 17 year olds in Great Britain.[1] Of these, more than 60 per cent had been unemployed for less than 6 months and more than 20 per cent for less than 6 weeks. Bad enough, you may say – and with justification – but the extent of change since the late 1970s and early 1980s, when the equivalent statistics peaked at over 350,000, is revealed when one discovers that, while in June 1983 there were 188,409 young people in youth training placements, the figure had risen to 307, 946 by May 1987.[2] This is eloquent testimony to the state's success in dealing with – if not solving – the problem of youth unemployment.

What this success has meant, however, is that it is now the 18 to 25 year olds who are the publicly obvious problem with respect to youth unemployment. Looking at the official unemployment statistics for Great Britain, which, with respect to the age of claimants, are divided into 5-year blocks, the 20- to 24-year-old category is far and away the largest, at 581,596 in July 1987 (20.9 per cent of the total). Eighteen to 24 year olds accounted for 29.4 per cent of the unemployed during this period. As a result we also have to be cautious in talking about *youth* unemployment. It is, in fact, the mass unemployment of young adults with which we are now concerned. At a time when the overall national unemployment rate was 10.4 per cent (July 1987), the rate for 20 to 24 year olds was 15.4 per cent and for those between 18 and 19, 17.2 per cent.[3] It remains to be seen what impact Employment Training, the new unified adult training scheme, will have upon this situation.

The final change to be noted with respect to the unemployment of young people concerns the degree to which their *long-term* unemployment has become an integral part of the social landscape. Although there has been a small decline, mirroring wider labour-market trends, of the unemployed population under 25 years of age, the proportion who have been on the dole for more than 6 months has remained fairly steady during recent years at just under 50 per cent. The percentage who have been unemployed for over a year dropped slightly from 28.46 in July 1985 to 27.16 in July 1987.[4] The social consequences of this situation are what this book is about.

In the 1970s the problem facing young people was perceived by researchers and commentators as *the transition from school to work*. How to cope with a situation in which the 'normal' process of moving from education to employment was interrupted for a sizeable number of, typically working-class, teenagers? Although this interruption was seen as potentially disruptive of life-course patterns in the long term, it was, in the first place, conceptualised as a hiatus or interlude which for most youngsters would be resolved one way or another as time passed. As the recession has deepened and hardened up into grudgingly accepted semi-permanence, and the nature of the youth labour market and the education and training system altered, perceptions of the problem have gradually shifted. Now the situation is increasingly discussed in terms of *the transition from youth to adulthood*. What is going to happen to the large numbers of young people who are experiencing long-term unemployment at just that stage in their life-course when they might conventionally be expecting (in whatever order) to leave the parental home, establish a household of their own, find a partner and, possibly, start a family? In short, how does long-term unemployment affect the assumption of adulthood?

These are the social changes which prompted the research discussed in the chapters which follow, and the intellectual developments of which it is a component. However, this study was also a response to our evaluation of the adequacy of the literature and research concerned with young people and (un)employment.

Broadly speaking, the extensive literature which has been generated by the 'youth unemployment problem', excluding those texts which offer an overview of the topic (Roberts 1984), is concentrated in five definite areas. First, there are discussions, typically either pragmatically evaluative or politically critical, of post-secondary-school training or educational provision, for example Bates *et al.* (1984), Cockburn (1987), Eggleston (1982), Fiddy (1983), Finn (1987), Gleeson (1983) and Rees and Atkinson (1982). The number of references provided here is indicative of the fact that this is possibly the most densely populated area of research and debate.

Second, and deriving some of its intellectual vigour from a critical reaction to an older tradition of research into 'troublesome' youth and delinquent subcultures, there is a genre of studies concerned with the culture or life-styles of young people, for example Coffield *et al.* (1986), Griffin (1985), Jenkins (1982, 1983), Lees (1986), Wallace (1987) and Willis (1977). One distinguishing feature of these studies is their qualitative orientation. There is also a characteristic use of observational techniques – ethnography – in addition to the more usual interviewing strategies. Much of this research bears directly upon the transition to work and/or unemployment.

Third, there are a number of important studies which have examined various aspects of the labour market for young workers; examples are the work of Ashton *et al.* (1982, 1986), Livock (1983), Roberts *et al.* (1981, 1987) and Wells (1983). Frequently explicitly policy-orientated, among the substantive issues examined in these studies are wage levels, selection and recruitment, non-registration, the provision of careers advice and the structure of the youth labour-market.

Fourth, there are those studies which are concerned with the psychological consequences of youth unemployment, for example Banks and Jackson (1982), Branthwaite and Garcia (1985), Breakwell (1985) and Jackson *et al.* (1983). These typically emphasise the loss of self-esteem and increase in minor psychiatric disorders which apparently accompany extended unemployment.

Finally, a certain amount of attention has been focused upon the social consequences of the disproportionately high unemployment levels which are visited upon young black people, for example Cashmore and Troyna (1982), Cross and Smith (1987), Dex (1982), Sillitoe and Meltzer (1986) and Solomos (1985). The level of concern manifest about the plight of black youth is, at least in part, related to the level of concern about sporadic disorder in inner-city areas. The 'riots' of 1981 and 1985 served to concentrate the public mind wonderfully; it is less clear what the positive consequences of this attention have been for young black people themselves.

Just as clear as the areas of concentration in the literature, however, is the neglect of certain topics. First, it remains the case, despite the work of some of the authors referred to above, and others, that comparatively few of these studies either pay much attention to young women or are specifically concerned with issues of gender. Despite the increasing number of studies (e.g. Cockburn, Griffin, Jenkins, Lees, Wallace, etc.) which have taken note of this rather obvious criticism, we still know more about young men than young women. Second, and closely related to the point about gender, most research, certainly until comparatively recently, has concentrated upon those young people – typically males – who are visible as an obvious 'problem'. If for no other reason, this was largely because these were, until recently, the category of youth most likely to experience unemployment. 'Ordinary kids' remain, by and large, invisible. With the exception of the work of authors such as Coffield and his colleagues, Jenkins and Wallace, much of the literature remains firmly cast within either the 'youth as a social problem' mould or its mirror image, 'working-class youth as romantic hero'. Neither of these images corresponds to the mundane reality of the lives of the majority of young women and men.

Looking at those pieces of research which have attempted to go beyond the necessary superficiality of the large-scale social survey, most have been carried out within the confines of restricted institutional settings, typically schools or youth service projects. As a consequence, we know all too little about the effects of the long-term unemployment of young people upon family and peer-group relationships. The work of Coffield and his associates, Jenkins and Wallace, as already referred to, and Walsgrove (1987), are perhaps the best examples of community-based research. When we started this research, there were only three research projects of which we were aware in the United Kingdom which were specifically concerned with the effects of young people's unemployment upon their families: the work of Allatt and Yeandle (1986), Wallace (1986, 1987) and McRae and White (McRae, 1987a, 1987b). Our research was planned from the outset as a supplement to these studies and an extension of their concerns.

Finally, as we have already suggested, the 'problem of youth' has ceased to be mainly defined as the transition from school to work. Instead, commentators are more likely to adopt a broader framework, talking about the transition from youth to adulthood instead. Surprisingly, however, with the conspicuous exceptions once again of the studies by Coffield *et al.*, Jenkins, McRae and White, and Wallace and the impressive programme of research led by Willis in Wolverhampton (Youth Review Team 1985), the over-18s as a category, and the movement into adult life as a process, have yet to figure in many published studies.

This is a thumb-nail sketch, superficial but, in its outlines, essentially accurate, of the current state of British research into unemployed young people and their problems, excluding some areas, such as delinquency and substance abuse, which are only peripheral to our concerns. Inasmuch as the study which forms the basis for this book is concerned with 'ordinary' or 'non-problem' young people, with young women as well as young men, with family relationships and with the transition to adulthood, we hope to contribute towards a fuller understanding of what it means to be moving into adulthood in modern Britain.

We also hope to illuminate a small corner of the experience of parenthood: the problems and possibilities which are bound up with having a young adult son or daughter in the present climate of economic recession and social uncertainty. Those of us who grew up and entered the adult world during the 1950s, 1960s and early 1970s did so – or so it seemed at the time – in a climate of prosperity and apparently unlimited horizons. In historical retrospect, that period may yet turn out to have been exceptional, almost an illusion. Many of the parents in this study, in coming to terms with the burdens under which their children labour, are also having to come to terms with that fact.

The research agenda

It is one thing to indicate the general subject-matter with which we are concerned, quite another to produce a set of actual research questions. At the start of the project, while we were framing applications for funding and carrying out the pilot interviews, we had three topics in mind: the effect of the long-term unemployment of young adults upon, first, their family relationships, second, their parents and, third, their courtship and marriage strategies. As the research progressed, however, these were elaborated and other topics emerged as equally important. In writing up the research we have identified six substantive issues or questions as central to our analysis. Each of these broad headings subsumes under it a number of separate and more specific topics for investigation.

The first question concerns the effect of long-term unemployment upon the family relationships of young people. How does unemployment affect the relationships which exist between young adults and their parents, siblings, their grandparents and their wider network of more distant kin and affines? To what extent does the unemployment of young adults create conflict within families and households? How do families cope with situations of this kind? What is the relationship between individual and collective responses to long-term unemployment and how is this potential conflict of interests worked out within families?

Second, there is the issue of the transition into adulthood. Has the hurdle of long-term unemployment interrupted the passage into adult life for many young people in contemporary Britain? In the absence of an adult wage, how are young people to construct for themselves an independent life-style, autonomy within a social sphere of their own choosing? What is the relationship between the family of origin and the peer group in this respect? Issues such as these beg the larger question of what it actually means to be an adult in our society. What are the socially recognised criteria of adulthood and how are they acquired?

Intimately related to the first two, the third topic concerns the implications of unemployment for courtship behaviour and marriage patterns. Is marriage being deferred for some young women and men as a consequence of their unemployment? Is it, perhaps, even being rejected altogether? To what extent is it possible to establish a connection between increases in cohabitation and unmarried parenthood, single or otherwise, and the long-term unemployment of young adults?

The fourth question overlaps with, and is generally implicated in, the previous three: how are young people's experiences and perceptions of long-term unemployment mediated and shaped by gender relations and categories? How is long-term unemployment different for young men and young women, and how is it the same? Is the 'traditional' order of gender roles – either within or without the family and the household – changing with changed circumstances?

On a different. tack altogether, we also become interested, fifth, in differences in the experience of unemployment between localities. This was partly as a consequence of developments within sociology, which has witnessed a resurgence of interest in . comparative area-based studies, whether they be of regions, communities, local labour-markets or whatever, and partly a result of the development of our own ideas during the fieldwork. Recognising the impact of economic inequalities and class relationships upon residential patterns, this topic has of necessity led us into a consideration of class differences in the experience of unemployment.

Finally, we have also tried to look at some of the wider social consequences of the long-term unemployment of young adults. In particular, we are interested in the possible political consequences: is the long-term unemployment of significant numbers of young adults likely to lead to their rejection of politics altogether, or will they move towards more radical politics, whether of the left or the right? If disaffection is a result of unemployment, what form will it take: apathy or rebellion? How do young adults and their parents – for their political stance, too, is at stake here – explain unemployment, and how is this related to their understanding of other issues? These are, of course, difficult questions, to which straightforward answers are likely to prove elusive. The search for such answers, however, whether ultimately fruitful or not, may reveal something useful.

Taken together, we recognise that these questions and topics are an ambitious research agenda. Some readers may consider it to be over-ambitious for a largely qualitative study of a relatively small number of people. We would suggest, however, that, inasmuch as the issues which we have outlined above are inextricably interlinked in the lives of those people, a more limited focus would not only have been inappropriate, it would have been an impediment to our understanding of the situation. There is, for example, no sense in attempting to analyse courtship and marriage strategies in isolation from family relationships, notions of adulthood or gender roles. Similarly, the nature of relationships between, for example, an unemployed young woman and the members of her family is likely to be influenced, or so our material suggests, by the way in which unemployment, in her case and more generally, is understood and explained by those family members. This in turn is related, at least in part, to local labour-market conditions, economic and social history and experiences of employment and unemployment. These, in their turn, have more than a little to do with political orientations. In short, we are dealing with a complex and interconnected skein – although cobweb may be a more appropriate metaphor, for that is how it has sometimes felt – of social relationships, culture, attitudes, material constraints and external contingencies, which demands to be treated as such. This is what we have tried to do in the analysis which follows.

Such an approach derives in part from the social anthropological traditions in which both authors have their roots. We are, in this sense, almost 'naturally' inclined to adopt a relatively open remit upon commencing field research and to follow up connections between facets of the social reality in question as they present themselves. However, our theoretical predilections are also important here. Drawing some of our general orientation from the work of such diverse authors as Berger and Luckman (1967), Bourdieu (1977), Cicourel (1964, 1973) and Giddens (1976, 1979, 1984), we have written this book from a perspective which emphasises the social construction of everyday life and 'reality' in and through the routine and extraordinary practices of individuals and collectivities. Social practices take place within, and contribute towards the production and reproduction of, a formal and informal institutional context which is hierarchically structured with respect to the allocation of resources and the distribution and exercise of power and authority. These practices and institutions are only meaningful in an established social and cultural context: to nod in the direction of Marx and Engels, men and women may make their own history, but they can only do so in circumstances which are neither of their own making or choosing. Writing a sociological account within a broad theoretical framework such as this, one must beware of oversimple interpretations of social reality and attempt to present as much of the complexity of everyday life as appears to be relevant and is practically possible. This is a further justification for the approach to our material which we have discussed above.

Fieldwork in Swansea and Port Talbot, 1985–6

The research has its origins in the appointment in October 1983 of one of us, Richard Jenkins, to a 'new blood' lectureship in sociology at University College, Swansea. Biased heavily in the direction of research, central to the new post's job specification was a requirement to undertake an investigation of 'the effects of high rates of unemployment on social life'. A study of the impact of youth unemployment upon family relationships, building in part upon previous experience of a study of young people in a Belfast housing estate in the late 1970s, developed as one of the major elements in the new lectureship's research portfolio.[5]

Susan Hutson became involved in the planning of the research towards the end of 1984. Following the refusal of two committees of the Economic and Social Research Council to fund the proposed study, Susan was appointed as a part-time research officer, funded out of the residue of the University Grants Committee 'new blood' allocation, to collaborate on a six-month pilot project between February and July 1985 (Jenkins and Hutson 1986). In the meantime, several foundations and charities were approached with applications for funding. The Joseph Rowntree Memorial Trust expressed strong interest, and in March 1985 they confirmed that they would fund a two-year project starting the following September.

As is the way with many research projects, our thinking has shifted considerably as the study progressed. What began life as a study of two 'respectable' working-class housing estates in west Swansea, finished as a comparison of families from three localities: 'Abbeyview', a large council housing estate in Port Talbot; 'High Oak', a smaller council estate in west Swansea; and 'Ty-Gwyn', a tract of owner-occupied private housing, also in west Swansea. Further details of the three areas – and these names are, of course, fictional – are given in the next section of this chapter. The shift to a three-area comparison was partly to do with our growing interest in class- and locality-derived differences in the experience of long-term unemployment, partly a response to the serendipities of the research process which provided us with contacts in Port Talbot.

We began this project with a point of view which stressed the importance of the family as the basic unit of our analysis. This has remained our view throughout. A total of fifty-eight families were involved in the study: twenty-six unemployed young women, thirty-seven unemployed young men, thirty-six mothers and twenty-eight fathers. With five exceptions (17 year olds who had been unemployed for over 6 months), all of our unemployed respondents were between 18 and 25 years old. The great majority had been unemployed for more than six months at the time of interview. A further ten young people – partners or siblings – were formally interviewed and we also had informal discussions with a number of parents. Further details of the individuals and families involved can be found in the Appendix. We interviewed a smaller number of unemployed young women largely because, in reflection of local labour-market conditions (discussed in greater detail in the next section), it proved more difficult to find them in sufficient numbers, particularly in Ty-Gwyn. A small number of interviews, undertaken outside the final study areas during the pilot phase, were discarded for the purposes of drawing up our main samples. They have only been used occasionally in the account which follows.

During the pilot project, our sampling strategy was a crude snowballing method in which one contact led to another. Initial contacts were typically obtained through the researchers' own networks. This approach continued to be useful during the main research period. It was, however, primarily a supplement to our major sampling method, which was devised by Susan Hutson. By going back through the old electoral registers for the areas concerned, which specifically identify new young voters (i.e. those young people whose eighteenth birthday falls during the year concerned), it was possible to locate households which had members aged between 18 and 25. Clearly, of course, in the interim period some families had moved; furthermore, many of the young people who we did locate were employed. There are also many households which, for a variety of reasons, will be overlooked by this method. None the less, it proved to be a useful means of drawing a sample. A lot of futile door knocking was thereby avoided. Using this approach, we screened all of High Oak and enough of Abbeyview and Ty-Gwyn to provide us with acceptable-sized samples. Including the pilot phase, fieldwork took place between February 1985 and November 1986. Susan undertook the bulk of the interviewing.

The degree to which we were granted access to families was variable, as is clear from the Appendix. In some cases we only interviewed the young person themselves. In one case we interviewed the young person and their partner of the moment, both of whom were unemployed. In the majority of the families, however, we interviewed the young person and at least one parent. In many cases we saw both parents and more than one young person. In one family, we managed to interview both parents and the girlfriend of the young man concerned. He, however, refused to have anything to do with us, largely, it seems, because he was too busy surfing. Waiting for the best wave conditions on the Gower coast can be a serious and absorbing business! It must be born in mind, therefore, when interpreting some of our findings, that we discovered a great deal more about some families than others.

The interview itself was a fairly loosely-structured occasion. In the pilot phase we relied on note-taking; later, tape recorders were used. An interview schedule provided the basis for the conversation; supplementary questions were asked, depending on the progress of the discussion, to explore particular topics in more detail when appropriate. The aim throughout was to keep the enquiry as 'natural', as close to 'normal talk', as possible. As a consequence of this approach, not all of the questions on the interview schedule were put to all of our research subjects. Wherever possible, the data from the interviews have been supplemented by information gathered observationally and during other, more casual, conversations. This has been particularly useful in writing the case studies.

In addition to the actual interviewing, several other research strategies were adopted. First, a number of group discussions were held with pupils and students from a west Swansea comprehensive school and Swansea College of Further Education. The central theme of these discussions was an exploration of the topics of unemployment, courtship and marriage and family relationships. Second, a number of wider-ranging discussions took place with youth workers, careers officers and teachers in Swansea and Port Talbot, concerning many general aspects of the youth unemployment situation as well as more specifically local topics. Contacts with some of these individuals continued throughout the research. Third, during 1985 both researchers had useful liaison with Rights of Boarders, a local pressure group campaigning against national changes in the Department of Health and Social Security's board and lodgings regulations, which threatened to make some of the local young unemployed – those living in bed and breakfast accommodation and lodging houses – homeless. Finally, there was a residual category of research activity, such as collecting newspaper clippings, attending public meetings and so on. Although we may not always draw on data from the above sources during this account, they provided us with invaluable background information.

There is, of course, another kind of data, to which we have not yet referred: statistics drawn from official sources and other published material. In the final section of this chapter we will draw upon statistics of this kind to place the study areas in their local and wider contexts and highlight the similarities and differences which exist between them.

Abbeyview, High Oak and Ty-Gwyn: a comparison

If nothing else, social anthropology teaches us that just as, in particular respects, all communities, all groups, all social situations, have something in common with other communities, groups and situations, so also do they differ. In this the final section of this chapter, we shall attempt to place the areas which we studied in Swansea and Port Talbot in their appropriate comparative contexts.

The first such context is the national. South Wales, when viewed in the national (i.e. in this case, and with apologies to Welsh nationalists, British) context, is clearly a part of the disadvantaged, marginal 'other nation'.

Following the large-scale decline in South Wales during the 1970s and early 1980s of mining, iron and steel and manufacturing, the regional economy has been characterised by high levels of unemployment and changing patterns of labour-force participation. Port Talbot, for example, according to a recent comparative study of local labour-market areas (LLMAs) in Great Britain, has bestowed upon it the following dubious distinctions: it was among the most severely affected with respect to declining male economic activity rates; it suffered the fourth most severe rate of employment decline between 1971 and 1981 (13,000 jobs lost, a net decline in jobs of 27.2 per cent); the sixth worst overall unemployment rate nationally in 1981 (17.5 per cent); the fourth worst national increase in unemployment rate between 1971 and 1981 (+ 10.54 per cent); and it qualified as the twelfth worst LLMA with respect to general local economic performance (Champion *et al*. 1987: 55, 65, 79, 80, 105). In the same survey of the available statistics, Swansea is revealed as having one of the highest national increases between 1971 and 1981 in the participation of married women in the labour force, with Port Talbot not far behind (*ibid*.: 52). In another comparative study of LLMAs, 'Swansea, Port Talbot and Neath' has been characterised as suffering from 'marked decline': low migration, a marked recent rise in unemployment and a similarly marked substitution of male by female unemployment (Owen, Gillespie and Coombes 1984).

As Fothergill and Gudgin's study of regional employment trends in the United Kingdom makes clear, the relative disadvantage of Wales, and more specifically South Wales, is not a recent phenomenon (Fothergill and Gudgin 1982). Following the impact of the Great Depression, and designation as a 'development area' in the post-war period, South Wales experienced an economic improvement in the 1960s. Successive regional policies have, however, failed to provide a secure basis for long-term self-sustaining growth. Particular problems may be identified as a heavy reliance on the declining coal industry (and this problem has become even more severe in the wake of the disastrous 1984 national mining strike) and an over-representation of subsidiary organisations, dependent upon development and investment decisions which are taken elsewhere.

This long history of economic depression is summarised by Chris Harris and his research team in their discussion of the background to the redundancies at the British Steel Corporation works at Port Talbot in 1980 (Harris *et al*. 1987: 44-63). Looking at their recent data for the West Glamorgan labour market, which includes Swansea and Port Talbot, there is a picture of significant job losses during the 1970s in construction, mechanical engineering and metal manufacturing, offset to only a small extent by limited gains in other manufacturing industries. Important advances were made in service-sector jobs, most of which were filled by women. Because of the importance of manufacturing employment, and the disproportionate local reliance upon one employer, British Steel, Port

Talbot was particularly severely affected by this process of decline and change. However, due to a number of factors, including the withdrawal from the labour market of many of the older ex-steelworkers and the earlier impact of the worst bite of the recession of the late 1970s and early 1980s in Port Talbot, the latter area has recently, somewhat paradoxically perhaps, suffered from lower rates of male unemployment than Swansea. Lest it be thought that this betokens a significant 'improvement', however, it is worth pointing out that unemployment rates remain stubbornly set well above the national rate (Table 1.1). The higher rates of female unemployment in Port Talbot than in Swansea which that table reveals are a consequence of the town's recent historical domination by the steel works and the resultant underdevelopment of women's employment opportunities.

Table 1.1   Unemployment rates in Swansea, Port Talbot, Wales and Great Britain, July 1987 (seasonally adjusted)

	Overall	*Unemployment rates (%)* *Male*	*Female*
Swansea	15.2	19.1	9.9
Neath and Port Talbot	14.8	15.9	12.5
Wales	12.7	14.7	9.4
Great Britain	10.4	12.2	7.9

Source: Department of Employment, Office for Wales, press release, July 1987

With respect to long-term unemployment, the situation is very much in accord with what has been said so far: both Swansea and Port Talbot are severely affected, with Swansea more severely so in recent years. For example, in July 1983, 39.2 per cent of the unemployed in Swansea had been on the register for more than 12 months, by comparison with 37.2 per cent in Port Talbot. By January 1986, and allowing for a change in the boundaries of the travel-to-work areas for which statistics are available, Swansea's figure had risen to 46.0 per cent. The figure for Neath and Port Talbot at this time was 36.7 per cent.[6]

So far, then, we have sketched in something of the national, regional and local contexts within which our study took place: economic depression, high male unemployment, changing patterns of female economic participation and a degree of local economic differentiation. At this point, however, it is important to remember that it is not Swansea and Port Talbot as such with which we are concerned. The research is about young people from three specific, and very different, areas, and it is to a comparison of Abbeyview, High Oak and Ty-Gwyn that we shall now turn.

Impressionistically, the three areas are poles apart. Abbeyview is a flat sprawl of post-Second World War council housing, originally built to house the influx of new workers attracted by the expansion of employment following the completion in 1952 of the Abbey Works of the Steel Company of Wales. Many of these workers were not local, some coming from as far afield as Scotland and Ireland. To the intrepid outsider, trying to find his or her way around Abbeyview by car, one street can look very much like another. In the winter, in particular, the wind whistles straight in from the nearby sea and in and out of the streets and houses. In Port Talbot and further afield, Abbeyview has a reputation in some quarters as at best, down at heel, and at worst, 'rough'. It is, however, a reputation which, although accurate in a general sense – Abbeyview *is* run down, there *is* high unemployment, many youngsters do get involved in petty crimes, the housing stock *does* leave much to be desired – conceals a considerable amount of internal diversity. The values and traditions of the 'respectable' Welsh working-class – hard-working, God-fearing, non-conformist and Labour-voting – are alive and in good hands in many households and streets in Abbeyview.

Moving across Swansea Bay to High Oak, here we see a very 'respectable' place indeed. In terms of its public reputation it is one of the two most desirable council housing estates in Swansea – the other is not far away, also in west Swansea – with a long waiting list of people looking for a house there. Although it is, like Abbeyview, close to the sea, in High Oak the houses are situated on a gentle slope and are not as densely packed together. Some of the houses have views of the sea which might be the envy of many an owner-occupier. Built in a number of phases between the immediate post-war period and the 1960s, High Oak has a high proportion of pensioners and mature family households, with grown-up and teenaged children who will probably have lived there all their lives. It is, in local terms, a 'tidy' place, eminently respectable, somewhere to aspire to. Mildly malicious local rumour has it that High Oak, and its nearby equivalent, were built as much to introduce Labour voters into the previously Tory-held parliamentary constituency of Swansea West as anything else. What they vote these days is anybody's guess. Many of the residents have recently bought their homes and the area is surrounded on all sides by middle-class families living in their own houses. Children from High Oak go to school with children from these neighbouring areas, the young people grow up together. However, as we will see, when we look at the Census material (e.g. Tables 1.2 and 1.3) it remains very much a working-class estate.

Ty-Gwyn, the third area which we looked at, differs from Abbeyview and High Oak inasmuch as it has no such easily defined geographical identity. It is not an 'estate'. It is, rather, an apparently unplanned sprawl of private, owner-occupied housing. Around the kernels of the original villages and hamlets of a once rural area, houses have been built and new roads created in a succession of small to medium speculative developments and individual initiatives. In style, the housing varies from late-nineteenth-century terraces of working people's cottages (often 'done out'), to semi-detached villa residences of the 1930s, to the 'Wimpey House'-style economy housing of more recent years. There are pleasant cul-de-sacs of bungalows and

detached houses set in their own small gardens. The countryside is not far
away, but neither is the centre of Swansea. The overwhelming majority of
Ty-Gwyn's inhabitants travel, even if only a few miles, to their place of
work. It is commuterised suburbia.

So much for impressions. At another level, we are fortunate enough to
have been provided with the 1981 Census Small Area Statistics by West
Glamorgan County Council's research department. Using this information
it is possible to delineate some fairly clear 'objective' contrasts between the
three areas, as in Table 1.2.

Table 1.2   Abbeyview, High Oak and Ty-Gwyn: selected indices of comparison

	Abbeyview	*High Oak*	*Ty-Gwyn*
Economically active population actually seeking employment (%)	23	10	6
Economically active population out of employment (%)	30	12	7
Married women in employment (as % of women over 16)	22	23	35
of these, % full time	47	32	51
% part time	53	68	49
Households without a car (%)	51	35	9

Source: 1981 Census Small Area Statistics

The picture which the Small Area Statistics paint is reasonably
straightforward. Abbeyview suffers from much higher levels of unemployment than High Oak, which in turn is somewhat worse off in this respect
than Ty-Gwyn, although the differential in this case is smaller. Looking at
the unemployment figures for Port Talbot and Swansea during 1981, and
ignoring the problems involved in a comparison of Department of
Employment and Census figures, these data indicate that the unemployment rate in Abbeyview is a little higher than the overall rate in Port Talbot;
by contrast, High Oak and Ty-Gwyn are well below the Swansea rate. Using
possession of a car as a crude indicator of prosperity, the Census material
illustrates a marked hierarchical economic gradation between Ty-Gwyn
(prosperous) and Abbeyview (relatively disadvantaged).

A different perspective, yielding a comparable set of distinctions,
however, can also be found in the Census statistics. Using the Registrar-
General's classification scheme as a rough means of illustrating social class
divisions, a crude contrast can be drawn between the three areas, as in Table
1.3. From this table it is clearly seen that Abbeyview and High Oak are both
overwhelmingly working-class districts. The differences between them are,
however, important: 41 per cent of the population in Abbeyview are

classified as 'semi-skilled' or 'unskilled', compared to only 15 per cent in High Oak, which also has a higher proportion of non-manual workers. High Oak is, furthermore, characterised by large numbers of retired people. Looking at Ty-Gwyn, however, the area's class composition is different again. Here, 44 per cent of the population fall into one or other of the non-manual categories, a further 26 per cent being classified as 'skilled manual'. Taking into account the predominance of home ownership in Ty-Gwyn it is reasonable on the basis of these data to classify the area – as, indeed, one would in commonsensical terms – as largely middle-class with a substantial leavening of skilled working-class people.

Table 1.3   Abbeyview, High Oak and Ty-Gwyn: social class composition

Social class		Abbeyview %	High Oak %	Ty-Gwyn %
I-II	Professional, managerial, intermediate	3	9	26
IIIN	Skilled non-manual	5	17	18
IIIM	Skilled manual	31	22	26
IV	Semi-skilled	20	14	6
V	Unskilled	21	1	4
	Armed Forces	1	–	2
	Retired	19	37	18
TOTAL		100	100	100

Source: 1981 Census Small Area Statistics

How are these differences revealed on examination of our own research data? The answer is, with reassuring clarity. The significance of the 1980 British Steel redundancies to the people of Abbeyview, for example, is obvious. The fathers of at least five of the young men and women to whom we spoke in Abbeyview were made redundant by BSC at that time. More generally, something of the nature of the social and economic differences which exist between the three areas is apparent in our material concerning household income sources. These data are summarised in Table 1.4.

As Table 1.4 shows, there is a contrast in our sample, between the Abbeyview group, with a majority of households solely reliant upon state welfare benefits, and the respondents from Ty-Gwyn, where a similar-sized majority of households had parents who were both employed. High Oak occupies an intermediate position between these poles: the majority of households had *either* no one working *or* both parents employed. These data are a stark illustration of the polarisation between 'no wage' and 'two-wage' households, which is, we suspect, increasingly a defining feature of British society.

Table 1.4 Household income sources: Abbeyview, High Oak and Ty-Gwyn (percentages in brackets)

	State benefit only [a]	One parent employed [b]	Two parents employed [b]	Total
Abbeyview	12 (67)	3 (17)	3 (17)	18 (100)
High Oak	10 (45)	3 (14)	9 (41)	22 (100)
Ty-Gwyn	2 (11)	5 (28)	11 (61)	18 (100)
TOTAL	24 (41)	11 (19)	23 (40)	58 (100)

Notes:
[a] Includes sickness benefit and invalidity pension.
[b] Includes part-time employment and self-employment.

It should be remembered, however, that while this polarisation is a feature of our material, and while Ty-Gwyn and Abbeyview are, in some senses, polar opposites, the three areas must be conceptualised as sited along a continuum between relative disadvantage and prosperity with many shared areas of overlap. In all three areas, for example, skilled manual workers are the biggest single social-class category, albeit in differing proportions. Even in Abbeyview, many more people are employed than not. Although the three areas are very different in some respects, in others they are strikingly similar. It is this very fact which makes them such useful places from the point of view of our comparison.

There is one final question to consider: what do our samples represent? Answers to a question like this in our kind of research are often necessarily imprecise, and to an extent, this is true of our work. However, we have every confidence that the groups we interviewed are fairly representative, as a whole, of families with unemployed young adults from the areas where we did our research. This is clearly so for High Oak, where we surveyed the entire estate. Given our sampling procedure for the other two areas, we have no reason to doubt the general representativeness of our final samples. Given also that the three areas are, in many respects, similar to other localities up and down the country, we suggest that our findings are likely to be broadly representative of an important aspect of social life in modern Britain. That having been said, however, South Wales *is* South Wales, Port Talbot *is* Port Talbot, Ty-Gwyn *is* Ty-Gwyn, and so on. They all have their peculiarities. In supplying as much detail as possible in the account which follows, it is our hope that readers will be able to judge for themselves the distinction between the locally particular situation and the generalisable pattern.

In this chapter we have set out something of the social and intellectual background against which this research was conceived and subsequently carried out. As a consequence of change with respect to the first, and deficiencies with respect to the second, there remain important gaps in our understanding of the process of the transition from youth to adulthood in contemporary Britain. In certain respects, which we have discussed above, the account which follows is intended to remedy in some small way those shortcomings. In Chapter 2 we shall begin by examining the impact upon family relationships of the long-term unemployment of young adults.

2

FAMILY RELATIONSHIPS

No matter where they live, no matter the culture or the historical period, the vast majority of people are born into, grow up within and take some important aspects of their social identity from a kin group of one sort or another. To adopt a sensible basic anthropological definition: 'Kinship ties serve ... to define the unique position of each individual in his or her social world – to establish strands of mutual amity and obligation in that individual's own group and in other groups' (Keesing 1975: 14). For most people in the industrialised societies of the European-dominated continents, that group is, in the first instance, the nuclear family. It is also, for most of the life-course, the characteristic and 'normal' domestic group or unit of residence in these societies. Extended kinship ties are of great importance – and for some cultural groups they are of primary significance – but in places like South Wales the nuclear family, a parent or parents and children,[1] may be considered the basic kin group underpinning the extended family network (Rosser and Harris 1965). Both kinds of kin relationships – within the nuclear and extended families – will be discussed in this chapter and Chapter 3.

The family, therefore, is a source of social identity. It is a node in the network of relationships which serves to link family members to other families and their members. It is also, certainly in our modern bureaucratic societies, an officially recognised and constituted social unit. As writers such as Donzelot (1980) and Meyer (1983) have recently reminded us, the family is enmeshed in another network, this time of state agencies and agents. Family membership serves, along with other things, to locate individuals within this network. They are thus placed within the reach of the state and its regulatory powers.

Informal and formal social identity, relationships of right, of duty and of expectation – these are all important reasons for being interested in 'the family' (or, more correctly, *families*). There is, however, another set of reasons as well. The family is generally the arena of primary socialisation. It is also, ideally, the well-spring of emotional security, first as the family of origin and subsequently as the family of partnership and parenthood. That, at any rate, is the model, the way things are supposed to be: the 'happy family' is the 'normal family'.

In considering the role of the family as a source of contentment and happiness, it is possible to identify two polar positions in the social science literature. At the risk of simplifying matters more than is perhaps warranted, these can be characterised as 'the family as a secure foundation and refuge' and 'the family as a burden and liability'. Around and between these poles there are many different positions, varying according to the discipline and predelictions of the authors concerned. Here we shall only consider briefly some of the better-known.

The notion that the Western nuclear family provides its members with a secure emotional and moral foundation (perhaps *the* secure foundation) and a refuge from the pressures of the 'outside world', is one which is firmly rooted in a taken-for-granted conservative consensus in British society. It is a central theme of established modern Christianity, and there are, for example, very few politicians who, even were they so inclined, would dare to publicly dissent from such a view.

Within sociology one of the best-known articulations of this model can be found in the work of Talcott Parsons, who considered the family to be functionally uniquely adapted to the requirements of modern industrial society (Parsons 1954: 69–88, 177–96; Parsons and Bales 1955). While Parsons did recognise the existence and force of tensions within the family, in particular with respect to contradictory evaluations and expectations of the 'traditional' female role, it is also clear that he considered the 'structurally isolated' nuclear family, with its sharply differentiated gendered division of labour, to be supremely functional with respect to both primary socialisation and the satisfaction of adult emotional needs. Similar views about the solidary family can be found, either explicitly or implicitly, in the writings of authors as diverse as Bowlby (1953), Fletcher (1973) and Goode (1963). Viewed from a somewhat different perspective, there is, as Harris has pointed out, a functionalist Marxist model of the family which stresses its role in providing an emotional shelter to mitigate the worst oppressions of capitalism and a particularistic focus of identification to obstruct the development of class solidarity by the working class (Harris 1983: 179). In this sense, the 'bourgeois' nuclear family is conceptualised as specifically functional for capitalism (Zaretsky 1976).

What of the hostile view of the family? One of the best-known attacks on our traditional evaluation of the family was mounted by Edmund Leach in his 1967 Reith Lectures: 'Far from being the basis of the good society, the family, with its narrow privacy and tawdry secrets, is the source of all our discontents' (Leach 1968: 44). In Leach's view, the inward-looking xenophobia of the nuclear family fosters emotional stress and conflict: 'The strain is greater than most of us can bear.' Perhaps the most extreme version of this thesis is to be found in the work of psychologist R. D. Laing. He argues that personal relationships within the nuclear family, particularly between parents and children, are largely about, and constructed within a framework of, power and domination. As such, they are profoundly dysfunctional with respect to 'healthy' psychological and emotional development (Laing 1971; Laing and Esterson 1970). From a more sociological perspective, the feminist critique of conventional family arrangements has centred on the consequences for women of 'the anti-social family' (Barrett and McIntosh 1982). In this view, the family serves as the medium through which men control women's reproductive powers, sexuality and labour, and is the institution wherein patriarchal gender identities are forged and maintained. Recent social trends with respect to easier and more prevalent divorce notwithstanding, the family remains, for many feminists, the focal point of women's oppression and the lynchpin of patriarchy (Smart 1984). Once again functionalism rears its head.

Of course, just because an explanation or a model is functionalist in certain respects does not necessarily mean that it is *wrong*. Nor is it to somehow imply that it is, by definition as it were, inane or lacking in sophistication. The contrasting perspectives which we have summarised above have all been criticised, by commentators sympathetic and hostile alike (for a summary of these debates, see Robertson Elliot 1986: 115–33). There remains, however, a good deal which one can, with caution, usefully appropriate from each position or pole in the argument. It is reasonably clear, for example, that, as an accepted way of organising domestic life and childrearing, the 'traditional' nuclear family harmonises with, rather than undermines, a partriarchial system of values and gender relationships. Similarly, associated with these family arrangements is a domestic division of labour which 'fits' the labour market requirements of industrial, capitalist society. These two points are, what is more, related: the domestic division of labour is specifically gendered – men do one thing, women another – as are labour markets. They are also, of course, historically contingent. It is for this very reason that one of our interests in this research is the potential for change in family relationships and domestic arrangements during a period of change in the labour market.

So far, so good. At the level of the logic of 'the system', one can accept elements of both poles of the argument. What, however, of the more intimate level of social interaction within the family, as Morgan has put it, 'the psycho-social interior' of the family (Morgan 1975: 131)? Here it is more difficult to simultaneously accept elements of opposite positions in the argument: there is either harmony or conflict. These are, however, simplistic alternatives. We suggest that it is much more convincing instead to argue that,

familial conflict [is] a necessary moment in the full realisation of the

emotional potentialities of both parents (qua parents) and children. ...
The family is not based on natural affection; it is the natural locus of
the generation of the whole range of human feeling.

(Harris 1983: 183)

Faith Robertson Elliot has also proposed the adoption of a similar
perspective on the private lives of families:

attention to the nurturant and supportive as well as the oppressive sides
of families is not just an ambivalence. It is, in part, a recognition of the
fact that family life may be experienced in different ways by different
people and, in part, a recognition of the tragic paradox that security in
personal relationships implies a commitment and loss of freedom. It
recognises that not only love and altrusim but the whole range of
human feelings find expression in family life.

(Robertson Elliot 1986: 133)

The understanding of the family and its internal emotional dynamics
which is outlined in the quotations above, and which we adopt in this book,
is not merely a compromise between the poles of 'harmony' or 'conflict'.
What we are proposing is that harmony and conflict – in different mixes,
according to the personal histories of individuals and the developmental
cycle of the domestic group concerned – are, in principle at least, likely to
co-exist within families. Both are 'normal', even, perhaps, necessary. They
are not, in any strict sense, alternatives. Families are typically structured in
a non-egalitarian fashion. They are, with respect to both sex and age,
'structures of dominance'; this hierarchy is, however, the site of *two-way*
conflict and struggle, albeit not between equals (Collins 1975: 225–85). It is
also the site within which emotional support and fulfilment are to be found
– along, of course, with their opposites.

One consequence of this approach to the topic is the de-pathologising of
important areas of family conflict. Some conflict within families should not
be viewed as necessarily deviant (which, if it needs saying, is *not* to argue for
the acceptability of, for example, child abuse or male violence against
women). The sources of conflict in this respect are various. Gender is a
fairly obvious one, particularly (although by no means exclusively) in a
period during which gender roles have become an issue and 'traditional'
notions are changing or under pressure, whether from inside or outside the
family. Similarly, generational differences are a likely source of
disagreement and disharmony, and have been, it sometimes seems, in all
contexts and at all times, albeit perhaps in differing degree (Eisenstadt 1956;
Erikson 1968; Frith 1984; Musgrove 1964). The developing accommodation
between declining parental control, on the one hand, and burgeoning
adulthood and social maturity, on the other, is fertile ground for inter-

personal tension within the framework of the 'normal' developmental profile.

Gender and generation are structuring principles in which conflict may be necessarily implicated. There are also, however, day-to-day or situational sources of conflict which may, none the less, be specified in the abstract. First, there is the straightforward fact that families are emotionally-charged and tightly-knit social networks. Family members generally matter to each other (whether for good or ill) and they usually see a lot of each other. *Some* conflict over *some* things is probably not to be avoided. Second, there is the gap which may open up between collective goals (regardless, for the moment, of how those are defined and by whom) and the goals of individuals. Third, related to the previous issue, there are questions of equity, efficiency and organisation in the context of domestic management: who does what, when and to what effect. Fourth, and also related to its predecessors, the allocation of resources, particularly money, is central to any attempt to understand family relationships. The family is, if it is nothing else, a primary institution for the provision of economic support, both across generations and – particularly during the child-bearing/rearing phase – between men and women. Finally, it is important to remember that external sources of conflict may frequently impinge upon the internal relationships of the family, although these are extremely unlikely, in our view, to be wholly divorced from the sorts of issues which we have been discussing so far. Examples of such external factors might be religious or political differences. Unemployment, the role of which we intend to examine in this chapter, is another such external problem.

Having put forward our argument so far, it is not, however, our intention to suggest that family conflict, if conceptualised as the dominant tenor of interpersonal relationships within the family, should be treated as either inevitable or the 'norm'. It is just as important to consider sources of consensus, solidarity and harmony. Emotional ties of affection and dependence between partners, parents and children and siblings are obviously important in this respect. In addition, the 'conventional' ideology of gender roles is, as Parsons recognised, a source of social consensus, if left undisturbed by alternatives. Shared collective goals – once again regardless of who defines them and how – can also contribute to familial cohesion. From another perspective, there is a matrix of need and dependence in the material sense which also serves to bind family members together. Finally, there is, in a very real sense, a specific family ethos or ideology which brings family members closer: 'the family' is a 'good thing', it is 'normal'. Its absence is, for most people, almost unthinkable. It is an axiomatically legitimated part of most people's lives. Whether they think about it or not, the 'happy family' is, for, most people, the pinnacle of interpersonal achievement (Study Commission on the Family 1982). Those who do not so conform to this ideal are, at best, regarded as being out of the ordinary; at worst they are stigmatised. While the disjuncture between the ideal model of domestic bliss and the unhappy reality of many families is, in itself, a potent source of distress, the normative power of the model remains.

In closing this section, one thing remains to be said. On reviewing the discussion immediately above, it is clear that, within families, conflict and consensus, disagreement and solidarity, are intimately related to each other. They often derive from similar, if not the same, sources. Of particular significance in this respect are emotional needs and ties, gender relationships, generational differences and the organisation of the physical reproduction of the family group. All of these things contribute to the production and reproduction of a hierarchical system of relationships of power and authority within the family which is typically structured by gender, age, personality and resources. We shall now turn to the interview material to see how these issues and problems are worked out by the families with which we are concerned.

The nature of family conflict

Although we have just argued that conflict and harmony should both be seen as lying within the normal distribution with respect to family relationships, we are going to concentrate in the discussion which follows largely, although not solely, upon conflict. The primary reason for this focus is that this is where the major problem is perceived to lie: does the long-term unemployment of young people cause or exacerbate tensions within families? This is the question to which we need an answer. It is also as good a way into the topic as any. There are, however, practical issues of method which indicate that such an approach is perhaps the most sensible. Inasmuch as harmony and good relationships are viewed in everyday life as the normal state of affairs, they are largely taken for granted. Conflict – an argument, a fight, even 'an atmosphere' – is easier to talk about than good times, a point which has also been made by Coffield *et al.* (1986: 124). Conflict is interesting, it is a problem for the protagonists themselves (frequently one which arouses deep concern), it is often a specific event. As a consequence it is easier to interview people about than 'normal' harmonious family matters. Hence the emphasis, in the research and in the following account, upon disharmony and tension.

Accepting such an emphasis, however, it is immediately necessary to qualify this approach, in at least three senses. First, the very fact that conflict is easier to talk about than other, less disrupted periods of family life means that one must strive not to overlook or underestimate non-conflictual family relationships, if at all possible. Second, while it is relatively easy to talk about conflict in one sense, it must also be recognised that many people would rather avoid the subject, precisely because it *is* a problem for them. It is therefore likely, even allowing for sympathetic interviewing, that the extent and severity of personal conflict within the families with which we are concerned will be underestimated. What is more, the fact that the majority of our young informants were still living in the parental home suggests that we have missed those young people who have left home due to family conflict and stayed away. This is another sense in which we are likely to underestimate family conflict.

Finally, and it is a more intractable problem, we do not unfortunately, possess unambiguous definitions of either 'harmony' or 'conflict'. Is harmony, for example, simply the absence of conflict, or must we conceptualise it as something more positive than this? On the other side of the coin, does conflict of necessity entail open tension and confrontation, or do less obvious undercurrents of strain and unhappiness qualify for inclusion in this category as well? These are not questions which permit of an easy resolution. Perhaps the best solution, which we have adopted here, is to accept some kind of commonsense definition of 'conflict' and allow our research subjects' testimony to sketch in the outlines of what it means for them. It is, however, an issue to which we shall return later in this chapter.

What, then, was our commonsensical definition of conflict? In the first place, we simply asked people if they had rows or arguments, and, if so, what about. Many said no, and the matter was generally left there, although contradictory evidence sometimes emerged from other parts of the interview. From the answers of those who admitted to conflict or tension of this kind, it is clear that, as indeed might be expected, there is a wide spectrum of situations which fit into the category of 'rows or arguments'. Some idea of this variety may be gained from the quotations below.

(1)
I think we got on one another's nerves more than anything. It sort of flared up and then it was all forgotten, like, you know ... It was never, it was never sort of, held a grudge and carried on for days ...//... and we had a bit of a row here one day, she went out with her friend and she didn't come back for 2 days.

(Mr Victor Ballinger, Abbeyview)

(2)
I mean, we have four girls sharing a bedroom no bigger than this. You can imagine the tight space we're in ... 'You've got my blouse on, get it off' ... 'You've got my socks on, get them off' ... 'I've done the washing this week' ... 'Look here', sort of thing, 'you're awfully untidy'. I'm a very tidy sort of person. I like everything to be in a nice neat pile, put away, you know.

(Paula Jones, Abbeyview)

(3)
We've only had one row. It ended up with him [her son, Simon] getting

so upset that he nearly burst into tears and he went into the garden to pull himself together ... And I thought, never again, it isn't worth it.

(Mrs Doreen Preece, High Oak)

(4)
Particularly now and again their worry comes to the surface ... There have been rows. Not many, three or four since Christmas. There was one particularly nasty one where I stormed out and the rest of it. I just stormed out [laughing].

(Steve Anderson, Ty-Gwyn)

(5)
My parents knew that they could throw me out and the dole would put me in somewhere. That happened regularly ... 'Go now!' I'd get a bag, go and stay with my friend, back up the next morning, 'Sorry, I didn't mean it' ... My father never hits me or my brother, but sometimes, when he gets in a very bad row ... like one night we had a stupid row and he was hitting me. He broke my tooth. My friend started, 'God, I wouldn't put up with that. You should move out'.

(Diana Fullerton, Ty-Gwyn)

These are some of the more obvious examples of family conflict – ranging from the relatively trivial to the serious – to be found in the interview material. Looking at the answers of those who professed not to have rows at home, it is, however, clear that not only can family conflicts be minor, and be perceived as such, but they are often talked about in language which presents them, in fact, as something *other* than conflict, as *not really* disagreements or fights.

(6)
There have been little tiffs, no rows. She [his daughter, Caroline] said once she would leave home in a row, but it was not serious.

(Mr George Young, High Oak)

(7)
Arguments all the time, but not rows ... Sometimes Melanie will fly up in the air.

(Mrs Violet Reilly, High Oak)

(8)
We don't have any rows. We're easy-going. We might have a little misunderstanding, we're not saying that.

(Mrs Mary Sullivan, High Oak)

(9)
It's not rows, just an atmosphere

(Mrs Horner, Ty-Gwyn)

(10)
I used to sulk. Get fed-up and bored.

(Shiree Vivian, Ty-Gwyn)

There would appear, then, to be a continuum of definitions or understandings of family conflict. In order of declining severity, 'fights' and 'rows' are most problematic, then there are 'tiffs' and 'arguments', followed by 'misunderstandings' with 'an atmosphere' or 'sulking' occupying the other end of the spectrum. These categories do not exhaust the possibilities, of course, but they do provide us with an understanding of the range of family conflict situations and the ways in which they are talked about.

It is, in fact, likely that the way in which people talk about conflict is also a means of dealing or coping with it. The same set of events may be described in different ways. The words which actors use to locate an event in their day-to-day life will clearly make a difference: if an exchange is seen as a 'row', then it must be managed in one way, whereas if it is thought of as a 'tiff' or a 'misunderstanding', a different response is appropriate. An extreme example of this kind of strategy may be found, perhaps, in (5) above: Diana Fullerton says that her father 'never hits' her. In the next breath, however, she describes an incident in which 'he was hitting me' and 'broke my tooth'. The violence can be rendered less problematic because it is treated as exceptional behaviour; her father, after all, 'never hits' Diana. The fact that this episode is regarded as an exception – which, to be fair, it may have been, although the interviews with Diana and her mother point to a very stormy set of family relationships – may serve to confirm Diana's model of the relationship with her father as non-violent.

The different labels which attach to family conflict also open the possibility – no, the likelihood – that different people will see the same situation in radically different lights. This may serve to limit conflict or it may exacerbate an already difficult state of affairs. It also means that the researcher must be perpetually sensitive to the contingent nature of the accounts which interviewees are offering. In the extracts below, Mrs Pauline Ace from High Oak is discussing her daughters, Theresa, 19, unemployed, sporting a mohican haircut and living in a bedsit nearby, and Kelly, 22, employed and living at home; Theresa and Kelly also offer their views.

(11)
SH: What about rows?
Mrs Ace: Every day.
SH: About what?
PA: Kelly. Everything from, how could I say … They're over nothing. She finds anything to pick on. It could be her tea. She didn't want salad today, the next day she does … She's always been difficult. Yes, ever since she was born. It's been one long nightmare … It's in the family, on my husband's side. …//…
SH: Do you ever have rows about her [Theresa's] hair?

PA: No, except my mother and Theresa. It ends up in a row because Theresa doesn't like it.

(12)
SH: Do you ever have rows?
Theresa: I can't think of any. I get on pretty well with my mother. She may make the odd poke about my hair, but nothing that makes me think, well ...

(13)
SH: Have you ever thought of leaving home?
Kelly: No, not really. I'm quite happy now. I've got a job and a boyfriend.

It is always difficult to know what to make of conflicting accounts, particularly when, as in this research, there is little in the way of observational data upon which to fall back. It is clear that Mrs Ace and her daughters see things from different perspectives. What is less clear, however, is which, if any, of them is the more 'correct' and exactly what are the consequences for their management of their relationships of their different understandings of those relationships.

So far, then, we have looked at the range of conflictual situations and relationships which exist in the families we interviewed. There is a broad spectrum of possibilities, from severe conflict and violence to apparent tranquillity. Family conflict may also take a number of forms. On reviewing the interview data from a different perspective, it is equally clear that there are many causes of, and reasons for, tension and conflict within family relationships. An analysis of the stated reasons for rows and arguments in these families yields the following hierarchy of apparently causal factors.

The most important nexus of family tension seemed to be unhappy personal relationships between family members, typically, in this context, parents and children or siblings. Of the fifty-eight families involved in our study, twenty-seven (47 per cent) mentioned this kind of situation as a point of conflict. As the quotations below illustrate, and also (2) above, it is a category which encompasses a variety of actual situations.

(14)
GT: There are rows, with my big mouth.
SH: What about?
GT: Answering back mainly.

(Gwyn Thomas, Abbeyview)

(15)
The trouble with Hugh and his dad, is they've never been able to have a real conversation. He's [Mr Reynolds] always been away playing

rugby. There's a lot of tension between me and my husband anyway ... But I do try and side with Hugh, its maternal instincts, you protect your kids ...//... Hugh has been marvellous lately, tension has been building up. My husband hasn't got time for us.

(Mrs Diana Reynolds, High Oak)

(16)

Its stupid things, like the dog or something ... My father's always got to be polishing or putting things away. He says, 'Oh, I didn't move it' ... Never big arguments.

(Melenie Reilly, High Oak)

(17)

If I do anything around the house and I do it faster, like. I painted the house in a few days. My father thought it should have taken several weeks. So there was a row ...//... There was another row when I took the car to pieces. He thought I wouldn't be able to put it together again. He gets annoyed when I'm better than him at something.

(Arthur Evans, Ty-Gwyn)

With respect to personal relationships within these families, it is worth drawing attention to the fact that the interview data suggest that there may be gender differences in the nature of family conflict. Fewer sources of conflict emerge in the families where it is a daughter rather than a son who is unemployed. There is, what is more, also a difference between the three study areas. In the Abbeyview families where the son is unemployed, the number of identified sources of conflict averages out at 1.2 per family; for the equivalent families in High Oak and Ty-Gwyn it is 1.3 and 1.7, respectively. Looking at those families with unemployed daughters, the figures are 1.1 (Abbeyview), 0.9 (High Oak) and 1.0 (Ty-Gwyn). We are, of course, talking about small numbers of families here; these figures should be treated with corresponding caution. Two tentative conclusions may be offered, however: family relationships with sons appear to be more problematic than with daughters, and the difference between sons and daughters in this respect widens from Abbeyview to High Oak to Ty-Gwyn.

It is difficult to know how these findings, such as they are, should be interpreted. A number of explanatory possibilities come to mind. In the first place, it may simply be the case that parent–daughter relationships are generically better – for whatever reasons – than parent–son relationships. We know, for example, from a number of classic studies of family life, that the mother–daughter relationship, in particular, is often intimate, warm and abiding (Rosser and Harris 1965: 218–21; Willmott and Young 1960: 61–76; Young and Willmott 1957: 44–61). There are also the myth of Oedipus and Freudian theories of generational rivalry, particularly between fathers and sons, to be considered (Connell 1987: 114).

These notions offer us interesting, and perhaps useful, explanatory possibilities. They do not, however, help us to understand the difference between Abbeyview, High Oak and Ty-Gwyn. The figures for the families with unemployed daughters are much the same for each area; for families with unemployed sons, however, there is an increase in the number and spread of sources of conflict between Abbeyview and Ty-Gwyn, with High Oak (once again) occupying an intermediate position. A plausible explanation of these findings may relate to social perceptions of unemployment: female unemployment may be seen as less of a problem than male unemployment, and male unemployment may be less acceptable in west Swansea than in the Abbeyview families. This is something to which we will return later in this chapter.

After 'personal relationships', the next most important perceived sources of conflict were unemployment (in 36 per cent of the families) and money (in 18 per cent). Although it is possible to differentiate these two topics for the purposes of producing a ranking such as this, considerable caution – and scepticism – must be exercised in doing so: unemployment and money are inextricably implicated, the one in the other, in the day-to-day experience of the young people about whom we are writing. The role of unemployment in the genesis of family conflict will be discussed later in this chapter, and money matters form one of the central topics of Chapter 3.

The last important area of tension within these families may be characterised as to do with 'life-styles', in particular parental disapproval of the life-styles of their sons and daughters. This, of course, is the stuff of which much generational conflict is commonly supposed to be made. It is therefore interesting to see how relatively minor this factor turns out to be in our data: in only ten families (12 per cent) did this figure, although it is likely that this category overlaps in important respects with the earlier category of personal relationships between family members. Something of the flavour of these life-style conflicts may be gauged from the quotation below:

(18)

AB: If I stay out late she [her mother] doesn't like it.

RJ: And what about when you were unemployed?

AB: All the time, because of the time I was coming in. I didn't get in 'til seven. Well, she went mad. She can't understand I've been with Andrea and we are just talking. Mind you, I know how you'd feel if your daughter came home and told you ... I don't think you'd believe her either.

(Audrey Ballinger, Abbeyview)

(19)

The kids, my sisters [aged 11 and 13] ... The eldest one now, she smokes. She drinks and she's out all hours. The little one tries to follow her. They're always in trouble ... not bad trouble. They wear their new clothes, they come in stinking. That sets the old man off. That sets me off ... When I was 17, 18, I wasn't allowed to discos, Cinderella's [a local night club], anything. In the end, I said, 'Bugger this, I'm going'. No more was said about it. I go out when I want, come in when I want.

(Jonathan Alexander, High Oak)

There are two interesting features of the above interview extracts. First, as in (19) it appears that disagreements over life-styles and behaviour may occur *within* as well as *between* generations. This is a good example of the overlap between conflict within personal relationships and conflict over life-styles. Second, listening to Audrey Ballinger in (18), there is the suggestion that the issue of unemployment is somehow bound up with the conflict with her mother over what time she should be in at night. In the next section of this chapter, we will examine in more depth the relationship between family conflict and the experience of long-term unemployment by the young women and men who we interviewed.

Unemployment, locality and family relationships

It is clear, then, that in these fifty-eight families there is a range of differing degrees of conflict, that conflict can take many shapes and is understood in different fashions, that conflict is associated with or arises from a number of factors and that it is not always easy to disentangle one such factor from another in the ebb and flow of family life. The unemployment of young people contributes to family conflict, that much is clear. Other researchers have also provided evidence that this is the case (Brah 1986: 66–74; Coffield *et al*. 1986: 144–6; Wallace 1987: 94–8). However, the manner and extent of that contribution is worth a closer look.

In the first place, what do the interviews tell us in this respect? The quotations below have been selected to illustrate the kinds of situation in which the unemployment of sons and daughters entered into or appeared to cause conflict within these families.

(20)
SH: Are there any rows about unemployment?
PF: Oh yes ... The fact that the boys wouldn't look for work.
SH: And after the rows?
PF: Oh yeah, they go out then ... The Job Centre or the Steel Company.

(Mrs Pearl Francis, Abbeyview)

(21)
RH: Oh yes, my dad come up on it [laughs] ... 'Get out and look for a job.'
RJ: But the row wouldn't be about that?
RH: No. It would come up, like ... You can't keep it in.

(Rebecca Hughes, Abbeyview)

(22)

It's his lack of worrying about it. I can understand people trying and not getting jobs. If someone won't even look for a job, he'll never get one ... It leaves a heavy atmosphere for a couple of days.

(Mr Michael Lynch, High Oak)

(23)

I feel it's centred around unemployment. I feel, if he was working, earning a wage, he would probably be somewhere of his own at 21 years of age. The fact that he's here, it's like having another adult in the house. He's a typical kind of boy. He doesn't do anything in the house unless he's driven to.

(Mr Fred Mansel, High Oak)

(24)

There's never anyone else in the house involved. I've had to put my foot down ... Like I told you, he won't go up to the counter in the Job Centre. And there's a Job Library and he won't go in and sit down and talk to the woman there. He wouldn't buck up his courage ...//... It isn't the money ... I don't want him to get into such a rut that he won't have the guts to go for an interview.

(Mrs Doreen Preece, High Oak)

(25)

There are rows, but not specifically about unemployment ...//... But it does come in. Usually dad. He gives me a lot of stick ... Not actual rows. We do have some, but not over unemployment.

(Matthew Griffiths, Ty-Gwyn)

(26)

Yes, but again it wouldn't be the kernel of why he [Matthew] was getting a row. It would be a side issue ... Irresponsibility, bad habits ... Unemployment wouldn't be the ... It may have been because he lost the job ...

(Mr Paul Griffiths, Ty-Gwyn)

(27)

I've been a bit touchy in the past about what I've been doing and when they've asked questions ... I suppose they have a right to know ... They've asked questions which I've regarded as silly. I've been touchy ...//... they don't want to drive me out. Neither do they want me still here, doing what I'm doing now [composing and recording electronic music in his bedroom], at the age of 43 or whatever.

(Steve Anderson, Ty-Gwyn)

(28)

My mum used to go on at me all the time to get a job, get a job ... She used to go on saying you shouldn't have left your other job, I just closed my ears to it.

(Kelly Hildreth, Ty-Gwyn)

A number of themes can be extracted from this material. First, what is often at issue is not so much the state of being unemployed *in general*, but rather, as in (24), (26) and (28), *specific* events: losing a job, not being sufficiently assertive in the Job Centre, or whatever. Second, in many cases it appears – see (21), (25) and (26), for example – that unemployment is not the actual *cause* of the problem. It seems instead to be handy ammunition once an argument or a row has already begun (although one must accept the possibility that unemployment is an 'underlying cause' in these cases; how, however, is one ever to tell?). Third, it is probably also true to say that what is at stake in many of these tense episodes is as much symbolic as anything else. It is important that young people are *seen* to be 'making an effort', whether they actually find employment or not; issues of this kind can be seen in (20) and (22). It is an aspect of the situation which we will discuss further, and in greater detail, in the next chapter. Extracts (26) and (27) illustrate, fourth, another dimension of the problem, one to which we have already alluded. Here there is a degree of overlap between two nominally distinct issues: unemployment, on the one hand, and parental disapproval of the young person's life-style, on the other. These quotations, along with (24), make another point, that parental worry or anxiety about their sons' and daughters' future prospects may often become manifest as conflict and confrontation. Viewed from the perspective of commonsense psychology, if nothing else, this kind of response is very much what might be expected. Finally, as implied by Mr Mansel in (23), domestic responsibilities and the problems attached to 'being around the house' can also create tension. We will discuss this further in Chapter 3.

Another cause of family conflict arising from the unemployment of young people is not mentioned in the above quotations and in fact may not be easily alluded to in front of an interviewer, namely the financial hardship which unemployment often involves. Few of the families with which we are concerned, particularly in High Oak and Abbeyview, appeared to have the kind of economic resources which would allow them to absorb easily the needs of an unemployed young adult (and many were, in fact, suffering considerable economic hardship, if not poverty). It is another subject to which we will return in Chapter 3.

At this point we should, perhaps, remember those families in which the long-term unemployment of a daughter or a son did *not* appear to be a germ of tension. A few illustrations will suffice to make the point:

(29)
If I was out of work and I was too lazy to look for work, bone idle, I suppose there would be rows. But my father knows there's not enough work about. He's very understanding.

(Gwyn Thomas, Abbeyview)

(30)
SH: Do you ever have rows about unemployment?
EK: None at all ...
GM: We're all in the same position.
                    (Elizabeth King and Mrs Glenda Miller, Abbeyview)
(31)
It's not their fault. If it was because they were lazy and didn't want to work, then there'd be a few rows about it.
                              (Mrs Glenys Haig, High Oak)

Two things may be said here, both of which will surface on other occasions later in the book. As with the material relating to the link between unemployment and conflict, so with its reverse; questions of explanation and the allocation of responsibility are at stake. *Why* are these young people unemployed? And whose *fault* is it? If it is not perceived to be their's, then it is less likely to be a focus of conflict. This, of course, explains some large part of the importance attached to 'making an effort'. Another important factor is the social context within which unemployment is experienced and understood. In a family where everyone is unemployed, as in (30), for example, unemployment may – on the principle that people who live in glass houses should not throw stones – be less available as fuel to stoke the fire during family arguments and confrontations.

Looking at the ethnographic extracts above, and reading through the detailed interview records from which they have been drawn, it is clear that simply being unemployed is not a major source of conflict *in itself*. It seems to be the case that it contributes to, and is experienced in the context of, the existing multiplex web of relationships of conflict and solidarity within families. In some cases people are pushed further apart, in others it may bring them closer together. Our argument here can be related to current debates concerning the psychological effects of unemployment. Until recently, the accepted wisdom was that these effects proceeded, as a general rule, in phases, from initial optimism to apathy and resignation (Kelvin and Jarrett 1985: 18–26). A number of studies have now suggested that, rather than unemployment having effects *sui generis*, the psychological impact of unemployment is to some degree contextually defined, differing from place to place, person to person and time to time (Fineman 1987; Fryer and Ullah 1987; Hartley and Fryer 1984)

It is equally clear that, more often than not, the 'problem' of unemployment is crystallised, where it does create conflict, in the shape of particular events or specific difficulties. Often what young people are criticised for is not so much their *state* of unemployment as their *response* to it, although, as in (20) and (22), there is an explicit recognition that the two are closely connected. Of course, in the case of Kelly Hildreth (28) the tension focuses on her having left a job and thereby precipitated herself into unemployment. Here unemployment *per se* is more directly a cause of conflict. Once again, however, this must be understood in the context of the individual's biography and the particular situation.

With respect to the unemployment of other family members, we have already mentioned one of the social contexts within which unemployment is experienced. Another important social context in this sense is the neighbourhood, locality or community. In Chapter 1 we drew a distinction between our three study areas: Abbeyview has very much higher levels of unemployment than High Oak, which, in turn, has higher levels then Ty-Gwyn (Table 1.2). This contrast is mirrored in our samples: a large majority of the families we looked at in Abbeyview were wholly dependent on state benefits of one kind or another, while in Ty-Gwyn a similarly large majority of households had both parents in employment. The High Oak sample lay somewhere between these extremes (Table 1.4).

Is it possible to relate these differences to our material on conflict within the family? We have made what is an admittedly crude attempt to establish such a relationship in Table 2.1. The information which forms the basis for this table derives from two questions: about rows in the family and about the reaction of parents to their daughter or son's unemployment. 'Serious conflict', in the terms of Table 2.1's categorisation, means that respondents reported rows *and* unhappy parent–child relationships. 'Some conflict' means that respondents reported minor rows and slightly poor relationships, or reported rows *or* unhappy relationships, but not both. Returning to our earlier discussion concerning how one should define 'conflict', we are not suggesting that we have, in Table 2.1, overcome the definitional difficulties which were there outlined. Our categories of 'severe conflict' and 'some conflict' are, however, defined according to explicit criteria which, if nothing else, allow the reader to understand the basis of our comparison.

Table 2.1 Respondents' perceptions of family conflict: Abbeyview, High Oak and Ty-Gwyn

	% of young people and parents reporting serious conflict	% of young people and parents reporting some conflict	% of young people and parents reporting no conflict	Total %
Abbeyview	18	59	24	100
High Oak	28	36	36	100
Ty-Gwyn	46	49	5	100
TOTAL %	30	46	24	100

The second point to bear in mind with respect to Table 2.1 is that, for the purposes of this exercise, the family is not in fact the unit of analysis.

Because different people may often see the same situation in different lights, it would have proved difficult to establish a secure evaluation of the presence or absence of conflict, or – more to the point – its severity, in the case of particular families. As a result, we have simply treated the three sets of families as samples of individual respondents and proceeded accordingly.

Bearing these qualifications in mind, Table 2.1 reveals an obvious hierarchy of family conflict. The Ty-Gwyn group clearly experiences more, and more serious, family tension than either of the other two. While High Oak has the largest percentage of respondents who claim to experience no family conflict, a greater proportion of the High Oak interviewees reported the presence of severe conflict than was in the case in Abbeyview, where nearly 60 per cent of the young people and parents gave answers which we have interpreted as indicating 'some conflict'.

Bearing in mind that the Abbeyview and High Oak samples were, overall, economically much less well-off than the Ty-Gwyn sample, with more housholds reliant on benefit, and that housing conditions were significantly worse for the Abbeyview families (at the impressionistic level, the Abbeyview houses were overcrowded by comparison with High Oak and Ty-Gwyn), this is, perhaps, a surprising finding. Conventional wisdom might suggest that material hardship and residential overcrowding would engender more rather than less conflict.

One factor which may help to explain the contrast between Abbeyview and High Oak, on the one hand, and Ty-Gwyn, on the other, is the experience of and attitudes towards unemployment in each area. It was obvious when talking to informants that unemployment was publicly a more routine fact of collective life in Abbeyview than it was in west Swansea. One reason for this, of course, is the large-scale redundancy exercise from the steel works in Port Talbot in 1979. Many families experienced unemployment at this time. The way in which unemployment has come to be seen as a feature of community life was expressed by one Abbeyview mother, Mrs Rosemary Hughes, who felt sorry not only for Rebecca, her 23-year-old daughter, but also for the other young people she saw on the streets:

(32)
I've been lucky with the children having jobs. When I see other children going around. It hurts you ... all these children, they've grown up and you've seen them grow up. And what are they doing? Walking the streets. They should be working. Well I feel for them. I do, 'cause I've known them since they were born.

In Ty-Gwyn in particular, however, one might expect that a young person who is unemployed will fall shorter of the expected mark. More young people in this area go on to further and higher education. Those who we interviewed were generally those who had fallen through the streaming system of the local comprehensive school and ended up unemployed. Most of their parents were in employment as were the overwhelming majority of their siblings and contemporaries. They were, quite simply, moving in a social context which was different from that of their peers in Abbeyview and High Oak.

However, the interview material – such as it is – does not unambiguously support the notion that youth unemployment is significantly more communally stigmatised in west Swansea. Only one family in Abbeyview and three in High Oak reported adverse neighbourly comment on the unemployment of their son or daughter. None of the families in Ty-Gwyn reported this. The latter finding may in part be explained, however, by the strong impression which one gains from the interview material that there is less neighbouring of any kind in Ty-Gwyn than in the other two areas. It is very much more a place where people keep themselves to themselves. It is not surprising, therefore, that there should appear to be less public comment about the unemployment of young people from neighbours.

Returning, however, to the internal social context of the family itself, it may be possible to relate the data presented in Table 2.1 to the pattern of employment and unemployment in our families. In Ty-Gwyn all of the fathers and the majority of the mothers who we interviewed were in employment. This is a situation which might make the unemployment of a son or daughter a source of family conflict, whether that conflict finds its expression as being 'about unemployment' or not. Conversely, in Abbeyview, with a majority of families without a parent in employment, the son or daughter is less likely to be censored for their unemployment. The situation in High Oak is, in all respects, more heterogenous.

There is, as we have already argued, a gender dimension to these inter-area differences in the severity and sources of family conflict for unemployed young people. What, however, is the place of unemployment as a focus of conflict in this respect? Looking at the families with unemployed sons, in three (33 per cent) of the Abbeyview families, as compared to five (41 per cent), from High Oak and six (46 per cent) from Ty-Gwyn, the young person's unemployment turned up as associated with or causing tension within the family. Looking at the families with unemployed daughters, this was the case for three (33 per cent) of the Abbeyview families, three (30 per cent) of the High Oak families and one (20 per cent) of the Ty-Gwyn families.

Now these are very small numbers and very small differences. We are handicapped in particular by the small numbers of unemployed young women who were interviewed in Ty-Gwyn. As a consequence the usefulness of any conclusions which we might draw from them is strictly limited. That having been said, however, it appears that the conflictual salience of unemployment for the young men in our samples *increases* as we move across the bay from Abbeyview to west Swansea. Bearing in mind the relatively small number of young women interviewed in Ty-Gwyn, the safest conclusion perhaps is that the level of unemployment-related conflict for young women is much the same in each area. This supports the suggestion made earlier that male unemployment is most likely to be perceived as a problem in Ty-Gwyn, followed by High Oak and Abbeyview in that order, a set of differences which is likely to be related to the severity of unemployment in each locality. Female unemployment, however, may be generally perceived as less of a problem than male unemployment, regardless of its severity in particular areas. Despite changes in women's rates of economic participation during the 1980s, it appears to be still the case that employment is thought to be more important for men than for women.

There the matter must be left. The evidence concerning unemployment, conflict, locality and gender is merely suggestive, and our interpretation tentative. At best, our discussion highlights the topic as a worthwhile area for further research. It is, however, possible to be more definite about the relationship between unemployment and family conflict in the three areas under consideration. Certainly, within the families concerned, the greater impact of parental unemployment in Abbeyview and, to a lesser degree, High Oak, is likely to be important in minimising the possibilities for conflict arising from the long-term unemployment of a son or daughter. It may also be the case that the communal experience of employment and unemployment contributes to the amelioration or exacerbation of the situation. The nature of local differences in these and other respects will continue to be a focus of our attention in subsequent chapters.

In this chapter we have discussed something of the nature of family conflict as it is revealed through our interview material. Unemployment is not the most important source or locus of family conflict. This is *not* to say, however, that long-term unemployment has no pernicious effects on the quality of family relationships. Our argument, rather, is that its impact should not be understood in a vacuum. Existing family relationships and the 'external' social milieu provide the contexts within which the effects of unemployment should be understood. By and large, the families with which we are concerned are managing – and this is the 'taking the strain' of our title – to *cope*. In the next chapter, we will look at some further aspects of *how* they cope.

| 3 |

GETTING BY

In looking at conflict in the previous chapter, we adopted a somewhat static approach to the internal relationships of the family group. However, conflict – no matter how it is defined – is not something which is 'just there' (or not). There is always a process whereby the character of emotional and interpersonal relationships between family members is produced and reproduced. This may be conceptualised as, in part, a management process in which, given the hierarchial age structure and gendered division of family roles and responsibilities, some family members exercise more power or authority than others. As in most managerial processes, control of outcomes and the securing of the consent of participants are the goals. Both symbolic and material resources are manipulated – in the shape of rewards and penalties – in the pursuit of those goals.

The management of the internal social and psychological climate of the family is the main subject of our discussion in this chapter. Four themes in particular will be explored in some depth. First, there is the centrality of money (and its absence) to this process. Second, there is housework and the salience in this context of gender divisions, particularly those between brothers and sisters. Third, we will discuss specific strategies or methods of conflict management. Finally, the first three topics coalesce in a consideration of the role of the mother as the most important manager of family relationships in most households.

'Money for nothing ...'

With due acknowledgement (and apologies) to Dire Straits for the use of the subheading, the issue of money – what you get it *for*, what you do *with* it and how much you *need* – lies at the heart of relationships between parents, children and siblings. If for no other reason, economic scarcity and plenty serve, in part, to characterise the experience of unemployment and employment for these young women and men and their families. Money is a source of domestic conflict. Within the hierarchical parent–child relationship, in particular, money is a medium of symbolic exchange, concerned with moral issues such as 'responsibility' and the negotiation of identity (most especially, adult identity).

The notion that money, the earning of a wage, is a central defining feature of employment and unemployment is hardly novel. Many sociological studies of the labour process and orientations to work have emphasised that for many people employment is, at best, a source of instrumental satisfaction (e.g. Beynon 1984; Blackburn and Mann 1979). Rather than having a *necessary* intrinsic value, employment is often primarily a means to an end, that end being the money with which to buy things. Bearing in mind the marked rise in the level of consumer spending in the United Kingdom since the early 1980s (*Social Trends* 17: 106-7), this materialist or instrumental evaluation of employment may be becoming even more significant than has previously been the case. The fact that higher unemployment has resulted in a diminished capacity for the exercise of choice by many job-seekers and more family poverty (inasmuch as worklessness tends to be concentrated, both, geographically and socially) is likely only to further emphasise this attitude to employment. One of the things which most people conspicuously do *not* have when they are unemployed is as much money as those who are employed. Full citizenship in the High Street is likely to be more important than job satisfaction.

There are two kinds of economic hardship: relative deprivation and absolute deprivation. While it is true none of the families we looked at appeared to be on the breadline – and if they were, they were probably not going to admit it to us – many, particularly in Abbeyview, were obviously hard up. Furniture, household decoration, clothes, the overall impression was often one of real if not abject poverty. Nor, as the quotation below makes plain, was hardship confined to Abbeyview. Living in owner-occupation in Ty-Gwyn could, when unemployment appeared, produce its own particular difficulties:

(33)
... we row a bit about money. Whatever we row about, it tends to boil down to that at the end. Mum and Dad [neither of whom were in employment] worry about the bills. I feel guilty about that, that I'm not paying enough. It's something we've learned to live with really. We try not to let it bother us. There's not much we can do about it really.
(Samantha Smith, Ty-Gwyn)

So much, then, for absolute deprivation. Few people go hungry – not to the point of starvation anyway – and children no longer walk barefoot to school. The hardship is, none the less, real and the consequences telling. There is no reason to dwell on it here because once the realities are stated, there is, in fact, little more to tell that is startling or novel.[1] That, in a sense, is one of the central tragedies of unemployment in Britain today. Most of the long-term unemployed are living in drastically reduced circumstances, their health and the health of their children suffer, they are poor; they are not poor *enough*, however, for anybody to *have* to do anything about it. The experience of deprivation is alienating and socially divisive, the social cohesion of the poor and the unemployed is too fragmentary to provide the basis for collective action. Historically high levels of unemployment have achieved the ghastly status of some kind of normality.

Samantha Smith's testimony in (33), however, alerts us to the difficulties involved in attempting to draw too sharp a distinction between absolute and relative deprivation. The Smith household, by Ty-Gwyn's standards, are suffering close to absolute hardship. Compared to many households in Abbeyview, however, they may not be too badly off. In this sense, deprivation always has an element of relativity about it. Hardship may be evaluated according to two criteria. First, there is social context, the living standards of significant others (these may be the neighbours or they may be the imaginary inhabitants of advertising's Never-Neverland). Second, each person's history and experience is relevant. It is in the interaction of these two factors that expectations emerge:

(34)
TF: If you wake in the morning and go down the shops you always see them. You know the unemployed ones and the working ones.
SH: How?
TF: You just look. They only buy a paper and that's it. With the working ones, he's got the money and he can buy what he wants from that shop. Unemployed people have got to save up to buy what they want. If you're working you can just buy it from your wage.

(Thomas Field, Abbeyview)

(35)
I don't know how long it is since he [his son, Jonathan] had a Chinese take-away. When he worked in the Club he had one every night.

(Mr Thomas Alexander, High Oak)

(36)
RP: I need to go out on Friday nights, Saturday nights. I haven't been out since I left work. It's fifteen pounds, twelve pounds you need to go to town. You go down the pub here first. You catch a bus in. A pint can cost you a pound in there. You may have something to eat. Taxi home ... I've no money to buy anything in town. No point in looking round the shops ... you sort of give up [looking for a job].
SH: What starts you off again?
RP: It's pressures, and they build up. You say, I've got to get a job', and you go down the Job Centre and it all starts again.
SH: What pressures?

RP: Pressures for money. Money matters. Money is all that counts, isn't it?

(Richard Pugh, Ty-Gwyn)

It may not be able to buy you love – it may even be the root of all evil – but, for some, 'money is all that counts'. As *what*, however, does it count? We have already seen that not having money means that the young person is prevented from doing things which he or she may have been accustomed to doing, which other people do, or which may be viewed as reasonable possibilities. For the family, a shortage of money may bring a whole train of consequences, from no longer being able to afford beef on Sunday to no longer being able to pay the mortgage.

A shortage of money does not simply result in economic deprivation, of course, whether absolute or relative. As a medium of exchange, money is also inextricably caught up in a culturally defined complex of notions about reciprocity, notions which are themselves concerned with a further set of ideas about honour, status and appropriate behaviour (Mauss 1954). Exchange relationships – whether we choose to view them as strictly 'economic' or not – are basic to social interaction and the production and reproduction of social groups, large and small. Exchange is also, however, about hierarchy, power and social control (Blau 1964; Ekeh 1974).

As an *abstract* medium of exchange, money is particularly well-suited to the demands of complex, changing situations; the social meanings which are attached to it are arbitrary and manipulable. Hence, in a sense, the ambiguity which invests many of our attitudes to money: it is both a curse and a blessing. Money is the most useful thing in our world, and it has no *intrinsic* uses at all (Simmel 1978: 325). To add to the ambiguity, there is a widely recognised distinction between professional services, performed for money, and personal services, ideally paid for in kind, if at all (Douglas and Isherwood 1979: 59).

This is also the distinction between market relationships and relationships which are governed by norms and customary obligations, such as kinship, friendship or community. The distinction is not as clear as this in day-to-day social practice, but it remains of considerable significance. When *personal* services are paid for with *money*, there may be confusion and conflict. This is what happens in many families without unemployed daughters or sons. It is likely to be an even greater source of difficulty where there is an unemployed young person less able to afford to make a financial contribution to the household. Bearing in mind that many of the families we looked at were solely dependent upon welfare benefits, they could not afford to do without such a contribution. The quotations below illustrate something of the uncertainty and ambiguity inherent in this aspect of family life:

(37)

He [her son, Hugh] gives something and I do take it off him ... But he gets it back by the end of the fortnight. But you have to, to give him a sense of responsibility, don't you?

(Mrs Diana Reynolds, High Oak)

(38)

SH: Does he [Anthony] pay back what he borrows?

CL: Well, the thing is, he offers it back but, the thing is, if he gives it back, a couple of days later he's borrowing it again, so I don't take it. As long as he's offered to repay it, I think then, 'Well, he's offered'.

(Mrs Christine Lonsdale, Ty-Gwyn)

(39)

This is the hard part. I can't get it over to him [his son Timothy]. Because he's in all the time, the heating, lighting, phone calls, and so on. It's a hidden thing. You don't realise ... Like yesterday I took him into town, took him back from town. When I came in ... the record player's been on all day. The television on in here. The phone ... all those things. Things he could have helped a little bit with. I don't want him freezing. If it were five pounds a week less on heating, that's a holiday abroad. We could do more things together.

(Mr Wynford Owens, Ty-Gwyn)

(40)

It works like a circle. There's my mother, my mother-in-law, us and Gary [Johnson]. We've got money on different days and we borrow each other's money. Tomorrow, my mother-in-law and mother says to Kevin, 'Pay our rent'. We get that back on Thursday. Mandy and Kirk [Gary's unemployed sister and brother] paid for practically everything we had for Christmas. They bought wallpaper and Gary and Kirk did it ... Mandy goes up the shop and buys something for Sunday dinner.

(Mr Johnson, Abbeyview)

(41)

SH: Do you borrow off your father?

PB: No, mostly off mates.

SH: Does your sister [Michelle Vivian, also unemployed] borrow?

PB: Oh yes. She borrows off me. I think she borrows off father. I'm not quite sure. They keep that secret.

(Phillip Broughton, High Oak)

These quotations illustrate a number of more general issues. The Johnson family and extended family, in (40), are trying to hold things together at the economic level, operating a 'roundabouts and swings' system of exchange in order to manage their money. In the process there is also an active affirmation of family solidarity and membership. This is one sense in which money transactions are also centrally concerned with things other than the economic exchange involved (or, at least, that is how they are presented). Mrs Reynolds, in another example (37), is trying to impart a sense of 'responsibility' to her son. Mr Owens, in (39), is suggesting that if Timothy were to contribute to a reduction in households costs, the family would be financially enabled to 'do more things together'. As long as Anthony Lonsdale *offers* to repay a loan, his mother is satisfied (38). It is as if it is not acceptable for parents to take money off their children solely to satisfy economic ends. Nor, however, is it the right thing *not* to take this money: responsibility, independence and financial management skills have to be encouraged, and how else is this to be done?

There is something of a dilemma here, for parents in particular. Moral imperatives appear to play an important – perhaps even a pre-eminent – role in financial transactions between parents and their unemployed offspring. The symbolic load upon the exchanges between the generations in this respect is important. Even in those families where, in purely economic terms, it was not strictly necessary to exact a contribution from the unemployed family member, it was generally seen to be the 'right' thing to do anyway. There are two, potentially contradictory, themes which can be teased out of our material in this respect.

In the first place, parents may be anxious that their sons or daughters should not be deprived – or *too* deprived – as a result of their unemployment. Clearly this will depend upon a number of factors, such as their economic circumstances and the manner in which they explain their child's unemployment (about which more will be said in Chapter 6). That notwithstanding, we have much evidence from our interviews to support Leonard's finding that in general many parents in South Wales 'spoil' their young adult children, in an attempt to 'keep them close' and prevent them from leaving home (Leonard 1980: 61-5). Claire Wallace has, however, come up with broadly similar findings from the Isle of Sheppey (Wallace 1987: 94-7). In her material this subsidy is specifically in the context of youth unemployment. Where a family could afford support of this kind, it seems that the young person was more able to maintain an active social life and avoided the worst psychological effects of unemployment.

Returning to our material, sometimes this support may take the form of accepting only a token sum, such as five pounds for example, for the young person's 'keep' or 'lodge'. Ten pounds was the average weekly lodge payment for an unemployed son or daughter in the families we looked at, the same figure as Coffield and his colleagues report for north-eastern England (Coffield *et al.* 1986: 125-6). In other cases, parents may simply buy some of the young person's necessities, particularly clothes or items such as cigarettes, razor blades, sanitary towels or tampons, which could easily be absorbed into the overall housekeeping budget. Another tactic for cushioning the impact of unemployment is either giving or 'lending' the daughter or son extra money whenever their benefit runs out. As in (37), above, it is often explicitly recognised that, in this respect, what is happening is that the parents – usually the mother – are saving the money they are given as 'lodge', only to give some or all of it back later in the fortnightly cycle of benefit payments. Such is the difficulty which may surround these transfers, that sometimes they are shrouded in attempted, if not real, secrecy, as in (41).

The second concern which parents have is that their children should learn how to handle money. This has two aspects, the pragmatic and the moral, both of which meet, however, in the notion of 'adult' behaviour. Pragmatically, it is important that young people should learn how to manage money, how to budget. This is an important aspect of the transition to adulthood. The young woman or man should learn the independent, 'sensible' way to manage their finances, as one of the major practical accomplishments bound up with being an adult. It is necessary for them to have not only their own ingoings – benefit, in this case – but also their own outgoings, their 'lodge'. The attempt to foster as much independence as possible is another reason for restricting the amount of subsidy the young person receives, as 'loans' or whatever. The contrast between 'good' and 'bad' managers can be seen in the examples below.

(42)
Well she's a sensible girl [her daughter, Rebecca] as far as money's concerned. She can work out her money and live on her money. She's penny-pinching. She can't have what she wants. She's not had a lot of things since she's had the baby ... Like every mother should be, she [Rebecca's infant daughter] comes first. She's a good manager, she'll do very well. But it's so frustrating for her. She knows she can do better.

(Mrs Rosemary Hughes, Abbeyview)

(43)
I buy all his [her son, Hugh's] clothes, and it's, 'Lend me a pound here and there mum?', but I never get it back. He gives me his twenty pounds [fortnightly lodge money] and he thinks he's paid me back ... Before Christmas, he had no money to buy Christmas presents, so I bought some for him ... He must owe me about two hundred pounds altogether. Before Christmas he was paying me a fiver [weekly lodge], but since then he's been giving me ten, to pay it off, or so he thinks ... He's got to learn that you just can't keep taking money off me without giving something back. He's giving me twenty pounds every fortnight, hoping I'll give him ten pounds back, but I don't. I know he'll get it back by the end of the fortnight anyway.

(Mrs Diana Reynolds, High Oak)

The pragmatic side of money management is, at least in part, to do with household economics. To quote Mrs Georgina Griffiths of Ty-Gwyn, talking about her eldest son, Matthew, 'It puts pressures on our finances as well as his'. Mrs Doreen Preece of High Oak put the problem into sharp focus:

(44)
DP: He gives me five pounds a week.
RJ: Does he ever get money from you?
DP: Five pounds last week for his darts, because I felt sorry for him. Not regularly ... Oh no! Oh God ...//... he seems to manage on it very well, but, of course, *I* lost his maintenance and his family allowance ... I make up for it because I go out to work.

The three ethnographic extracts above illustrate the difficulty – experienced by the parents concerned and by us as researchers – in clearly distinguishing the moral from the pragmatic in this context. The domestic or household economy is also a moral economy, a system of symbolic transactions. Words such as 'sensible' are laden with a variety of meanings. The notions of reciprocity and fairness which are invoked, either implicitly or explicitly, are clear enough. It is equally clear that one feature of adulthood – which sons or daughters have to learn to accept, just as their parents did before them – is that the seemingly unlimited horizons of youthful aspirations and demands must be set aside in the knowledge that you can't always get what you want. Many people never do, falling perpetually short of even the modest satisfaction of their needs.

There is, therefore, a notion of 'fairness' – in this context between family members – bound up in the handling of money in an adult fashion, as encapsulated in the notion of 'independence'. This has also been documented by Allatt and Yeandle in their study of youth unemployment and family life in north-eastern England (Allatt and Yeandle 1986: 108–10). While recognising that there are limits to the pursuit of independence for a young person living at home on a low income, many of our parents were concerned that their son or daughter should learn 'the value of money', both to themselves and, crucially, *to other people*, particularly their parents and siblings.

The parental desire to cushion the young person from the worst economic deprivations of unemployment may often sit uneasily beside the attempt to encourage independence and a knowledge of the 'value of things'. It is a real moral dilemma, experienced as such by many parents. Here, for example, is Hugh Reynolds' mother again, talking about her problems in trying to ensure that he does not 'go without':

(45)
Anybody would want to, if they were a good parent ... But you've got
to try and teach him the value of money, and how to manage it, on the
other hand.

Several parents felt in addition that their children would be driven into
employment by their need for money. One father, for example, felt that if
he made things too comfortable for his 20-year-old son, he would never
look for a job. As he said, 'I keep him a bit hungry'.

There is thus created something of a moral ambiguity for many of these
parents: how to provide for their sons and daughters in what they regard by
their lights, as the 'proper' fashion, without pampering them and
undermining their, difficult enough, assumption of adulthood? How to
provide support, without breeding dependence and encouraging apathy and
sloth? This is the difficult balancing act which many parents see themselves
facing.

There are a number of solutions to the problem, none of them perfect.
Reductions in 'lodge', or small extra financial subventions, may, for
example, be justified as exchanges for jobs done or services performed
about the house. Alternatively, gifts in kind, particularly of clothes, seem to
be more acceptable, because they are not cash transactions. These may be
explained away as 'presents' or 'extras'. An interesting variation on this
theme is the increased significance which 'Christmas and birthdays' have
come to assume for some of the young people we interviewed. These are
occasions, clearly marked as special and out of the ordinary, upon which it
is morally defensible for economic exchanges, whether in cash or in kind
to take place between parents and their unemployed children. Such
transfers are, indeed, *required* for the proper fulfilment of the parental role.

Returning briefly to the subject of deprivation and expectations, it is clear
from our data that both are relative with respect to gender. Fairly
predictably, given the well-attested fact that women are generally paid less
than men (Martin and Roberts 1984: 43–6), many of our informants – both
parents and young people – felt that young men need more money than
young women do when it comes to 'going out' and meeting the opposite sex,
and therefore, suffer greater deprivation as a consequence of their
unemployment. Similar views have been reported by Allatt and Yeandle
from the North-East (Allatt and Yeandle 1986: 104). We will look at the
topic further in the next chapter when we discuss courtship and marriage.

We have already suggested that there are likely to be differences between
our study areas with respect to local perceptions of needs and material
expectations. This is one of the most obvious senses in which deprivation
can be said to be relative. If it is the case that the threshold beyond which
deprivation is subjectively experienced by unemployed young people is
lower in Ty-Gwyn than in Abbeyview, for example, this might help to

explain why there are higher levels of conflict in the former area even though the families there are, in absolute terms, more affluent.

Despite the devices which we have described for the resolution of the problem, it is apparent from our interview material that the moral dilemma concerning financial transfers between parents and children is not easily solved. The internal moral economy of the family is not just, or even mainly concerned with money. Goods and, possibly most important of all, services are also involved. This latter, domestic labour and housework, is the subject of the next section.

Housework and the domestic division of labour

Housework is, by and large, *women's* work. Day-to-day observation and research evidence (Gavron 1966; Myrdal and Klein 1968; Oakley 1974a, 1974b) both insist that this is the case. The organisation of domestic work is embedded in an emotional division of labour in which women are categorised as more 'warm' and 'caring' – and, incidentally, less 'rational' – than men (Finch and Groves 1983). Housework is an important – perhaps, in fact, the *most* important – dimension of the public social role of 'wife' and 'mother': cooking, cleaning, washing, sewing, ironing or whatever. The production of an acceptable domestic environment, for external as well as internal presentation and consumption, is 'what women do'. This extends, what is more, to daughters (Coffield *et al*. 1986: 63–8; Griffin 1985: 36–43; Thorogood 1987; Wallace 1987: 97). In addition, an important part of the female domestic role, particularly as wife and mother, is bound up with the socialisation of children and the provision of emotional support. This is something to which we will return in the closing section of this chapter.

Men, of course, also do work in the household. It is, however, work of a particular kind, and they generally do less of it. 'Real' work for men is typically employment, carried on away from the household, whereas women, because their 'real' work is domestic, remain responsible for housework whether they are in employment or not. Men's household work (for it would not, strictly speaking, be accurate to call it housework), as conventionaly construed in South Wales, includes such things as house maintenance, fixing the car and vegetable growing. Evidence from other research for example, suggests that, as one might expect, this applies both to young men and to other parts of Britain (Henwood *et al*. 1987: 9–18; Youth Review Team 1985: 102–3). The gendered division of domestic labour is, of course, informed by and informs wider social definitions of gender roles, particularly those which are bound up with the occupational segregation of the labour market into male and female jobs (Dex 1985; Hakim 1979).

It must be recognised, however, that the 'traditional' gendered division of domestic labour is a statistical norm. Not all households are organised in this fashion. As Pahl's research in the Isle of Sheppey has convincingly demonstrated, there is a range of variation with respect to the distribution of household tasks between men and women (Pahl 1984: 254–76). Some similar findings have been reported from the United States (e.g. Lein 1984; Pleck 1984). Changes in women's consciousness and in the nature of socially acceptable gender roles have had an effect, albeit small and in differing degrees, upon the allocation and performance of household responsibilities. It might also be thought that increased female labour-market participation and chronic male unemployment would contribute to a renegotiation of the domestic division of labour in favour of women. This indeed has been suggested by Laite and Halfpenny (1987) on the basis of research in Macclesfield and Bolton. However, the majority of relevant studies – including research carried out in Port Talbot – suggests that male unemployment does not in fact lead to a more egalitarian distribution of household duties, much less the assumption by men of the major responsibility in this respect (Clark 1987; Harris *et al*. 1987: 169–72; Hartley 1987; Henwood and Miles 1987; Jackson and Walsh 1987; Morris 1985a). Housework is apparently no substitute, for men, for *real* work.

How was housework organised by the families we looked at? At one level, our material reveals a very conventional scene indeed: women did the housework. What is interesting, however, is *which* women. Although it is certainly the case that the unemployed young women we interviewed did more about the house than their male peers, most of them actually did very little. The unemployment of young people, whether male or female, does little to relieve the domestic burden on 'mam'. In this respect our material indicates, once again, that little has apparently changed since Diana Leonard's research in Swansea in the late 1960s (Leonard 1980: 57–60). Seventeen (61 per cent) of the unemployed young women and eighteen (38 per cent) of the unemployed young men about whom we have information appeared to do *some* work about the house. With a small number of conspicuous exceptions, often rooted in specific circumstances such as the death or absence of one or both parents, this contribution to the housework was, as we shall illustrate below, minor and sometimes done with a bad grace:

(46)
RJ: Does Audrey do any work around the house?
VB: Oh no ... that's the gospel truth [something which Audrey confirmed in her own interview].
RJ: Has she ever done any work around the house?
VB: No. If she came in by here, and she'd say ... she might do it, she would, would you like a cup of tea? That's all ... But I'd have to ask her.

(Mr Victor Ballinger, Abbeyview)

(47)

SH: Do you do any work about the house?

EP: My mother would say no ... I do my bedroom. My bedroom's a mess. I wash dishes. I should do more to be honest. I wipe up. The usual things.

SH: Not regularly?

EP: No.

(Elaine Peters, Abbeyview)

(48)

He [her son, Malcolm Rees] keeps where he's been clean ... Now he's inclined to take his cup and wash it, since he left home. I was surprised to see him cooking.

(Mrs Gwyneth Lynch, High Oak)

(49)

HR: I tidy the bedroom, make the beds. Then I have breakfast and wash my own dishes. I polish, Hoover, do the washing ... everyone's clothes. I do it two or three times a week, in the twin tub, I have to stand over it.

SH: And in the afternoon?

HR: I do ironing, knitting, watch television.

(Helen Roderick, High Oak)

As Helen Roderick makes clear, some young people we spoke to did make a sizeable contribution to the housework, particularly young women. As is equally clear from the other quotations, however, many did not. In Chapter 2 we described conflict about 'personal relationships' and 'life-styles'. Housework, done or undone, was often a contributory factor in disputes or tension of this nature. The quotations below from our interviews with the Anderson family of Ty-Gwyn are an illustration of such conflict. They are also a good example of something we have noticed in other contexts, the gulf which may exist between the perceptions of the same situation by different family members. First of all, then, Steve Anderson:

(50)

SH: Do you do much about the house?

SA: Not a lot. Mainly ... when Dad was off he did and he was glad to do it, because he wasn't really engaged in anything else ... I will probably have to do more now that he's at work. We haven't really evolved any new routine to cope with the new situation.

SH: Do you keep your bedroom tidy?

SA: After my fashion. We don't row over it so much now. We used to row over it a lot ... The big problem is the airing cupboard is in my room, so she comes in all the time and sees it ... It often has a lot of junk lying around, books, papers.

Compare this with, in particular, his mother's view of the situation:

(51)
Mrs Hilda Anderson: He does absolutely nothing.
SH: Does he make his bed?
HA: No.
Mr Alun Anderson: Don't say 'never'.
HA: Well, if we have a row ... He doesn't do the sheet underneath, he
    just pulls the duvet up.
SH: Does he tidy his room?
HA: Only under protest.
SH: And Hoovering!
HA: What's a Hoover?
SH: What about shopping?
HA: He will go over the local shop.
SH: And the main shopping?
HA: No, no. We wouldn't particularly want him to.
SH: Does it ever cause rows?
HA: It has sometimes. When I've come home tired.
AA: It does with his mother, not with me.

It is tempting to read into evidence such as this more than one perhaps
should: the concern with physical cleanliness and symbolic boundaries, the
attempt to maintain order, the struggle over what counts as adequate
tidiness ('my fashion'), the mother's control over the definition of
adequacy in this respect. What *is* certain, however, is that domestic work,
like money, can be a potent focus of conflict.

There is a dilemma here too, this time particularly for the mother. It was
obvious to us that many of the mothers to whom we spoke did not really
want their children to do much housework. That was *their* responsibility, an
important aspect of their identity, and one which they were not yet prepared
to abdicate. Daughters and, particularly, sons were likely to do it wrong,
without sufficient care, sloppily. Fathers could also take a similar view with
respect to their, more limited, sphere of domestic activity. One father, for
example, told us that his son would do the painting and decorating if he was
allowed to, but that he was worried about 'drips of paint everywhere'. As a
result the father did it himself. Echoes of a similar situation can be heard in
extract (17) in Chapter 2.

On the other hand, however, sons and daughters could not be permitted
to laze around the house doing nothing either. A routine had to be kept.
They had to do something with their day. They could not be allowed to get
used to doing nothing, to get out of the habit of working. Between the horns
of this particular dilemma, between the encouragement and the discourage-
ment, lies both a source of conflict and its possible solution, something we
will discuss in the section following.

Looking at housework immediately brings gender differences into the spotlight. We have already seen that with respect to domestic work, while the young women did more than the young men, neither, in fact, did very much. What, however, about gender difference within the household with respect to other matters?

We began the research with the conventional expectation that gender would be one of the most important factors structuring the lives of unemployed young people and their parents: 'commonplace relations, experiences and representations of youth are quite crucially related to questions of the masculine and the feminine' (McRobbie and Nava 1984: ix). And, in one sense, this remains our view. However, what is interesting is the fact that gender relations are not uniformly important in all situations. The important questions then become: *which* gender relations, *how* important, and in *what* contexts?

Within the family of origin we were particularly surprised to observe that, in many important respects, it was the similarity in the parent's treatment of young women and young men which was most striking. Some notions of gender equality – and we stress, *notions*, not necessarily actual practices – were current in many of the households which we visited. Daughters and sons were generally seen to have similar kinds of needs in terms of their finding a job, their moral standards, their friends, having a good time, and their need of love and security. Nor, in so far as we can tell, are there major gender differences with respect to attitudes to money and its handling or to attitudes towards leaving home. The major exception in this respect, which we mentioned earlier and which we will examine in detail in a subsequent chapter, concerns financial needs with respect to courtship and 'going out'.

It must be remembered, talking about leaving home, that the study was concerned primarily with families where long-term unemployed young adults were living with their parents. As a consequence, we have probably, for example, missed those young women, who, if Christine Griffin's findings are at all representative (Griffin 1985: 48–9), leave the home in the wake of violence or other forms of abuse, typically at the hands of their fathers.

Our experience, then, is that within these families it was personality characteristics – as attributed and interpreted by family members – rather than gender stereotypes which appeared to be most influential in determining the quality of relations between parents and their unmarried children. This, however, is not to suggest that gender was *never* relevant. Far from it: as we have seen, the daughters we interviewed generally contributed more, for example, than their brothers to the domestic labour needs of the household. We have also speculated in the previous chapter about a gendered 'division of conflict' within the families we studied. Further dimensions of the salience of gender in these young people's lives will be discussed, as appropriate, in subsequent chapters.

In many of the families we looked at, there were apparent conflicts which may be impressionistically described as more or less severe. In many others there were less serious tensions, but tensions none the less. We have discussed this in detail in Chapter 2. The presence of conflict is, of course, not in itself particularly unusual in families with adolescent or young adult members. Unemployment certainly contributes to the severity of family conflict, but we do not think is it likely to actually *cause* it in most cases. We have already suggested that a degree of conflict within families – sometimes a considerable degree – must in some senses be conceptualised as within the normal distribution of possibilities.

Conflict is, perhaps, all the more to be expected if *some* notions of gender equality are current at the level of day-to-day life within the families in question. Such egalitarian ideas are likely to be at considerable variance with another set of notions, largely taken-for-granted and historically deep-seated, concerning male roles, rights and responsibilities. In Chapter 4 we shall examine this contradiction in so far as it affects courtship strategies and marriage. In the next section of this chapter we will examine some of the ways in which the families in our samples attempted to cope with or resolve conflict.

The limitation and control of conflict

What are the implications of adopting, as we have in this discussion, a view of domestic life and family relationships in which harmony is not accepted as the taken-for-granted normal state? From such a perspective, relatively harmonious co-existence is not something which just happens. It must be actively produced by family members, it is an emergent property of the practices of family members. Perhaps the most important practices from our point of view are those which are aimed at the prevention or amelioration of tension and disharmony. It is possible, on reviewing our interview material, to identify a number of strategies for the limitation of conflict.

Basic to our understanding of these strategies is the notion of *domestic bargaining*. In many of the families we looked at, a bargain is being struck between the generations within the household. 'Good behaviour' on the part of the son or the daughter is exchanged for a measure of greater independence. One of the best illustrations we have of this is a quotation from a young woman, the eldest of two daughters – both unemployed and living with their father – who were interviewed as part of the pilot study but were not included in the final samples:

(52)
As long as I do my bit, I can come and go as I please ... Before, when I did nothing, relations were bad. Now I do my bit, it's okay.

As we have seen in the previous section, and as implied in (52), domestic work is an important element in these unspoken contracts betwen parents and children. Precisely because these bargains are typically struck implicitly, the possibility that one party to the contract – usually the son or daughter – may be unaware of its existence is a real one. Similarly, inasmuch as the criteria for the bargain's fulfilment are also likely to be implicit, and almost certainly vague and imprecise as well, the potential for disagreement is considerable. It is under these circumstances that contracts break down and conflict may result.

Implicit agreements can be detected with respect to conflict limitation as well. For example, it appears to be the case that in many families large issues, the sort of major problems which might lead to the serious disruption of family relationships, are avoided wherever possible. Petty issues become the focus of disagreements:

(53)
We row about silly things, nothing big.

(Alan Sweetman, High Oak)

(54)
Well ... I argue with my sister sometimes. Little things ... Alison mostly. She annoys me sometimes, like ... I annoy her.

(Chris Bishop, Ty-Gwyn)

We are not suggesting that this is necessarily a conscious strategy for minimising tension (although it may be). It is, however, related to something which we have already discussed: the significance of what conflict is called – the distinction, for example, between a 'row', a 'disagreement' and a 'tiff' – for the manner in which it is handled and the interactional construction of it as experience. Niceties of this kind are another important dimension of conflict limitation, and they indicate another kind of bargain, an agreement over definitions and appropriate words.

Something else to which we have alluded, both in this chapter and in Chapter 2, is the role of symbolic gestures, with particular respect to financial transactions and housework. If money is lent, it is important that the son or daughter should at least *offer* repayment. Some *attempt* should at least be made to make the bed or Hoover the living room. In both cases parents, in particular, are caught in a double bind. In the case of money, there is a contradition between the wish to protect one's own from hardship, on the one hand, and the attempt to prevent the work ethic being undermined by spoiling, on the other. With respect to housework, mothers may find themselves expecting that unemployed daughters and sons should do *something*, rather than 'lazing around the house all day' (once again it is the work ethic which is at issue here). On the other hand, however, if they do *too* much, then the boundaries of the mother's domestic role and identity may be transgressed.

Between the one hand and the other there is, in each case, a potential for conflict. Equally, however, therein may also be found a solution to the problem. This is where the symbolic gesture, the token offering in the realm of appearances, comes into its own. What is important is not so much what is done, as what is *seen* to be done. It is another aspect of domestic bargaining: a calculus of expectation and offering, the creation and maintenance of a fiction. Like most such fictions, however, if explicitly acknowledged the effect would be spoiled. It must therefore remain tacit, an exercise in mutual confidence (in both of the word's meanings).

Inasmuch as the situations which we have been discussing are bargains, and generally implicit bargains at that, they may be broken, misunderstood or one-sided. This is all the more so since, within the family's hierarchy of age relations, it is typically parents who are in a position to define the canons of acceptability and appropriateness, the rules of the game which set the limits and procedures within which the deal is done. Control of family relationships is at stake here. Once again this process is likely to be largely implicit, which is where sons and daughters may find themselves in a double bind, failing to satisfy conditions or demands of which they are insufficiently, if at all, aware. In some situations, therefore, attempts to minimise conflict may actually contribute to its exacerbation. A failed attempt to keep the peace may be more painful than no attempt at all.

There are, perhaps, other bargains or agreements which are more open, if not necessarily more easily struck. In particular, as young people get older, more autonomy is granted to them by their parents in specific areas of their lives. This is emphatically not something which is peculiar to the young unemployed – indeed, it is for most young people a process which begins some time before school-leaving – but it is, none the less, of importance in this context as a further means of reducing tension. It is, however, something which is perhaps best understood as an aspect of the transition to adulthood generally. We will, therefore, discuss it further in Chapter 5.

Sometimes, of course, misunderstandings or tension cannot be successfully contained. Open and serious conflict is the usual result. Both words and punches may be thrown. Sometimes the upshot is that the young person either leaves home, or considers the possibility:

(55)
GW: I have thought of it several times. I went up to my sister's once after a row here with my father ... Not over anything special. I stayed 2 or 3 weeks.
SH: Why did you come back?
GW: Because of my mother. I know which side's my bread's buttered.
                                        (Geoffrey Wallis, Abbeyview)

(56)

DF: I have done [left home] ... Into a flat, house with two mates. Two years ago. I was there for a year. We were thrown out ... the landlord. We were drunk ... Council flat. This woman, she rented it. I don't know if she was allowed to.

SH: Did you leave home because of a row?

DF: Yeah ... lots and lots, and building up.

SH: Did you get on better when you were away?

DF: Yeah.

SH: And why did you come home?

DF: I had nowhere to go ... it was all right then. Now it's started again.

SH: Would you go again?

DF: If I could find a decent place.

(David Francis, Abbeyview)

(57)

SH: Why did you move out?

DF: It was lack of privacy for a start ... Me and my father were fighting. My mother was nagging me non-stop ... I just wanted to be on my own.

(Diana Fullerton, Ty-Gwyn)

In Chapter 2 we have already seen that the incidence and severity of reported conflict varies between our Abbeyview, High Oak and Ty-Gwyn samples. As can be seen from Table 3.1, this is also true with respect to attitudes towards, and experience of leaving home. On comparing Table 3.1 with Table 2.1, in which respondents' perceptions of conflict are compared by area, it is, however, clear that there is no straightforward correlation between them. For the High Oak sample the match is quite good. In Abbeyview, however, where only 18 per cent of respondents reported 'serious conflict', 57 per cent of the young people we interviewed had left home at some stage. In Ty-Gwyn, by way of a contrast, 37 per cent had left home but 46 per cent reported 'serious' conflict. How to explain, then, the apparently inverse relationship between leaving home and reported conflict in our Abbeyview and Ty-Gwyn samples? There are three likely (and complementary) reasons for this pattern in our data.

First, leaving home may actually be a means of limiting or ameliorating conflict. Getting out before things become unbearable, or in order to allow the temperature at home to cool down, may be the response of some young women and men to a difficult situation. A period of absence may allow the heart to grow fonder or provide the necessary distance to put matters in perspective. Thus a higher incidence of leaving home in Abbeyview may, in part, account for a lower level of perceived conflict.

Second, given that in many cases housing conditions are worse and families significantly more impoverished in Abbeyview, there may be less

Table 3.1 Young people's attitudes towards leaving home, by area (percentages in brackets)

	Never thought of leaving home	Thought of leaving home but had not done so	Had left home at some stage	n.
Abbeyview	4 (19)	5 (24)	12 (57)	21 (100)
High Oak	9 (39)	7 (30)	7 (30)	23 (100)
Ty-Gwyn	4 (21)	8 (42)	7 (37)	19 (100)
n.	17 (27)	20 (32)	26 (41)	63 (100)

there to hold sons or daughters in the home. It is certainly clear that many of the young people from Ty-Gwyn knew when they were materially well off. Sean Evans is a good example:

(58)
SH: Have you ever thought of leaving? Perhaps a flat in Swansea?
SE: Yeah.
SH: But you never have?
SE: No.
SH: Why not?
SE: It's so much of a hassle on the dole. You go down, find a flat, then get them to pay. A couple of my mates have got flats. I couldn't afford it anyway. You just don't get enough money.

Parents often subsidise their unemployed children, whether directly or indirectly. The subsidy in Ty-Gwyn may have been enough to keep more young people at home than in Abbeyview. Some parents were explicit that their subsidy was designed to achieve this end:

(59)
It would be a bad start. He would be on drugs, sleeping all day ...//... There's too much going for him. If he did not get on with us so well he might go.

(Mrs Anthea Roberts, Ty-Gwyn)

However, at the risk of adding more twists and turns to the analysis, the ambiguities surrounding money transfers and 'spoiling', combined with the fact that economic self-interest keeps more young people at home (and under their parents' feet) in Ty-Gwyn, may actually create conflict. There is, therefore, no necessary contradiction between higher levels of conflict and lower levels of leaving home. They may, in fact, be closely (and causally) connected.

Finally, and it is a related point, it must be remembered that there are reasons other than conflict for leaving home. This is particularly the case where there is economic hardship and/or poor housing conditions. The desirability of leaving home is, at the risk of stating the obvious, relative to the desirability of staying. Given such conditions young people may also, self-interest aside, see themselves as a burden which their parents can ill afford. Similarly, if local employment prospects are perceived as sufficiently bad moving away, which, by definition, means leaving home, may appear to be the only solution.

Diana Leonard, in the study to which we have already referred many times, found that in the 1960s nearly all young people in Swansea stayed in the parental home until they were married. As Table 3.1 demonstrates, however, things have changed since she did her fieldwork. It is likely that youth unemployment has been a catalyst in producing this change. Many of the young people to whom we spoke were – when explicitly asked about the issue – willing to leave the local area if a job and accommodation were available elsewhere. Only one that we know of, however – Audrey Ballinger from Abbeyview, who went to London shortly after being interviewed and is still, in July 1988, there – has subsequently found these conditions. Youth unemployment, however, is not the only factor influencing young people's decisions to stay at home or leave. There is an increasing amount of evidence to suggest that, for a number of reasons, more young people are leaving the parental home before marriage to set up independent households (Harris 1983: 219–22; Jones 1987). We will discuss the relationship between unemployment and changing family relationships in the next chapter.

Most of the parents to whom we spoke expressed strong feelings about young people leaving home. Most disapproved. Several mothers told us that they deliberately tried to avoid family arguments so that their sons and daughters would not be tempted to leave. Thus, the fear of the young person leaving may also serve to inhibit conflict.

Why do feelings about leaving home run so high? Part of what is being expressed here is the feeling of loss which a mother or father may often feel when a child leaves home. Here the situation is worse, however. In at least half of the twenty-six cases which we were told about, the departure of the young person had been precipitated by a row. Local cultural norms do not expect that an unmarried child should leave home before marriage. If they do, it is often taken as an indication of some breakdown in family relations. As our material suggests, in many cases such an interpretation is correct.

There may also be the fear that a young person, particularly if they are unemployed, will fall under the spell of an 'alternative' life-style, in which work and material goods have less importance than hedonism and the temptations of drugs and alcohol. Once in receipt of a social security housing allowance, some parents (and, in fact, some young people) fear that there will be less incentive to take a job. To set against this worry, however, we must also mention a small but not inconsiderable group of parents and young people who viewed leaving home as a good thing, easing family tensions, allowing the young person greater independence and constituting a definite step forward into adult life.

There is a dilemma between, on the one hand, providing protection for one's children and, on the other, granting or encouraging them independence, of which many parents will be aware. This dilemma is complicated by youth unemployment. Family tension may increase; it becomes more difficult for young people to attain satisfactory financial independence. These are additional problems, contributing to the age-old life-course pattern of families breaking up as new ones form.

Leaving home is therefore not a simple situation. It may have a number of causes or antecedent factors and be indicative of a number of family situations. Even where conflict is the reason for packing one's bags, we have argued that this conflict is also a complex of many different factors and problems. One relatively straightforward response to conflict, or approach to its limitation, which we have yet to discuss, is arbitration or 'peacemaking'. Where this happens it is typically the mother who is the mediator. It is to her role, in this and other respects, that we now turn in the final section of this chapter.

Mothers and family management

Money, gender relations and conflict management are topics which converge on the central role which mothers play in each. The mother is, to use a theatrical metaphor, the director (if not the producer) of the negotiated order of family relationships in many households. There is a considerable body of literature which discusses the role of wives and mothers in domestic management. With respect to financial responsibilities, it appears that the extent to which women have managerial authority above and beyond the weekly housekeeping budget is dependent upon overall household income levels and the employment and financial status of the woman herself. However, in low-income families – and many of the families in Abbeyview and, to a lesser extent, in High Oak, fell into this category – wives appear to have the most responsibility for making ends meet (Pahl 1980, 1983; Wilson 1987). Such authority as women do exercise with respect to the disposition of domestic budgets, and it may be considerable, exists – lone parents aside – in the context of a set of family power relations in which the husband or father is typically dominant in the economic domain.

Although male unemployment or increased female economic participation might be thought to undermine this state of affairs somewhat, we have already seen that there is a sizeable research literature which insists that the domestic division of labour, for example, remains largely undisturbed: women still have primary responsibility for housework. Nor is this aspect of the role of wife and mother challenged significantly, in the families we looked at, by the long-term unemployment of daughters and sons. However, it is clear from a number of research reports that women do assume a major responsibility for the management – both financial, social and psychological – of their husband or partner's unemployment (Clark 1987; Hartley 1987; McKee and Bell 1985; Morris 1985b; Popay 1985). To appropriate a memorable phrase coined by Lorna McKee and Colin Bell, *his* unemployment is *her* problem (McKee and Bell 1986).

In part, of course, this is an aspect of the more general role of women, particularly wives and mothers, as carers (Finch and Groves 1983). There is a gendered emotional division of labour which, in this respect underwrites the wider division of domestic labour and is bound up with the biological realities of pregnancy and birth and the subsequent social construction of childcare and primary socialisation.

The centrality of the mother's role as the source of care and emotional support in the households which we looked at became clear to us during the course of the research. The problem of the son or daughter's unemployment, for example, in all of its aspects – emotional, financial or whatever – is one with which 'mam' copes (just as she would if it was her husband who was on the dole, as, for some of the women we interviewed, it was). 'Dad' was often something of an enigma to us, a distant figure whose presence was felt even though he himself was not seen. Mothers were more willing to answer our questions, or felt more competent to do so, and they were a majority of the parents to whom we had access.

To a degree, this represents no more than a reflection of their 'normal' responsibility for the primary 'woman's work' of childcare. This extends, as other research evidence has made clear, to the management and organisation of important life-course transitions for sons and daughters; marriage is a good example and the mother's role is important (Leonard 1980: 33–4). However, it is also likely to be a function of the wife and mother's roles in the management of the domestic budget, on the one hand, and as the 'caring' one in general, on the other. In this sense it is similar, as we have seen, to the job which wives do in managing or coping with their husband's unemployment.

There is, in addition, a second aspect of the mother's familial role as the 'carer' which is relevant here. She is typically – although not always – the one who attempts to prevent family conflict, the person to whom sons and daughters are most likely to turn in situations of stress or tension. A mother is expected – and, indeed expects herself – to keep the family ticking over as smoothly as possible. Witness the following conversation with Mrs Elsie Wallis, mother of Geoffrey Wallis, from Abbeyview:

(60)
EW: Well I try and help him as much as I can. I break my heart for

him, mind. Because he's the one now who's been with us the longest
... Lionel and Claire [older siblings] now, they've got their own
families, haven't they? We are more concerned now with Geoffrey.

SH: Your husband?

EW: Well, they're both here [Mr Wallis is on an invalidity pension].
They are bound to get on one another's nerves ... Well, you can say,
for the last 6 years for him, not for me, it's been awful.

SH: Why not you?

EW: Because I love him. I wouldn't say 'Having him at home, it's
terrible'. Not for me. Well, I'm his mother aren't I?

Even in the absence of the father, a mother could see her responsibility as
lying in managing her *own* relationships with an unemployed child. Take,
for example, Mrs Mason of Ty-Gwyn:

(61)

SH: How did you react to Kenneth's unemployment?

Mrs M: In the beginning it really did get on my nerves. And my nerves
are not very good as it is. But now we've got the added problem that
there's no father [Mr Mason died 4 years before]. There's a sadness
about it. So I've got a good temperament, being a nurse. That has
helped. So we, how can I say? ... Don't get in each other's way but
we go about our own little jobs. Some days I do get irritable,
especially if I'm doing night work. I say, 'Please go out'. All in all, if
I can pat myself on the shoulder, we get on very well.

Sociologists are not much given to talking about the emotions. Notions such
as 'love' and 'affection' are little in evidence, for example, in recent
sociological studies of the family (or, if they are, they are largely
characterised as ideology). If, however, we are to take seriously what our
informants say – and we should – we must recognise that love and affection
are important threads in the weft and warp of family relationships. Nor are
we particularly well placed to dismiss them as ideology.

   We are not, of course, suggesting that only mothers take care to manage
their relationships with their children. Nor, thank goodness, do women
have a monopoly on the more tender emotions. However, within the
conventional set of expectations which our culture provides for men and
women, it is the latter who are the designated carers. Most men, given the
presence of an appropriate woman, will withdraw from the public display
of tenderness or affection towards their adult or adolescent children.

   This brings us to the conflict which may exist between parents, and to the
other set of emotions which play an important part in the experience of
family life: hurt, hate and unhappiness. As Robert Connell has argued,
apparently incompatible emotional forces may not, in fact, be so: 'love is a

project that can be interwoven with the project of oppression' (Connell 1987: 216). Intervention on behalf of a son or daughter may be part of a wider pattern of conflict between a mother and a father, it may even cause it.[2] This is what seemed to be happening in the Reynolds family from High Oak, as illustrated by quotation (15) in Chapter 2.

Moving on from the mother's role as arbiter and carer, we have seen that, so far as housework is concerned, the significance of gender divisions for these young people was less than we have anticipated. However, this apparent (relative) equality largely reflects the centrality within the parental generation of a gendered division of domestic work. The fact that many of the young women we interviewed do little, if any, housework, is a function of its nearly total monopolisation by their mothers. One of the families from the pilot study illustrates well the unequal division of effort between working mothers and unemployed daughters. The mother described her daughter's day:

(62)
... she'll help round the house, do some of her hand washing. She's bored by midday. She does sometimes cook my lunch. She has a snack. This afternoon she'll go swimming. If Karen's off or Helen's home, she'll do Helen's hair.

Although partly domestic in its orientation, the daughter's day compares favourably with her mother's domestic commitments, which centre around the provision of food. After going out at lunchtime to supervise school dinners, her mother also goes out to clean the same school just before tea time. Her husband, who works shifts, prefers to have a main meal near midday whenever possible. The daughter and her boyfriend have their main meal, however, at five o'clock. During the interview the mother was cooking some chicken in a casserole for herself and her husband's midday meal. This was then to be turned into a different dish later for the daughter and her boyfriend's tea.

From our material, it can be seen that gender and generation interact within the family to produce a complicated hierachy of obligation and duty, on the one hand, and indulgence, on the other. The apparent gender equality of the young woman within the household – relative to her male siblings or peers – is likely to be as much a function of her position in the life-course as a reflection of 'new' notions about gender roles. She is, in a sense, 'on holiday' from her destiny as a woman. The indulged independent South Wales girl of 1987 will almost certainly, on becoming a wife and/or mother, assume the role of subordinate domestic worker and carer. She may also have to find employment in order to help make ends meet. Correspondingly, as a 'male breadwinner' in a family, a young man is likely to have a control over his life and that of his wife that, as a younger man, he would probably have neither expected or wanted over his sister's.

In Chapters 2 and 3 we have discussed a number of issues which are more or less related within the families we looked at. Conflict, for example, comes in many forms and degrees. Unemployment and money, themselves closely related, are inextricably bound up with family conflict. It is not, however, our view that conflict is often *caused* by unemployment, although it is obviously impossible to assert this with anything other than limited confidence. The patterns of causality of conflict within families are sufficiently tortuous to inspire circumspection in our conclusions in this respect.

None the less, we have little doubt that unemployment, particularly in the long-term, is an important strand in the multiplex relationships of conflict within the families we looked at. However, the problems posed for families by youth unemployment are embedded within, and in our view partly arise out of, an existing history of conflict or its absence. Marie Jahoda has argued that the effects of unemployment and its meaning for individuals can only properly be understood in the context of the experience and meaning of work and employment for those individuals (Jahoda 1982). Something similar can be said about family relationships and unemployment (Marsden and Duff 1975). The impact of unemployment upon such relationships in any particular case is best understood in the context of the family's psychological and social history and its present circumstances.

The family of origin is not, however, the only important set of family relationships for young people. This is also the period in their lives when they are beginning, if they have not already begun, to take the first steps towards establishing an independent family of their own. This process, courtship and marriage, is the subject of the next chapter.

| 4 |

COURTSHIP AND MARRIAGE

'The family in Britain is changing – in some respects quite dramatically.' Most readers will agree with this view, the opening sentence of a recent report entitled *Values and the Changing Family* (Study Commission on the Family 1982: 6). According to the report's authors, the most important of these changes are increased divorce, a concomitant rise in the numbers of single-parent families, shifts in the role and consciousness of women, a growing trend of remarriage and the greater popularity and acceptability of cohabitation outside marriage. They might also have added a small but definite rise in the age at which people marry, after a long period during which this had declined steadily (Harris 1983: 205–6).

We are not concerned with the full range of this broad spectrum of social change. Instead, we will concentrate upon three particular aspects of family life – or, more exactly, aspects of the process of family *formation* – courtship, marriage and cohabitation. The general problem which we have set ourself concerns the impact of the long-term unemployment of young people upon that process. We will start by establishing a baseline against which we can compare our research findings.

Love and marriage in South Wales

One of the most fortunate aspects of doing research into aspects of family life in the Swansea area is that there is a wealth of comparative material available from other research studies.[1] The first of these studies, deriving from the work of the Department of Research in Social Studies at the University College of Swansea between 1949 and 1953 has, however, only a little to say about such matters. For example, we learn that in 1939 in South Wales, a higher proportion of women were married than was the case nationally and that there was a 'relative scarcity' of women over 20 years of age: 'unless they married locally females left the area, presumably to work elsewhere' (Brennan and Cooney 1950: 14). This particular demographic pattern was presumed to result from a shortage of employment possibilities for women in an area dominated by mining and heavy industry.

After the war, however, industrial change in the region produced changes in gender relations (Brennan, Cooney and Pollins 1954: 3–8). A decline in the long-established metal manufacturing industry – the modernisation of steel production, in particular – and an influx of light industry undermined to a degree the 'traditional' model of 'men's work' and offered more employment and higher wages for women. In addition to a 'lowering of men's status in the community', these changes – in concert with broader, national social changes – led to generational conflict between parents and their young adult offspring, particularly their daughters. The foci of this conflict were life-style patterns, such as smoking and drinking in pubs, which were in sharp contrast to established standards of chapel-going 'respectability'. With respect to marriage, it is suggested that, whereas previously marriage had represented a sharp experiential break for women ('the chance to manage a home of her own with more money each week than she had previously handled in half a year'), it was increasingly true that women who worked before they married experienced marriage as something less than a new-found sphere of responsibility and relative independence.

Our next source of comparative information is Rosser and Harris's well-known *The Family and Social Change* (1965). With respect to courtship, perhaps their most important finding is that, whereas before the war the typical pattern was for relationships and marriages to be established and contracted within a very narrow locality – often focusing around a place of employment or chapel – during the late 1950s and early 1960s, when their research was carried out, these courtship patterns were becoming less predominant (*ibid.*: 239–49). Young people were increasingly meeting and marrying partners from elsewhere in Swansea, if not from outside the city altogether. This was related to the growing importance of the city centre as a place of employment and entertainment. There was also evidence to suggest that, in conjunction with a changing occupational structure and improved education, courtship and marriage were increasingly taking place across boundaries of class, religion, culture (i.e. language) and ethnicity.

Having tied the knot, the newly-weds in Rosser and Harris's account faced a problem which remains depressingly familiar today: housing, then as now, was in short supply (*ibid.*: 249–62). The majority ended up living, at least for a while, with parents, most usually the bride's parents. This was a pattern which had become more marked since the end of the war and represented a significant change from the 1920s and 1930s. In the process of social reorientation which followed marriage, it was typically the wife's kin group who became most important and the wife's relationship with her mother which exercised the strongest pull.

The social and affective strength of the mother–daughter relationship has been underlined by many studies of urban kinship in other contexts (e.g. Stack 1974; Young and Willmott 1957). It is also a central thread of the next Swansea study which we shall look at, Leonard's *Sex and*

Generation (1980). Specifically an examination of courtship and marriage practices in the late 1960s, Leonard's material provides the most direct point of comparison for the discussion of our interview material in the rest of this chapter.

At the risk of doing some injustice to the richness of Leonard's ethnography and the subtleties of the analysis, her conclusions may be summarised thus. For the young people of Swansea in 1968 and 1969, particularly for the young women, courtship (with the eventual, and not too distant, goal of marriage) was the dominant concern of their lives during the three to five years after leaving school. The process of finding a suitable mate and marrying was bound up with a complex of notions concerning 'moral decorousness' (*ibid.*: 256). Sexuality was only acceptably expressed within marriage (*ibid.*: 71); considerable stigma attached to unmarried pregnancy, which almost inevitably led quickly to the Register Office (*ibid.*: 102-5). There was a clear preference for 'white' weddings in church (*ibid.*: 115-17), one of the central components of an elaborate ritual cycle of prestation and counter-prestation between the two kin groups involved.

Parents, particularly mothers, often liked to spoil their young adult sons and daughters, with an eye to 'keeping them close' (*ibid.*: 50). It was almost unheard of for young people to leave home prior to marriage (*ibid.*: 61). If a son or daughter did leave home for single independence this was often viewed as a social failure – the breakdown of family relationships or an admission of the young woman or man's inability to successfully find a marriage partner. Marriage, then, was typically the route to housing independence; the majority of couples moved into 'a place of their own', whether rented or bought (*ibid.*: 51, 229). The new marital home was, however, typically relatively close to both sets of parents (*ibid.*: 238). The closest ties to remain, however, were those existing between mothers and daughters (*ibid.*: 239-41).

One of the key influences on the couple's living standard and the kind of accommodation they could afford was the nature of the courtship process; whether or not resources had been accumulated in an orderly and planned progression from engagement to marriage. The entry into adulthood was inextricably bound up with marriage; for men, in particular, this depended upon the assumption of the full adult wage in their early twenties (*ibid.*: 48). Marriage was taken for granted; it was a question of *when* not *if* (*ibid.*: 73). Getting married was axiomatically accepted as an inexorable fact of life. Not to marry was seen as a failure in the living of one's life.

Finally, an enduring theme of Leonard's analysis is the asymmetrical power relationship between men and women, both before and after marriage. Inasmuch as young women were paid lower wages than young men, they were willing to be 'paid for' during courtship; this indeed was an expectation (*ibid.*: 48). During courtship there was a gradual dropping off of the young woman's participation in her peer group, although the young man maintained his 'mates' (*ibid*.: 79–86).[2] This pattern continued after the wedding. Women were in effect barred from many areas of social life: going to the pub, for example, without a male escort (*ibid*.: 88). More generally it was simply taken for granted that, in courtship and in the marriage, it was the men who would take the initiative in decision-making (*ibid*.: 107).

So much, then, for our summary of Leonard's conclusions. In this chapter and the chapter which follows, we will be particularly concerned to discuss issues such as decision-making and financial arrangements in courtship relations, the 'balance of power' with respect to gender, attitudes to sex, cohabitation and marriage and the identification of marriage with adulthood.

Although Diana Leonard's research was undertaken in the late 1960s, the major published account of her findings did not appear until 1980. She argues (*ibid*.: 39) that the results remain none the less representative, in most important respects, of both Swansea and urban Britain in general. Leonard suggests two exceptions to this claim which are, for our purposes, significant: (a) a degree of sexual freedom or licence is now acceptable within 'committed' relationships, and (b) there has been a slight rise in the average age at marriage, with children being born later. The second trend she relates to a more depressed economic climate.

We have already seen, in Chapter 3, that there are clear-cut differences between Leonard's data, from the late 1960s, and ours, from the mid-1980s, with respect to young people leaving home. While the pattern of our material related to leaving home is clearly conditioned by our focus upon unemployed young people, we are confident that it also accurately reflects an important shift in attitudes in this respect.

Another shift since the period which Leonard has documented can be seen in Table 4.1. Had the pattern which she reports (*ibid*.: 72–3) remained in place unchanged, one might have expected, even allowing for unemployment, to find a greater proportion of steady relationships and engagements in a sample of young people the great majority of whom were over 18 years of age. The picture portrayed in Table 4.1 is, of course, in general accord with the earlier remarks about a rise in the age at marriage since the 1960s. Although it would be possible to break the figures down to provide finer comparisons by age and gender, we have decided, in the light of the small size of the sample and the correspondingly small number of cases per cell, not to do this. Nor is it possible to decide how representative our sample is in this respect, given the absence of comparative information about employed young people. Our results are, of course, coloured by the fact that this is overwhelmingly a sample of young women and men who are still living in the parental home. Suffice it to say that the evidence of Table 4.1 indicates that many of the young people who we interviewed appear to be less involved in courtship and marriage than their equivalents of 20 years ago. One sense in which our data is, however, broadly representative is in the relationship between age of marriage and class: the middle class marries later than the working class (Dunnell 1979) and this is reflected in the differences in Table 4.1 between Ty-Gwyn and Abbeyview with respect to marriage and engagement. High Oak occupies an indeterminate position.

Table 4.1 Young people's courtship and marriage status, by area (percentages in brackets)

	No present relationship	'Going steady'	Engaged	Married	Total
Abbeyview	6 (29)	10 (48)	2 (10)	3 (14)	21 (100)
High Oak	15 (65)	6 (26)	1 (4)	1 (4)	23 (100)
Ty-Gwyn	11 (55)	9 (45)	–	–	20 (100)
n.	32 (50)	25 (39)	3 (5)	4 (6)	64 (100)

Note: There are sixty-four young people in this table due to the inclusion of Gwyn Roberts from Ty-Gwyn, about whom we have information even though we did not manage to interview him personally.

The contrast between our findings and Diana Leonard's is in part a consequence of a general change in attitudes and behaviour and in part a reflection of the impact of unemployment upon the lives of the individual young people with whom we are concerned. Both factors can be seen at work in the quotations which follow:

(63)
I've no intention of getting married or having children. I couldn't cope with children. I just seem to have come out of school and done nothing. If you come out of school, have a job, get married and have children, it's the way it's supposed to go. You can't just come out of school and have children ... I want a job, a career ... If I could get into social work, it's a career. I could move up.

(Elaine Peters, Abbeyview)

(64)
Lots of people, well they are working, but they're in dead-end jobs. They're married 'cos they had to. Looking at it that way, I've got better prospects [being unemployed but single] than any of that lot.

(Neville Clifford, Abbeyview)

(65)
SH: What about your mates?
MB: They've all got kids. One has two babies. She had to get married. Then she had another one. Then her husband left her. One has got a baby, she's married but she didn't have to get married. She's happily married.

SH: And your prospects ...?

MB: Terrible. I'll end up like the rest. Having a kid, getting a flat, debts and debts. It will get harder and harder.

(Michelle Bowen, Abbeyview)

(66)

SH: Does unemployment affect your relationships with girls?

RG: Sometimes. You don't have enough to take them out. I don't like it at all [if they pay]. I don't ask her out if I don't have the money.

(Robert Griffiths, Abbeyview)

(67)

TA: He's never had a girlfriend, never.

SH: Because he's unemployed?

TA: Yes ... Because I said to him about a girl and he said, 'What's the point? I can't afford to take her out.' None of them have got girlfriends. There's only Nicky. He got married. They're all school-friends. Sandy [Nicky's wife] was one of the crowd anyway, so I don't suppose that counts.

(Mr Thomas Alexander, High Oak)

The testimony of Robert Griffiths and Mr Alexander indicate clearly one of the major ways in which unemployment has an effect upon courtship (and marriage). Members of the opposite sex, prospective partners, have to be encountered in order for the process to begin at all. With the decline in importance of church, chapel and club documented by Rosser and Harris, the major context for meeting the opposite sex, apart from school or college, becomes commercial leisure provision. There has thus been created a courtship market – or, to be more accurate perhaps, certainly if Swansea's nightclubs and discos are anything to go by, a sexual market-place (not for nothing does one hear a particular nightclub described as 'a cattle market') – in which an income of a particular level is a prerequisite for successful participation. The implications of this situation are discussed in the next section.

(S)he who pays the piper?

In looking at the relationship between unemployment, leisure participation and courtship, there are three separate lines of enquiry which can be pursued: first, what effect does unemployment have upon leisure activities and 'going out'?; second, what implications do those effects have for courtship?; and third, what strategies have been developed for coping with the first two problems? We will look at each in turn. Here are some examples of what 'going out' means for the young people we interviewed:

(68)

I go out with a lot of mates. Before we go out for a drink, if its early enough, we go to the 147 snooker club ... then to a normal pub ... Once every fortnight. Friday, I go to the Starlight, a disco. I go with mates and meet girls there. They come from Neath, Swansea, Cwmafan, Briton Ferry. I go once every three weeks, or when I can afford it. Saturday ... to town first with my mates. If I have money, I buy one or two records. Go back to my mate's house. Have a drink with him. We make arrangements first, where we're going in the night. We end up round Cwmafan, in a pub. That's all I keep my money for really, to go out with the boys.

(Robert Griffiths, Abbeyview)

(69)

Once a fortnight, that is, down the Raffles [local nightclub] ... When the cheque comes through. That's the only time I go out and I haven't been for the last 3 weeks.

(Helen Jones, Abbeyview)

(70)

I go out every other Friday, when I get my dole. To Mumbles [a local resort village]. To the pub, take it from there. If my mate down the road [Simon Preece] calls, I go with him.

(Philip Broughton, High Oak)

(71)

KM: We go out a couple of times a week. To town. To clubs ... I'm with the girls, but I do meet my boyfriend.
SH: Is he working?
KM: Yeah.
SH: Is it a problem? Going out without money?
KM: No, not really.
SH: Because boys buy you drinks?
KM: Yeah.
SH: And at the weekends?
KM: Yeah ... Saturday and Sunday. The same places.

(Katherine Mansell, High Oak)

(72)

There's nothing to take them [girls] out on. They have no respect for you when you're unemployed. Ken [his stepbrother] meets different girls. They tend to have council houses and children. They're unemployed. I just meet single working girls. They are sometimes living at home. I would like to meet them at discos. You have to have smart clothes in discos. They turn you out in jeans.

(Jason Wilding, Ty-Gwyn)

(73)

DF: I go out every night of the week. A nightclub, mainly the Mayfair [in Swansea]. If Charlie's at the door I get in free. Sometimes I go on my own, sometimes with a boyfriend. I see him Monday, Wednesday, Friday and Saturday. We go to a nightclub on Friday, usually a party on Saturday. He'll pay to get in. Then he'll buy two rounds and I'll buy one ... If I'm really hard up, then I won't go out. Wednesday, we usually go to the pictures, sometimes we go for a couple of drinks. When I'd been here several weeks and I was sickened with not going out, I dressed up and went down to a night club. Even if I didn't have money for a drink, if I could get in I could always get someone to buy me a drink.

SH: Is it easier for a girl?

DF: Yes, I've had a couple of boyfriends who've been unemployed. You go for just one drink then you come up here [to her lodgings] to watch television. You understand it then. Chris [her boyfriend] is earning sixty pound at the DVLC.

(Diana Fullerton, Ty-Gwyn)

Looking at this interview material, the first point which strikes one is the centrality of public houses and night clubs (which, in Swansea and Port Talbot, are essentially licensed dance halls, open after normal drinking hours, providing disco entertainment and occasionally live music) as arenas of leisure and 'fun' for young people. Cinemas are also important, but not to the same degree. These are the focal points of 'going out'. However, they all fit into the social whirl in a different fashion. Take pubs, for example: young men typically go 'down the pub' with their (male) mates, while young women may go as part of a boy-girl couple. It is increasingly the case that, particularly in the city centre, one can also see groups of women on a 'girls' night out' in public houses. Pubs remain, however, more a male than a female preserve and women on their own, without men, are still the exception in many pubs.[3] The point is that pubs are not primarily places for 'picking up talent'; *that* typically occurs in discos and nightclubs. The cinema, on the other hand, is somewhere to go with a boy or girlfriend once a relationship exists, or the possibility of a relationship has been recognised.

The second point, which is clear from all of the above quotations, is the necessity of economic resources – or access to them – for participation in leisure activities of these kinds. It costs money to drink and, in the case of nightclubs, there is also a cover charge. In addition, as mentioned in (72), a certain kind of clothing is required for nightclubs: 'no jeans or t-shirts' is a common dress policy. This also requires a certain basic level of expenditure. With the rise of the 'disco pub' – a cross between a pub and a club, often with bouncers on the door – the range of leisure venues to which restrictions of this kind apply is expanding.[4]

Third, there are gender differences in the use of and access to commercial entertainment facilities, and in the resources required. Young women, in particular, are at an advantage – albeit, perhaps, of a dubious kind – with respect to clubs and discos, for a number of reasons. Many clubs, for example, operate a selective admission policy: women may get in free on certain nights (typically the quiet nights from Monday to Wednesday) or before a set time, and they may get in cheaper the rest of the time. Men, of course, pay the full admission price. The rationale is obvious: women are the attraction to lure the men in. And the reason why that matters is that, as revealed in (71) and (73), it is generally men who buy most of the drinks. There is, of course, a fine line to be walked by any woman adopting such an approach, but drinks and entertainment may, with care and calculation, be had for next to nothing (or next to nothing in strictly financial terms, anyway). There is a three-cornered market operating; women are an important resource in the club owner's strategy for parting (male) punters from their money.

Finally, it also appears to be the case that unemployment, with its effects upon young men and women's social lives, also has implications for the social organisation of time. Given that 'the rhythms which govern social life are entirely conventional' (Zerubavel 1981: 11), it is clear from a number of research studies that employment is powerful among those conventions and that unemployment may, as a consequence, disrupt those rhythms (e.g. Bostyn and Wight 1987; Fagin and Little 1984: 33–6; Henwood and Miles 1987; Jahoda *et al.* 1972: 66–77). Our material indicates that one of the areas in which this disruption occurs is leisure and social life. Instead of the weekend being the fulcrum of the week, a brief holiday from work – and it should not be forgotten that 'the weekend', as distinct from the sabbath, is itself a relatively recent product of a struggle between workers and employers – it is every other weekend, as in (70). For Helen Jones (69) and Robert Griffiths (68) it may be every third weekend. And now, instead of being a respite from wage labour, the social weekend – 'going out' – becomes an interruption of boredom, a brief reinsertion into the normality experienced by other people, a short essay back into the courtship market. Once again, however, inasmuch as the possibilities for participation in that market are greater for women, should they so choose, the potential disruption to their social organisation of time may be less (or, at least, different: Diana Fullerton, going out 'every night of the week', may be experiencing no less a deviation from the conventional pattern than Helen Jones[5]).

The interview material presented above has been selected to give a flavour of the dominant themes running through our evidence. However, it *is* only a selection, and there are at least two important qualifications to be made to the generality of our arguments so far. As is abundantly clear from the evidence we have presented, there is a broad heterogeneity of experience of 'going out'. Helen Jones, for example (69), does not appear to exploit her sexuality in the same way as Katherine Mansell (71) or Diana Fullerton (73); Robert Griffiths (68) seems to manage to do more than Jason Wilding (72). The other point to remember is that although commercial leisure provision may now be pre-eminent for young people, other, less expensive avenues of leisure activity – everything from sport to motorbike racing – remain open, and some of these may permit the pursuit of relationships with the opposite sex (although many such organised activities are male-oriented, if not male-dominated; see Deem 1986).

What is more, although the youth club or the church may be less important than they once were, they are still significant for *some* young people. Peter Griffiths, for example, from Ty-Gwyn, is a 'born-again' Christian whose social life is based around a network of other young people in his church: on Sunday he attends worship, Monday he helps out at a 'Monday Club' for pensioners run by evangelical Christians, Wednesday is a 'house group' which meets for Bible study and prayer, on Thursday there is the Church youth club, and Friday and Saturday are taken up with the Young People's Fellowship. His girlfriend belongs to the same network. As his father said, being unemployed made little difference to Peter's social life: 'Everything he does is in a church setting, which is free.'

This brings us to our second question: what are the implications for courtship behaviour of the effects of unemployment upon leisure activities? Perhaps the most important of these is the disadvantage which is likely to be experienced by unemployed young men. This is obvious from quotations (72) and (73), but some further direct evidence may be useful:

(74)
It's a strain. Moneywise. Not being able to afford things I want, or take her where she wants to go ... she tends to want to pay a lot, which is embarrassing for me. I just feel ashamed. And she tends to get uptight if I refuse ...//... Her mother and father knowing I'm unemployed. That's also been a strain. You can imagine ... A girl brings a boy home and he's not working. There's no real future.
(Hugh Reynolds, High Oak)
(75)
He [Matthew Griffiths] probably would take her out more, wine and dine more, if he had money ...//... Mind, what her parents think of him is another thing. They're very middle-class, both work in a bank. Whether or not they approve of him, as an ideal son-in-law
(Mrs Georgina Griffiths, Ty-Gwyn)
(76)
On our side, it would be a great match, but I don't know about the other parents.
(Mr Paul Griffiths, Ty-Gwyn)
(77)
SH: Does a boy need money to go out with girls?
TO: Yeah, definitely.
SH: Are you at a disadvantage?
TO: Oh, definitely. I can take girls out and all this, but I can't spend anything in the week.

SH: Like?

TO: Well, I can't go to town to look for a job. It's mainly travelling and not going out with my friends.

SH: Is it worth it?

TO: I suppose so.

(Timothy Owens, Ty-Gwyn)

On looking at this material, and referring back to our earlier discussion, it is clear that the problem for unemployed young men with respect to courtship is threefold. In the first place, there is the issue of access to and full participation in the sorts of activities which are bound up with courtship or, at a less committed level, simply meeting girls or young women in a context appropriate to sexual advances and exchanges. Of the thirty-eight young men about whom we collected information, fifteen (39 per cent) either mentioned lack of money as an obstacle to 'getting off' with young women or had it identified as such by their parents. This problem is created in large part by a shortage of cash, but it is compounded by conventional expectations about 'who should pay' (i.e. males) and the consequent role of women in the marketing strategies of those who provide commercial entertainment facilities.

Second, within a relationship which is actually established, an unemployed young man may feel himself to be at a considerable disadvantage, as exemplified by Hugh Reynolds in (74). The issue here is not one of actual economic deprivation; it is, rather, the sense of failure and shame which comes from the inability to live up to the masculine self-image as the provider, the one who pays. This may be a source of considerable conflict within a relationship.

At this point it may be worth pointing out a contradiction of sorts in our interview material with respect to expenditure and gender. Many interviewees, both female and male, expressed with some force the view that there should be equity of expenditure in courtship. A considerable number of these then went on, however, to discuss the problems experienced by unemployed young men because, in fact, it was taken for granted that they should pay. Despite the importance of attitudinal changes, 'traditional' notions about appropriate gender roles exert a real and unmistakable force on the courtship process, stronger perhaps than in any other area of social life which we looked at: only 30 per cent of the young people we interviewed (the overwhelming majority of whom were, interestingly enough, women) thought that a young woman *ought* to pay for herself when 'going out' with a man. The power of these traditional role models is, however, coupled with a recognition of change and uncertainty; many interviewees, for example, prefaced their remarks on this matter with disclaimers along the lines that 'I know I'm old-fashioned, but ...'

Gender differences in patterns of leisure spending and consumption are related to the position of young men and young women in the labour market. Generally speaking in the United Kingdom, women earn less than men of the same age, the 1970 Equal Pay Act and the 1975 Sex Discrimination Act notwithstanding (Dex 1985: 112–42; Martin and Roberts 1984: 43–59). A young man who is in employment is generally able to bear the financial burden created by social expectations relating to courtship expenditure during that period of his working life before the acquisition of family responsibilities. We use the word 'burden' advisedly, to remind the reader that some working young men may find it difficult to compete adequately. It should also be remembered that patterns of expenditure within a stable or established relationship often shift towards greater equity and/or joint saving for 'a home of our own' once the initial period of attraction and attachment is over.

The position of a young man who is unemployed – particularly if his unemployment persists for any length of time – is different. His is a difficult situation. In the first place, he will simply have to subsist on a reduced income. This is a timely reminder that unemployment is about money, if nothing else; living on state social security benefits means a major reduction in one's circumstances at best, and poverty at worst. Now this, of course, applies also to unemployed young women. In the second place, however, unlike wages there are no gender disparities in the formal incomes of unemployed young adults: unmarried women and men with no dependants have the same benefit entitlement.

Gender equality with respect to social security for single people has its ironic consequences in a situation where there is no such equality in other contexts. We have already seen that some of the young men who we interviewed felt themselves to be at an economic disadvantage in terms of going out with women. This is all the more so given the importance of commercial entertainment venues as the terrain over which the local system of sexual exchange operates, the privileged position of young women within that system and the power of traditional expectations about 'who pays'. Viewed within these parameters formal equality may actually be experienced as substantive inequality.

The plight of the unemployed young man is rendered more severe by the nature of the local opportunity structure. As we have seen in Chapter 1, in both Swansea and Port Talbot female labour is more in demand than male (a situation not uncommon elsewhere). Not only, therefore, are unemployed young men at a disadvantage in terms of courtship and relationships relative to their female peers, but young women are less likely to be unemployed anyway.

The third problem which these young men have is revealed in quotations (74), (75) and (76). When it comes down to serious courtship, 'going steady' (and it must be remembered, of course, that often it does not come to this), the views of parents are still, despite changes in attitudes, of considerable significance. Particularly the views of the girls' parents. Many people recognise that unemployment is a widespread and obstinate social problem; many people have considerable sympathy for the unemployed. For many of the same people, however, it is a different matter when it is a potential son-in-law they are talking about.

Finally, the conversation with Timothy Owens in (77) reveals a further dimension of the situation. Should a young man decide to follow a life-style which includes the pursuit of young women, this may only be possible at the expense of other things. Perhaps even at the expense of job-seeking. Such is the complicated internal economy of unemployment.

There are a number of strategies, whether conscious or unconscious, for dealing with these problems of sex and courtship. Perhaps the most obvious is simply not to bother with it all: some young men just stick with their mates, 'having a laugh', some stop at home, some busy themselves with other things. Others may attempt to adopt a more cynical, predatory approach, as encapsulated in 'the three Fs': 'find 'em, fuck 'em, forget about 'em.' And some of the young men behaving in these ways might have done so anyway, of course, unemployment or no unemployment. It is impossible to know.

Another solution of a kind was to do without during the week, in order to allow for some degree of latitude at the weekend (or every other weekend). Timothy Owens, in (77), is a case in point. There is, however, a limit to the viability of such a strategy: some things, new clothes for example, you can only do without for so long.

For some young men a steady girlfriend was actually the solution, although this still raises the issue of how to *find* a steady girlfriend in the first place. In the context of such a relationship it is easier to lower consumption and expenditure to the level of the young man's income:

(78)
It helps. It depends where she wants to go. The girlfriend sometimes says 'Let's go for a Coke' ... and then she goes out with the girls.
(Neville Clifford, Abbeyview)

(79)
SH: Do you go out?
KA: Sometimes, once a fortnight [with her unemployed boyfriend]. It all depends how we're fixed. The Starlight, or the Grand in town.
SH: Is the Starlight expensive?
KA: It all depends if you're going up to the nightclub after. We don't. It's a quiet room. You just pay for drinks.
SH: Would you like to go out more?
KA: Oh, yes. To the Grand or the Plaza. There are good films on.
(Karen Anderson, Abbeyview)

(80)
I go out a couple of times a week. On my bike with my girlfriend and we go to a pub. It only costs £1. We went away last weekend to England ... it was bike racing. We took a tent ... It doesn't have to cost you a lot to go out. If you go into town like Nigel [his brother, also unemployed], to discos and nightclubs, that costs you. Nigel's different to me, he's into town, dressing up. I just wear faded blue jeans.

(Charles Mason, Ty-Gwyn)

Once a relationship is established, therefore, there may be less need for participation in commercial leisure. Within an established relationship, it is also possible for the woman to contribute financially to social activities; she may even be the main contributor to the expenses of these occasions:

(81)
RT: Sometimes my girlfriend takes me over the Starlight.
SH: She pays?
RT: Most of it.
SH: Do you mind?
RT: I did at first, to be honest with you, because it wasn't fair on her.
  But she insisted on it, so I thought, 'Well, why not?'

(Richard Thomas, Abbeyview)

This kind of subvention is often made either backstage, for example before the couple go out, or surreptitiously:

(82)
Sometimes girls [with unemployed boyfriends] go to the toilets and put a fiver in the boys' hands as they pass.

(Elaine Peters, Abbeyview)

As we have already seen, in the case of Hugh Reynolds (74), this can be a source of friction. Some young men are not prepared to be paid for; in other cases the manner of the transfer (e.g. if it is done too publicly) may be unacceptable and embarrassing. This is a situation which differs radically from that described by Leonard; the men in her research were, however, in employment, and it was nearly twenty years ago. Similar arrangements between employed young women and unemployed young men have been reported from elsewhere (Beuret and Makings 1987: 67–8); we will return to these research findings below.

The last solution to the unemployed young man's predicament with respect to the opposite sex is, in effect, to trade down-market. Several of the young men we interviewed were going out with girls who were much younger, still at school. While it is statistically and culturally normal for the male to be the older member of a couple, these relationships were sometimes seen as outside the usual range:

(83)
I do wonder, because the only girls he's ever interested in are girls in Helena's year at school [i.e. 15-year-olds]. To me, that's too young for Simon ... it never lasts long. It's never a date, never a proper date. He just meets them down at the Tivoli.

(Mrs Doreen Preece, High Oak)

Schoolgirls may have lower expectations about their social life, or be more restricted by parental constraint than their older equivalents. They are also unlikely to have more money than the young men. As a result, expenditure may be reduced and the relationship may be less threatening for the male partner; as such, this may be a satisfactory coping strategy for some young men.

Looking at the situation from the viewpoint of the young women we interviewed, it is clear that they do not – at least under many circumstances – experience the same degree or kinds of difficulties with respect to courtship as many of the young men. We do not, however, wish to present a picture of uniform male disadvantage and unalloyed female contentment. The situation is a little more complex than that and fraught with a degree of contradiction.

For example, a few of our interviewees claimed to be able to go out more while they were on the dole, because of increased free time and the fact that they did not have to get up in the morning to go to work. Claire Wallace has recorded something similar from the Isle of Sheppey (Wallace 1987: 75). Of the six who suggested that this was the case, four were young women, a finding consistent with our argument concerning relative male disadvantage. To underline this point, it should be noted that one of the two young men concerned was Peter Griffiths, whose entertainments were Christian and cost less.

A more important point perhaps, second, is the degree to which some of the young women who we interviewed felt isolated from their peers. It appears to be the case, from some research, that young women between school and the early twenties may find their friends largely through employment (Griffin 1985). By contrast, other research suggests a picture of active female peer groups which do not necessarily depend on social contact in the workplace (Coffield *et al*. 1986: 155-9; Wallace 1987: 75-6).[6] Most researchers are, however, agreed that unemployed young women are relatively more socially isolated than unemployed young men. Nine (36 per cent) of the young women we interviewed either spoke of themselves or were spoken of by their parents as isolated. Several others saw themselves as too dependent upon their boyfriends because of their lack of contact with their peers:

(84)

I depend on him for company. I'm just waiting for him. I am more dependent on him for company because I'm unemployed ... I wake up in the mornings sometimes, I look at my watch and think 'Two o'clock and he'll be home now.' You're just waiting for somebody else.

(Elaine Peters, Abbeyview)

A third perspective on our data which requires emphasis is the importance of the particularity of the experience of unemployment. There is pattern and there are general aspects of that experience; there is also a considerable amount of individual variation as well. In the context of courtship this is well illustrated by the contrast between two unemployed brothers from Abbeyview, Gwyn and Richard Thomas, aged 22 and 21 years respectively. Richard, in (81) above, does not appear to mind his employed girlfriend paying their way when they go to the Starlight. For Gwyn, however, who was always a bit tighter with his money, the effort to keep up with his girlfriend's demands looked likely to finish the relationship:

(85)

I can't afford to go out every time and withdraw from the bank ...//... This spend, spend, spend all the time. I saved for a reason [to have money behind him for a home and a marriage] – not to go out all the time and be drunk all the time.

Different young men, different young women, two totally different situations. It is important that the heterogeneity of experience within the patterns we are describing should not be lost to sight.

Finally, and in some senses following on from this point, it is interesting to note that many of our informants seemed to feel that a close male–female relationship, or indeed a relationship between mates or between parents and children, is somehow insulated from or untouched by external economic forces such as unemployment. A 'real' relationship – love – is something altogether different, protected and protecting:

(86)

TF: You don't need to take her out to have a steady relationship. If the girl cares about you enough, she doesn't care about the money. Some girls pay for themselves.
SH: Do boys mind?
TF: I don't mind. If you're caring about someone and you're steady ... they ask for equal rights.

(Thomas Field, Abbeyview)

(87)

SH: Where do you meet girls?

RP: Girls that you want a relationship with you mean? ... You accidentally bump into them ... They take an interest in you and you take an interest in them ... I wouldn't go up to a girl and start chatting her up. I know people who would.

SH: Does unemployment affect your relationships with girls?

RP: No, I don't think so.

John Jones: If you had a flashy car and you went up, you'd get ten or twenty.

RP: Oh, yeah, that would be different. Then they'd be jumping for money. Me personally, I don't think so. My relationship with girls when I've had a job and now being on the dole is exactly the same.

(Richard Pugh, Ty-Gwyn)

Now is not the time to discuss the roots and development of the notion of romantic love in Western society (see, for example, Macfarlane 1985; Stone 1977). There can, however, be little doubt that it is a powerful cultural ideal, widely circulated through day-to-day discourse, popular music and literature, the various media of advertising and telecommunications, particularly television. While accepting that it *is* an ideal – and an ideal, what is more, the naïve pursuit of which breaks many hearts and spirits – it is not *just* an ideal, nor is it fostered solely by propaganda. Many women and men have, or certainly appear to have, 'good', 'loving' relationships. Many do not, of course, but that is not the point. Hope springs eternal and a 'real' relationship is a legitimate and realistic aspiration. Nor, as the quotations above are designed to illustrate, is it an aspiration which is confined to women, although they might be more publicly committed than men to romance (Sarsby 1983). Either way, the quest for a 'real' relationship, the search for a romantic ideal, is an important counterweight to set beside our earlier image of the sexual market-place in arriving at a balanced view of the experience of courtship for the young people we interviewed.

The other theme which must contribute to that balanced view is an appreciation of changes in the gendered hierarchy of power relations within the courtship process. Thomas Field, in (86), gives us a clue when he talks about 'equal rights', as do the ethnographic reports of Coffield *et al.* (1986: 163–75) and Wallace (1987: 174–8): we found a complicated mixture of 'traditional' and 'progressive' views about relationships between men and women. On the one hand, for example, women should contribute financially; on the other, men often do most of the paying in practice. The taken-for-granted order of things has been somewhat undermined by gender equality in benefit payments for single people and higher unemployment rates for men. Some young men find themselves in the culturally novel situation of dependence upon their women.

Beuret and Makings, in their study of the effects of male unemployment upon courtship in Leicester and the North-East, provide the closest point of comparison in this respect for our material (Beuret and Makings 1987). It is clear that the young women they interviewed, all of whom were employed as hairdressers, while allowing the men to appear to be in charge of the relationship, consciously sought to control the relationship themselves through a process of manipulation. This applies both to who 'made the first move' during the phase of initial attraction and during any subsequent established relationship. At least in part as a consequence of their partner's unemployment, these young women are less dependent than they might have been in the past; they are also less committed to marriage, certainly in the short-to-medium term, than the young women described by Diana Leonard.

In all important respects our findings match Beuret and Makings'. In addition, it seems to be the case that less importance was attached by our respondents to courtship than might have been predicted in a sample of this age and composition: 64 per cent of the young men and women who we interviewed answered 'no' to the question 'Is a girl or a boyfriend important?' This is a bald question, of course, which does not begin to tap the complexities of the situation. It is, none the less, an interesting finding, and unexpected.

There may, therefore, be the makings of a shift in the 'balance of power' within the courtship process, a shift in favour of young women deriving from their relatively favourable position within the local labour market. For many young women *and* young men – both employed and unemployed – the realities of sex and courtship are very different from the experience of the immediately previous generations. It is much too early to speculate about whether or not orientations towards marriage, or marriage patterns themselves, will change in the long term. However, bearing in mind Wallace's arguments (Wallace 1987: 156–69), the possibility that increasing numbers of unemployed young people will opt for deferred marriage, or no marriage at all, is a real one. It is, in fact, already happening. Much the same can be said about the likelihood that more young women will set up in – and continue in – independent households, with or without partners and children. We will discuss these issues in more detail in the next section.

Love and marriage (again ...)

Only passing reference has been made so far to sex. This is an accurate reflection of the central emphasis of the interview. Generally undertaken in the young person's house, sometimes with a parent popping in and out – generally mother – the setting was not appropriate to the discussion of intimacies (although they did on occasions crop up). Nor was it easy to discuss such matters with parents themselves. By and large, the issue was only discussed if the interviewee raised it.

Beuret and Makings' research setting – the all-female, semi-confessional atmosphere of the hairdressing salon – was a much better venue. Their findings, of a self-confident female sexuality, explicitly concerned with the young woman's own satisfaction, albeit within the framework of love and romance (Beuret and Makings 1987: 71), is in broad harmony with other authors' data. Coffield and his colleagues, for example, while documenting the young woman's concern not to be labelled a 'slag' or a 'tart', are equally clear that female sexuality can be respectably and openly acknowledged within the context of an established relationship (Coffield *et al.* 1986: 157–9, 173–5). The gendered double standard of sexual propriety still applies – after all, boys *will* be boys – but there does not seem to be the obsessive female concern with sexual reputation to be found in the ethnography of authors such as Griffin (1985: 58–62), Lees (1986) or McRobbie (1978).

These differences are in large part ascribable to the fact that Griffin, Lees and McRobbie are concerned with younger subjects, girls, as opposed to the young women of the other studies. Our material, such as it is, agrees closely with the findings of Beuret and Makings and Coffield and his colleagues. Similarly, we did not pick up the atmosphere of sexual threat, harassment and tension manifest in the work of Griffin, Lees and McRobbie. This may also be due to the greater independence and self-confidence of our older research subjects; it may be a reflection of differences in the predelictions and interests of the researchers concerned. It is also, given that we did not tackle the topic of sexuality head-on, merely an impression. Since we are, however, in the business of interpretive sociology, we should perhaps be prepared to offer our impressions with a degree of confidence.

While we did not ask people directly about sex, we did, however, ask them their views about cohabitation. Overall, forty-four (70 per cent) of the young people who we interviewed thought that is was acceptable to live together before marriage. The overwhelming majority of these responses indicate a preference for cohabitation prior to entering into a legally binding commitment. For the parents, the corresponding figure is twenty-seven (42 per cent). One of the factors affecting the distribution of attitudes to this topic appears to be class, as revealed by area of residence (Table 4.2). It is clear from this table that cohabitation is more acceptable to both young people and parents in Abbeyview than in either High Oak or Ty-Gwyn. Given the aggressive public respectability of High Oak, this should not surprise us; what is more interesting, perhaps, is the apparent rejection of 'liberal' values by the parental generation in Ty-Gwyn. Bourgeois permissiveness is clearly not a universal phenomenon in modern middle-class Britain.

The acceptability of cohabitation varies, therefore, with age and class. What, however, of gender? Of the forty-four young people who regarded cohabitation as acceptable, fifteen (34 per cent) were young women. Within this category of respondents, nine (53 per cent) of the seventeen from

Table 4.2　Attitudes towards cohabitation, by area (percentages in brackets)

		Acceptable or desirable	Not acceptable	Don't know or no comment	Total
Abbeyview	Young people	17 (81)	1 (5)	3 (14)	21 (100)
	Parents	10 (59)	5 (29)	2 (12)	17 (100)
High Oak	Young people	14 (61)	1 (4)	8 (35)	23 (100)
	Parents	11 (41)	6 (22)	10 (37)	27 (100)
Ty-Gwyn	Young people	13 (68)	2 (11)	4 (21)	19 (100)
	Parents	6 (30)	9 (45)	5 (25)	20 (100)
n.	Young people	44 (70)	4 (6)	15 (24)	63 (100)
	Parents	27 (42)	20 (31)	17 (27)	64 (100)

Abbeyview were female, compared to five (36 per cent) out of fourteen from High Oak and only one (8 per cent) out of thirteen from Ty-Gwyn. This is a crude set of comparisons and its interpretation is not immediately clear.

What can be said with some small degree of confidence is that, first, cohabitation is – in theory at least – more popular or acceptable with young men than young women, and second, that gender interacts with class in this respect: whereas there is little difference between the young women and men of Abbeyview in this respect, the contrast in Ty-Gwyn is striking, with High Oak once again occupying an intermediate position.

These results probably serve to underline the continued importance of reputation for women – who have more to lose should cohabitation *not* become marriage – and the greater importance of that reputation in High Oak and Ty-Gwyn. It is instructive to compare these results with the conclusions of the team led by Frank Coffield:

> in working-class communities babies conceived or born out of marriage have usually been accepted into the family and the community with little comment. ... For at least two decades university students and middle-class women generally have had a freedom to experience sex before marriage. Living together and trial marriages have become commonplace among these groups and such practices are now becoming part of working-class life, although an element of social defiance was still attached to the women involved.
>
> (Coffield *et al*. 1986: 174)

The overall thrust of this conclusion – the greater acceptability of pre-marital sex, within the appropriate relational context – is indisputable. We would, however, take issue with the homogenous models of class and community being used: our material indicates that pre-marital sex is more acceptable in some working-class communities than in others, nor is it uniformly acceptable in all middle-class communities or families. More than that, it is, if our findings are at all representative, more acceptable for working-class young adults in South Wales than for their middle-class peers. Or perhaps it is just that the latter find it less easy to admit to or discuss. The safest conclusion is that overly-confident generalisations about class and pre-marital sexual behaviour should be avoided in the absence of further research (Study Commission on the Family 1982: 26-7). A further issue which we have not yet touched on – the deliberate move into single parenthood by unemployed young women – is discussed in the next chapter in the context of a consideration of the criteria of adulthood.

Asking questions about cohabitation is fairly straightforward in at least one important sense: people usually have relatively clear-cut views about it. They generally regard it as acceptable or not. Trying to fathom their views on marriage is a little more problematic, however. Nearly everybody *approves* of marriage, certainly nearly everybody in the areas we looked at. They may not be happy in their *own* marriage, they may not want to get married just *now*, they may not see it as strictly *necessary* in order to publicly share a bed with the person of their choice; none the less, the institution of marriage is generally taken-for-granted. For most of the young people in our study, as in Leonard's earlier study (1980: 73) and the more recent research of Coffield *et al.* (1986: 165-6) and Wallace (1987: 179), the ideology of marriage remains intact: it is usually a question of *when*, not *if*, even if the former may be at some indeterminate or unconsidered time in the future. There is, however, despite this core consensus, a variety of perspectives on marriage revealed in our interviews with unemployed young people:

(88)
I haven't thought about it [marriage]. I may be old-fashioned, but I wouldn't marry when I wasn't working, not 'til I can support her. It wouldn't be fair on her. She wouldn't be happy. She [his girlfriend of two-and-a-half years] agrees.

(Neville Clifford, Abbeyview)

(89)
Unemployment doesn't come into it. If a person is ready to settle down, he'll settle down with the girlfriend that he loves. But if he's working it doesn't make any difference. When I was working I wasn't ready to settle down.

(Thomas Field, Abbeyview)

(90)
KA: My boyfriend wants us to get married.
SH: What about you?
KA: Yes. We put money by this week for the first time ...
SH: Would you get engaged?

KA: It all depends how the money comes by when we're saving it ... If not, you get one ring ... I know my boyfriend's got his name down for a contract. God willing, something will come of that.

SH: When will you get married?

KA: When we can afford it. It could be this year, but then again it could be next year.

SH: Why don't you get married and just manage?

KA: [Laughs] Well, you've got to get the licence, and that's thirty or forty pounds.

(Karen Anderson, Abbeyview)

(91)

SH: What do you think you'll be doing in five years' time?

JA: Well, guaranteed I won't be married.

SH: Because you don't want to?

JA: Yeah ... I can't see myself in ten years having a mortgage and a house and kids and all that. I can't see that, but there again, you never know.

(Jonathan Alexander, High Oak)

(92)

SH: What about marriage?

HR: You should be at least 25. I'd like to be 30.

SH: Why?

HR: I want it to be for good. At 30 it's about half your life.

(Helen Roderick, High Oak)

(93)

MR: I knew her from school. She's just had a baby. They're all having babies.

SH: Do you want a baby?

MR: No.

SH: Do girls get caught?

MR: Yes, I think so, but it's just that I don't think I'd be able to cope with a baby at the moment.

SH: Do they get more benefit with babies?

MR: Alison's sister's got a little girl and she gets forty-five pounds a week. She gets a lot of help off her parents.

SH: Do people have babies to get benefit?

MR: No. They cost more than that.

SH: Is it okay just to live together?

MR: I won't get married. I'd live with someone. I'd have children. I'd do it [get married] if they really wanted me to. Eventually they would.

(Melanie Reilly, High Oak)

(94)

RP: I wouldn't get married if I didn't have any money. A lot of people do. They call it love, like. It's not for me. I've got to have money. I wouldn't like it in a council house with three kids. I know people like that ... Like my brother. He's buying a house down there. He's got a mortgage, he's getting married.

AL: It doesn't mean you can't have a family if you haven't got a job or if you're low-paid ... You can still be happy then.

RP: I can't ... It's completely up to the individual. That's my view of it.

(Richard Pugh and Anthony Lonsdale, Ty-Gwyn)

(95)

That's not part of the scheme of things at all. I've got so far as to tell my parents, largely to annoy them, that I don't even believe in marriage. I wouldn't see the necessity of taking marriage vows ... I say it as a reaction against what I see. Like now there are a lot of people from [his old school], not really people I knew, who seem to be getting married ...//... I just think, for a start, that going out of one family unit straight into another, seems to me they're not giving themselves a chance. I suppose I kind of see marriage as part and parcel of the whole job ... 2.2 children and all the rest of it. I might change my mind, but I don't see myself doing so.

(Steve Anderson, Ty-Gwyn)

(96)

DF: It [marriage] doesn't appeal to me at all. I don't want children. I don't fancy spending the rest of my life washing some man's socks. I don't think I could live with someone 'cos I'm so temperamental ...//... Me and my last boyfriend really finished 'cos he wanted to move in with me. My friend, now, she's been living with her boyfriend for a year ... She gets up in the morning. She tidies the flat 'for Nigel'. She makes dinner 'for Nigel'. She does the dishes 'for Nigel'. She's got to be home at 3.30 'when Nigel comes home' ...//...

SH: How many of your friends got pregnant without wanting to?

DF: Loads of them ...//... Not using contraception properly. Out of my friends, not one of them wanted the baby. They've wanted it when they had it, like. All my friends are dropping out like flies. They're either getting pregnant or engaged. It's terrible.

(Diana Fullerton, Ty-Gwyn)

Looking at quotations (88) and (94) above, and (66) earlier, it seems likely that unemployment is having some effect on views about marriage and possibly on marriage patterns. This is certainly the view of many of the parents to whom we spoke. Take, for example, Mrs Doreen Preece, mother of Simon Preece from High Oak:

(97)

Years ago, when we handed our keep in, parents, they used to save part
of that for when you got married ... He can't even give enough for
hiself, let alone for me to save for when he gets married ...//... How
could he ever, *ever*, get married? He'd have to live together, so she'd
get her dole and he'd get his dole ... It would have been a shameful
thing years ago ... but he'd have no choice.

Here one is afforded a glimpse of the fragile economic fabric upon which
working-class marriage rests, and how it can be undermined by unemployment. Mrs Preece's testimony also makes plain the rational economic
calculation – although she is mistaken in thinking that the social security
system works in the manner she is describing – which may lie behind the
decision to cohabit.

It is, however, difficult to avoid the impression that, while unemployment undoubtedly contributes, the attitudes towards marriage and
cohabitation expressed in (63), (64), (91), (92), (95) and (96) – so different
from those found among Diana Leonard's informants – are more a part of
wider undercurrents of social change than anything else. The last thirty
years have witnessed major changes with respect to sexual mores, gender
roles and courtship and marriage patterns (Henwood *et al*. 1987; Study
Commission on the Family 1982). These changes have occurred alongside
the continuation of other values and patterns of behaviour. It would not be
realistic to expect our informants to be somehow outside all of this.

The continuity of values and social arrangements is well illustrated in
Michelle Bowen's view of the inevitability of her likely fate, in (65), or by
Jonathan Alexander or Melanie Reilly, in (91) and (93), both of who go
some way to acknowledging the probable disjuncture between what they
want and what they will get. Even Diana Fullerton, (96), comments
gloomily and that her mates are 'dropping out like flies'. Similarly, in (85)
and (90) there is a model of engagement and marriage as an orderly process
which would in all probability be recognised and approved by Leonard's
couples: *plus ça change, plus ça la même chose.*

In this chapter we have discussed courtship and marriage. It is as clear to us
as these things ever can be that, while unemployment is having an effect
upon the situation with respect to deferred courtship and marriage for some
and the nature of gender relationships, these changes should be viewed also
in the context of a whole range of social changes in the areas of gender
roles, sexual behaviour, marriage and parenthood. These broader changes
can, at best, only be attributed indirectly to the effects of unemployment. A
variety of causes, from the increased availability of contraception to the
steep rise in house prices which has entailed a long period of saving for 'a
place of our own', can be pointed to. Such things have their historical roots

in the affluent 1960s and impinge upon the employed and the unemployed alike. The latter is also likely to be true if the 'new puritanism' of the post-AIDS social world becomes a powerful force for change.

Which brings us to our final point. From our review of the research literature relating to South Wales, it is clear that gender roles and courtship and marriage patterns have been changing – even if only in small degree – since the 1930s. The further back one goes historically the more one is forced to recognise that, certainly in the areas we are concerned with, sexual relations and family life, change is the norm not the exception (Marsh 1965: 19–58; Wall 1987). It is important, therefore, to talk about 'traditional' values or 'established' patterns of behaviour in only the loosest of possible senses. Change and continuity – each in differing degrees, depending on the specificities of the historical moment – are both routine or 'normal' aspects of social life. We will continue to explore this theme, in the context of a discussion of models of adulthood, in the next chapter.

| 5 |

INTO ADULTHOOD

One of the themes running through our discussion so far has been the transition from youth to adulthood. Implicit in that discussion has been an understanding of the meaning of adulthood as a social category. Up until this point, however, that understanding has been largely commonsensical and taken for granted. In many respects, this usage accurately reflects much of the wider sociological literature concerning youth and its many transitions.

It is possible, however, to be more specific or explicit about what one means by adulthood. In part, that is what we will attempt to do in this chapter. In order to construct a working definition, a coherent analytical model, the models of adult status which are current in society must be the starting-point inasmuch as adulthood, in our understanding, is a culturally and socially defined status (a facet of the life-*course*) rather than a biologically determined condition (a phase of the life-*cycle*).[1] Chris Harris has argued persuasively for the importance of making this distinction: the life-cycle is a recurrent unit of biological time between birth and reproduction and is shorter than the life-course, which stretches from birth to death – continuing beyond the period of parenthood and child-raising. The life-course, therefore, is a variable unit of social time and individual biography (Harris 1987: 22–3). A further argument for adopting the life-course as the appropriate sociological model for the passage from womb to tomb criticises the notion of the life-cycle because it 'implies fixed categories in the life of an individual and suggests a stable social system' (Cohen 1987: 2). It is the life-course rather than the life-cycle with which we are concerned here.

An understanding of the life-course as culturally or socially constructed, and hence variable, is central to the discussion which follows. In this chapter we will be examining two related topics: first, the nature of adulthood and the criteria which are used to mark off its boundaries in contemporary Britain[2] and, second, the impact of long-term unemployment upon the assumption of adulthood by young women and men.

Adulthood and unemployment: the argument

In Chapter 1 we suggested that the research agenda for a large slice of the sociology of youth has changed from the transition from school to work to a less narrow focus upon the transition from youth to adulthood. This is partly due to the gradual erosion of work by unemployment and the insertion of state employment or training schemes into the institutional network which mediates the passage from education to the labour market and partly because of a shift away from looking at 'youth as a problem' towards the analysis of the problems of youth. This latter has entailed both a relatively novel concern with 'ordinary' rather than 'troublesome' young people and a widening of the range of topics in which researchers are interested.

Paul Willis, in an influential series of short articles (Willis 1984a, b, c, d), was one of the first commentators to highlight the possible consequences for the transition to adulthood of long-term unemployment on a grand scale. His argument is as follows:

> In my view we are still failing to get to grips with the implications of unemployment ... most of the adult unemployed are already *culturally formed*. ... They are workers without work, wage earners without the wage, consumers without money. ... But for young adults the situation is qualitatively different, and in my view more open – both positively and negatively. This is because they are not yet fully formed. For them there are only broken transitions into the possibilities of adult roles. They have never experienced them. They are in suspended animation.
>
> (Willis 1984a: 18–19, original emphasis)

> To understand unemployment we need to understand what is missing – the wage ... the wage is still the golden key (mortgage, rent, household bills) to a separate personal household, away from parents and away from the boss. ... The loss of the wage also interrupts the main preparation for transition into the separate household: the formation of 'the couple' and preparation for a family. ... The wage finally, of course, permits the transition to being a consumer – having some real power in the marketplace.
>
> (Willis 1984b: 476)

> The disappearance of work and the wage is likely to produce a very particular crisis for [the] traditional masculine sense of identity and meaning. ... One way for young men to resolve their 'gender crisis' may be an aggressive assertion of masculinity and masculine style for its own sake. ... For young working-class women the case is somewhat different. Unemployment may well mean a deepening of their domestic duties and their oppression. The tradition role of housewife, child carer and support may be not broken but strengthened. ... If you can't escape

from home through the earning power of a young man, an alternative way to 'get your own place' may simply be to become pregnant ... child rearing offers a clear role for young women. You are meeting the needs of someone else, and you are achieving a transition to adult status.

(Willis 1984c: 13)

The reader will, we hope, excuse these long quotations from Willis. They serve to present, concisely and in his own words, the major points of his argument with respect to the assumption of adulthood. First, unemployed young people are, Willis suggests, in a state of 'suspended animation', condemned to a purgatorial appendix of the life-course – more than adolescents but less than adults. Second, there appear to be four major criteria of adulthood: employment and an earned wage (particularly for men), parenthood (in reality motherhood, for it is women to whom this seems to apply most), an independent household and market capacity in terms of consumption. Finally, the responses to the problem of 'broken transitions' by young people vary by gender and in terms of their effectiveness: young women may opt for motherhood as a route to adulthood (albeit passive and dependent on the state); for young men, however, there is only the boastful and troubled chest-beating of traditional masculinity. The responsibility of being needed by another dependent human being versus the fantasy and insecurity of redundancy.

This analysis has been supported by other researchers (Bostyn and Wight 1987: 142; Coffield 1987). According to Beatrix Campbell, in particular (Campbell 1984, pp. 57–79), unmarried single parenthood may be an escape strategy for unemployed young women looking for a route out of continual juvenile status and domestic oppression in the parental home. Campbell's argument has been endorsed in an impressionistic study of the lives of young women in Swansea; unfortunately, the author provides little in the way of supporting evidence (Windsor 1984: 56). The reports of Willis, Campbell and others seem to suggest a trend towards later marriage, or even the rejection of marriage, the creation of matricentric family units and the huddle into the collective solace of the peer group by unemployed men. The comparison with underemployed black communities in the United States is suggestive, although it probably should not be pushed too far.[3]

Claire Wallace's ethnography of the young women and men of the Isle of Sheppey provides us with a more rounded view of these issues than Willis offers (Wallace 1987). For the young men in Wallace's study there is the possibility of finding a limited haven in the male peer-group, with its compensatory ideology of *machismo* and sense of shared adversity; it is a defensive laager for a fragile and threatened masculinity. By contrast, unemployed young women often spend more time than they might otherwise in their family home, 'a form of extended adolescence' which is symbolised by their increased responsibility for housework (Wallace 1986: 109). This is in general accord with Barbara Hudson's argument that 'girls' attempts to be accepted as "young women" are always liable to be undermined (subverted) by perceptions of them as childish, immature, or any other of the terms by which we define the status "adolescent" ' (Hudson 1984: 31–2).

For some of the unemployed young women of Sheppey there does appear to be an alternative to dependency within their family of origin: a household of their own. What is clear from Wallace's ethnography, however, is that this is most often found in the context of marriage – although, as elsewhere in the United Kingdom, levels of cohabitation are on the increase. However, of the cohabiting couples in her study, the majority were both in employment (Wallace 1987: 156–69). Single parenthood remained very much a minority situation, and not one which appeared to be deliberately embraced as an alternative to unemployment. This also appears to be the case for the sample of young people in Wolverhampton surveyed by the team led by Willis himself, although in the absence of the quantitative data it is impossible to be completely certain (Youth Review Team 1985: 110–13). Such evidence as there is from recent research in Swansea supports an overall view that many young people – whether unemployed or not – *drift* into cohabitation, marriage and parenthood (Windsor 1984: 55–64).[4]

Marriage remains, therefore, the statistical and the cultural norm; nor does cohabitation appear to be particularly a response to unemployment. Rather, much as we argued in the previous chapter, there has been a range of major social and attitudinal changes with respect to marriage and sexuality which are, at best, only in small part bound up with unemployment. It is clear from Claire Wallace's material and our own fieldwork that there is no longer a uniform, neat, conventional progression from courtship to engagement to marriage to parenthood. For many young people this has been replaced by a passage from courtship to parenthood with cohabitation and marriage as important but none the less movable events. Parenthood is also coming later for many young adults, be they employed or unemployed, as a consequence of the wide availability of contraception, the changing expectations of women and the economic calculus of the housing market. However, a further aspect of Wallace's argument is equally clear: moving out into an independent household, usually in the context of a 'couple' relationship, is more likely to be an option for an unemployed young woman than for an unemployed young man. This has to do with the importance of money, the relative adequacy of male and female wages and social security regulations.

Wallace's research, while it adds considerably to our understanding of the heterogeneity of the process of transition to adulthood and the increased variety of life-style options which are now open to young men and women (whether they are unemployed or not), does not specifically address the issue of adulthood and its vulnerability during unemployment. In that sense, her analysis offers only an implicit comment on Willis's position. In an attempt to expose Willis's arguments to a more systematic critique, we shall discuss three distinct issues in turn: first, the conventional social meaning of adulthood in modern Britain; second, the meaning of adulthood for our young respondents and their view of its relationship to unemployment; and finally, the perspectives of the parents we interviewed concerning the adulthood of their sons and daughters.

The thresholds of adulthood

We have already suggested that the notion of adulthood as it is commonly used in the social science literature is curiously ill-defined; its definition is largely implicit and commonsensical. Willis, for example, in the articles discussed above, seems to suggest that – with differing emphases for men and women – the central criteria of adulthood are employment and the wage, a household of one's own, parenthood and independence as a consumer in the market. These are, for Willis, the major practical elements in the social and cultural formation of individuals as adults, the exercise of which constitutes the consummation of the transition from adolescence. There is, however, no attempt in Willis's discussion to deconstruct the notion of adulthood or map out its major contours.

Wallace offers a different view, distinguishing between official definitions of adulthood – whether legal, economic or whatever – and the perceptions, definitions and experiences of young people themselves (Wallace 1987: 2–3). While the official definitions are at present being redefined, the views of young people are also variable. The transition to adulthood may therefore occur across a range of ages, depending on circumstances. Wallace further suggests that the key factor defining 'youth', 'adulthood' and the threshold between them is employment and market capacity: the assumption of economic independence.[5]

In Allison James's discussion of 'the boundaries of adolescence', a yet more complex understanding of the meaning of adulthood emerges from her examination of the meanings of adolescence for the young people she studied (James 1986). First, she emphasises the importance of official definitions, tied closely to precise calender age, in defining the social experience of young women and men: 'For many adolescents the process of growing up represents ... the endurance of years until they are "old enough" ' (*ibid.*: 157). As Ariès has pointed out, one of the characteristic features of modern society is the recording of precise age (i.e. date of birth) and its use, in a variety of settings, for the categorisation and registration of individuals within the networks of the state (Ariès 1973: 15–18). Part and parcel of long-term historical processes of literisation and bureaucratisation, this is the source of the official definitions mentioned by Wallace.

Second, James points out that these official classificatory definitions are variable: different ages matter as definitional thresholds for different purposes. Gender is also a source of variation: there are some things, particularly with respect to sexual behaviour, that girls and boys can legally only do at different ages. Third, the physical body is, according to James, a source of categorical definition at the folk or popular level: 'the age, shape, size and functioning of the physical body have become important referential poles' (James 1986: 158). This may be the case for the transition between childhood and adolescence, marked in part as it is by the onset of puberty; it seems likely to be less important with respect to adulthood.

This is not to say, however, that the body and, more generally, the world of appearances, is unimportant: the use of *style*, whether behavioural, sartorial or physical, as a marker of life-course transition, particularly between childhood, youth/adolescence and adulthood, is too well documented to require much comment here (Brake 1980; Hebdige 1979). Robert Connell, for example, has emphasised the role of the body and its representations in the social construction of hegemonic male adulthood in the realms of work, sexuality and fatherhood (Connell 1983: 22–6). It is also clear that the use of language, particularly with respect to non-standard usage and slang, is age-related and may serve to mark the transition from youth to adulthood for many people (Romaine 1984: 104–11). All of these stylistic devices are aspects of the claim to adult status and are among the means by which that claim can be made: they are part of appropriate 'adult behaviour'.

The social recognition of reproductive capacity as part of the construction of 'youth' as a social identity, and the subsequent according of an expanding degree of sexual licence as a facet of the bestowal of adulthood, provide the terrain for generational conflict as well as thresholds of social status. The topic of generational conflict is, of course, a fairly well-worn sociological patch. More generally, so is the broader topic of the structuration of social relationships and institutions by age categories. One does not have to either accept or endorse the analyses of authors such as Mead (1942, 1943), Parsons (1954: 89–103), Eisenstadt (1956) or Musgrove (1964) – not to mention the psychoanalytic approach of Erikson (1968) – to acknowledge their importance in laying the foundations of a theoretically informed discourse about young people. More important, however, it is equally clear that, by comparison with the youth culture paradigm in particular, these older 'classic' authors are mobilising a broad and inclusive model of adulthood and its dimensions. Instead of a small number of criteria being used to model the transition to adulthood, as is the case in Willis's work for example, a wide range of factors is considered: institutional, interactional, psychological, and so on.

While we do not intend to go as far down that road as might be possible, such an approach must surely be right. A host of factors and processes contribute to the transition from youth to adulthood and a range of thresholds, criteria and signals serve to demarcate and distinguish one status from the other (Hogan and Astone 1986). Some of these have been mentioned above. It should now be possible to draw up the beginnings of a descriptive analytical model of the notion of adulthood in contemporary Britain.[6] The components out of which such a model must be assembled are, in the first instance, those models of adulthood which are current among actors in the social world 'out there'.

Among the most important of these are the official models or criteria which serve to delineate the steps along the way to full adult status. These are the various thresholds of adulthood which are defined by the state and which are reached at different ages. The profusion and inconsistency of these official models of age status – products of *ad hoc* legislative decisions over the years – results in a degree of legal and popular confusion:

> when is a child not a child depends upon what it is doing. For example, at five years of age children can legally drink alcohol in private but they cannot buy drinks in public places until eighteen. At sixteen, on the other hand, they can be bought beer, cider, wine or sherry to be drunk in public as an accompaniment to a meal. At seven years of age a child may withdraw money from his or her Post Office account but cannot earn money until thirteen and he or she can only work for two hours a day and one on Sunday. From birth a child may have a Premium Bond in his or her name, but cannot buy one until sixteen.
>
> (James 1986: 157)

Some readers may object that the above proscriptions and possibilities are relatively trivial. Be that as it may, they serve to illustrate the point: the official legal models of majority and minority are anything but clear-cut. They cover such non-trivial matters as criminal responsibility, sexual consent (which differs for heterosexuals and homosexuals by gender and between heterosexual and homosexual men), the conditional and the unconditional rights to marry, the right to drive a motor vehicle, medical consent, the right to vote, the right to accept paid, full-time employment (if you can find it, of course), the right – given individual entitlement – to welfare benefits, and the right to donate blood or organs for transplantation. Obligations are also involved of course: to register for National Insurance purposes, to pay income tax if in employment, or to attend if summoned for jury service, for example.

In many important respects, therefore, adulthood is legally and administratively defined by the state and recognised as a basic category of social membership. It is bound up, in a weaker or stronger sense, depending upon the particular criterion concerned, with citizenship, the pre-eminent category of membership. Most elements of 'official' adulthood – with the limited exceptions noted above – are not gendered: they are universally bestowed aspects of citizenship, involving and invoking rights and responsibilities. Not all, however, are automatically acquired: eligibility for jury service, for example, depends upon inclusion in the electoral register (something which, at the time of writing, is threatened by the introduction of the community charge or 'poll tax').

The official criteria of adulthood do not, therefore, coincide in a sharp or clearly defined passage from one legal status (childhood) to another (adulthood). Instead, there is a gradual and incremental inclusion into citizenship and the rights and duties of the adult world. For most people in Britain, this culminates at 18 years of age in political suffrage and the unrestricted right of marriage. We have also suggested, however, that the state or official models of adult status are not the only significant dimensions of adulthood. We will discuss the popular or informal models in the sections which follow.

Responsibilities and independence

In our brief discussion of the relevant literature, it became clear that in addition to its existence as an officially defined identity – something which an individual *is* – adulthood is also understood as a set of practical accomplishments, a repertoire of appropriate behaviour: something which the individual *does*. This is no more than Linton's classic distinction between status and role as aspects of social identity (Linton 1936: 113–14). As a theoretical formulation it is, of course, not without its problems or its critics (e.g. Jackson 1972); these concepts do, however, serve a limited purpose in this context by clarifying the analytical distinction between membership of a social category, on the one hand, and the expectations which attach to membership – in the eyes of both the individual concerned and other people, on the other. Furthermore, as Linton himself insists, status and role are, at best, only analytically separable; the reality of day-to-day social life is that they are not distinct. In the consciousness and practice of actors, they are simply part of 'being adult'. But what does 'being adult' actually mean?

This was a question which we asked when we talked to students at Swansea College of Further Education. Far and away the most important criterion was age: official models notwithstanding, between 20 and 21 years was seen as the point of transition. 'Being old enough to work' was also important. Another strong theme was the taking on of responsibility: 'being able to cope with life', 'making your own choices', 'being independent' or 'being mature enough to handle responsibilities'.

It was not just what *they* might do which was important to these young people, however. Other people's attitudes and behaviour were clearly also significant:

(98)
When you're working, you're with older people. That's got something
to do with it. If you're on the dole, you're staying with your mates all
the time.

The home was another important arena in this respect: 'Your parents'
reactions are important, especially if you're living under their roof ... How
they treat you'. So, the company of adults provides the appropriate setting
for the adoption of adult behaviour and the validation of the young
person's claim to adulthood. That behaviour and that claim are particularly
bound up with notions of responsibility and independence.

The same themes crop up in the interview material from Port Talbot and
Swansea:

(99)
SH: Do you see yourself as a child, or an adult?
TF: An adult ... 'cos I've got all the responsibility. If I was thinking of
   being a child I would say 'To hell with the responsibilities' and lose
   the house. Now I've got all the responsibilities of the house and
   whoever's in it.

                                          (Thomas Field, Abbeyview)

(100)
SH: Is Thomas a child or an adult?
AF: Adult ... he's taken on responsibility. He knows how to cook, he
knows how to clean. He knows how to do things. He knows what
trouble is. He knows how to look after people.

                                       (Mr Alexander Field, Abbeyview)

Mr Field is an invalid, his wife is dead; Thomas, the youngest child and the
only one still at home – 23 years old at the time of the interview – had taken
over the tenancy of the house and was now looking after his father. He has,
in a sense, had adulthood thrust upon him (although he could, presumably,
have insisted that one of his married sisters shoulder the burden instead).
His is an extreme case. However, as the material below illustrates, similar
issues are at stake – although the stakes are lower – for other young people:

(101)
SH: Do you see yourself as a child or an adult?
EP: A bit of both, I think. I'd like to think of myself as a fully fledged
   adult, but I'm not, I suppose. I still depend on my parents for a lot
   of things.
SH: What would make you?
EP: Getting a job and getting out, I think ... A bit more independent.
SH: And your brother [aged 18]?

EP: I think he's still a child. [Elaine is 19 years old.]

SH: What would make him an adult?

EP: I don't know. Being more independent. He relies on people a lot more than me.

(Elaine Peters, Abbeyview)

(102)

SH: Is Elaine a child or an adult?

Mrs P: Oh, adult. She was a young lady very early. You could never treat her like a child.

Mr P: She always told me what to do.

Mrs P: We've always listened to what they have to say.

SH: And Chris? [Elaine's younger brother.]

Mrs P: Still very young for his age. He's not responsible.

Mr P: Since he's had that job down there [a Council YTS scheme] he's changing.

Mrs P: He is answering you back, which he never did before.

(Mr and Mrs Peters, Abbeyview)

(103)

SH: What defines an adult?

AW: Well, to be an adult you'd have, you know, responsibilities and you'd be able to cope and look after yourself. Now I don't think I'd be able to do that.

(Andrea Watkins, age 20, Abbeyview)

(104)

SH: Is Malcolm [Rees, 20 years old] an adult?

ML: No, I don't think you can be an adult if you're not particularly bothered about what's going to happen. I don't see how he can be grown up with that sort of attitude. As long as he's got a couple of pounds to go out in the night ... If you can think, 'Good God, what's happening to me? I'm going to miss out unless I start doing something. The fellow next door's got a Capri. The guy down there's got a Capri. They're running about. I've got nothing. I want a Capri', you know? Then you start doing something about it. You start growing up.

(Mr Michael Lynch, High Oak)

(105)

SH: Are you an adult or a child?

RH: I'm in between. An adult means responsibility ... being married, kids, a steady job, a mortgage.

SH: Would having a job make you an adult?

RH: No, I'm not ready for those responsibilities.

(Richard Haig, age 23, High Oak)

(106)

HR: I'm an adult ...//... I can go where I want to. I can come in when

I want to. I don't have to answer to anyone.

SH: Does it involve responsible behaviour?

HR: I've never done anything out of the ordinary.

(Helen Roderick, age 22, High Oak)

(107)

Ever since I was a child I was an adult. My parents consider me a youth. If I waited for them I wouldn't be an adult 'til I was seventy. I can never tell my father what to do because I'm younger ...//... It would totally undermine me to listen to Radio One. I prefer Radio Four.

(Arthur Evans, age 18, Ty-Gwyn)

(108)

CE: He's been an adult ever since he was born, I think ... When he was born he looked three months old.

SH: What do you mean?

CE: He's always been, I think, serious-minded and mature in his attitude. He's never been, I would say, frivolous in the way children tend to be.

ME: He never played as a child. Always children came to play with him and his play was 'Watch me do this' ... He never played *with* the children.

CE: He sprayed the side of my car.

ME: He was three. He got a tin of paint and painted the wing of Clive's car ...//...

CE: I think he's an adult, therefore, he's perfectly capable of looking after himself. As capable as any young person. We've got confidence in him when he goes places.

(Mrs Megan Evans and Mr Colin Evans, Ty-Gwyn)

(109)

I had to grow up a lot since my father died. I've been through a lot of situations. I can't really say. People might say I'm a child, but I know I'm an adult, because ... it's the way I handle situations and stuff.

(Kenneth Mason, age 18, Ty-Gwyn).

A number of currents can be traced in the ethnography above. As we have already suggested, the importance of 'responsibility' – the accepting of responsibility for oneself or for others, the exhibition of responsible behaviour – should not be underestimated. Whether it be perceived as a general attribute, as in (101), (103) and (106), or, more specifically, as a particular way of responding to a difficult situation, as in (99), (100) or (109), responsibility – which is both something one can accept at need or an attitude one can just have – is a core component of adulthood. In the case of Arthur Evans, (107) and (108), for example, the maturity of his attitude to life is explained by himself and by his parents as a response in part to the difficulties involved in moving around the country and changing schools many times during his childhood.

There is, however, another theme in this material; related to the notion of responsibility there is an emphasis upon 'independence', of both thought and deed. This can be seen in (101), (103) and (106). Independence involves, minimally, the assumption of responsibility for oneself. Neither, however, is a hard-and-fast attribute: it is typically degrees of responsibility and degrees of independence which are expected and attainable. Total independence, in particular, while it is a seductive myth is exactly that, a myth; nor is undiluted responsibility – for either oneself or another – something which many citizens of a modern industrial society ever have to face up to.

Along with responsibility, the fostering of independence is also at the heart of financial dealings between parents and their daughters and sons. As we have seen in Chapter 3, mothers and fathers are caught between the attempt to encourage or teach financial and other independence, something which may necessitate the son or daughter experiencing a degree of hardship, and the understandable wish to ensure that not *too* much hardship is involved.

Independence and responsibility converge in the social security payments received by unemployed young people (or, if they are 'on a scheme', in their training allowance). There are a number of points here which are germane to this discussion. First, claiming benefit is an adult transaction between the citizen and the state, wholly independent, in the first instance, of mediation by parents or other adult representatives. It is something which young people have to do for themselves. And the money, the girocheque when it comes, is *their* money.

The second point is that, although benefit is not much, because it is their own money they can, within limits, dispose of it as they see fit. It is, as we have already seen, an important resource – in the shape of 'lodge' money – in the symbolic economy (and in many cases the subsistence economy) of the household and family relationships. It is a medium through which responsibility can be displayed: enough to scrape by on and enough to allow them to get into difficulties. It creates the possibilities of success and failure. It is an independent income for which they alone are responsible – very different from pocket money and greater than the wages of a Saturday job.

The receipt of benefit or a training allowance by a son or daughter is the precondition for a legitimate demand by parents for a contribution to the domestic budget. This is also an essentially adult transaction, signifying the end of shelter and succour within the family home *as of right* and without cost (which is, of course, not to say that parents would necessarily turn out a son or daughter who did not contribute). State benefits and allowances are meagre, they are not enough to permit a full life-style, they may often entail a degree of poverty – sometimes severe poverty – for young adults and their families. They are, however, better than nothing.

In this sense, it is possible to argue that the privations of youth unemployment provide the young person with both sufficient – if limited – resources and severe enough adversity to permit the satisfactory perform-ance of a degree of adult behaviour. What is more, as Helen Roderick suggests in (106), this behaviour is, in the context of widespread youth unemployment, 'ordinary': it is simply doing what is routinely appropriate, what lots of other young women and men are doing, getting on with as much of the business of life as is available to them. Perversely, as in the case of Elaine Peters' brother (102), this may include such apparently undesirable behaviour as starting to assert oneself by 'answering back', something which may be taken to indicate the beginnings of indepen-dence.

For the 17 and 18 year olds at the College of Further Education, age was the most important single criterion of adult status. They were going to get there, and quite soon. The sample members from Swansea and Port Talbot were, in the main considerably older and, for them, having reached the 'magic age' of 20 or 21, the simple fact of age in years was now less significant. They knew that it was also a matter of how they managed their lives. Parents also recognised this. Hence the meaning of descriptions such as 'still very young for his age' or 'adult ever since he was born'. Hence, too, the wry recognition by Richard Haig that, at the age of 23, he was 'in between' (105), old enough to count as an adult, but not yet ready or willing, as an individual, to accept the responsibilities involved.

One of the most interesting aspects of the interview material relating to models of adulthood is that it is, for most important purposes, undifferenti-ated by gender. Even in the case of Rebecca Hughes from Abbeyview, whose adequacy as a single parent was the subject of approving comment from neighbours and her family alike, the fact of motherhood was not what made her an adult. It was how she coped, how she responded to the challenge which having a baby had offered to her, which mattered. Her sister, it was thought, would not have done half as well:

(110)
RJ: Do you see yourself as a child or an adult?
RH: An adult.
RJ: And what is it makes you an adult?
RH: Well, especially since I had Jemma I've got more responsibilities. You know what I mean. I've got to watch her everywhere ... make sure she's all right.
(111)
RJ: Is Rebecca a child or an adult?
Mrs H: Rebecca's been more of an adult.
RJ: What makes the difference?
Mrs H: Well, Rebecca've been a very independent girl. Since she's been

tiny she've always known what she wanted to do and it's always worked out for her, see. I didn't think the other one [Rebecca's sister] would cope as well as Rebecca. They're two different girls ... Rebecca can be a problem to live with. She's too independent for the baby. Everything the baby has got, she's struggled to get.

What is important here is Rebecca's personality, her individual nature. This is something – the role of notions of individual responsibility in framing popular understandings of, and responses to, unemployment – which we shall return to in detail in Chapter 6.

The quotations from Rebecca and her mother illustrate another point: independence, one of the desirable keystones of adulthood, may also be a source of conflict when the young person concerned is living in a state of *de facto* dependence under the parental roof. Once again, there is the need to achieve a delicate balance between control and freedom:

(112)
I treat him like an adult, and there are certain things I don't really know about, you know. Whereas when they were younger you wanted to know everything they were doing so you could keep a check on them. Basically, he's now in activities I don't know much about ...//...
I feel if he was working, earning a wage, he would probably be somewhere of his own at 21 years. The fact that he's here, it's like having another adult in the house. He's a typical boy. He doesn't do anything around the house unless he's forced to it.

Here Mr Fred Mansell of High Oak is talking about his step-son, Philip Broughton, aged 21. Philip, too, had views on the appropriateness of continuing to live at home:

(113)
I think I'll leave home. There are a couple of flats in Mumbles ...//...
It's just a, getting older, a stage living with your father. The lady over the way she's still living with her parents, not married. I don't know how old she is. I couldn't face doing that. It's a cushy number, living at home.

Philip's half-sister, Katherine Mansell, aged 19 and also unemployed had a very critical view of her brother's life-style:

(114)
SH: Is Philip a child or an adult?
KM: Ah, now ... half and half, I think.
SH: What would make him an adult?

KM: He's more helpful when my dad's away. He does become a father figure ... or tries to be.

SH: Why is he a child?

KM: He doesn't face up to reality. He goes surfing and doesn't think about what's more important in the future.

SH: What is more important?

KM: I mean, if he were thinking about getting married. I mean, he's got to have a job if he's going to support a family.

In Chapters 2 and 3 we talked about the management of the family as a social group, something which is largely the responsibility of mothers. Parents – once again, particularly mothers – are important factors in their sons' and daughters' passage into adulthood. Whether we view this as 'pushing them out of the nest' or whatever, there is no room to doubt the importance of parental guidance and pressure, especially when the young person concerned is showing few signs of enthusiasm for the beckoning delights of adulthood. Even where this is not the case, however, many parents see themselves as having a role to play in this respect:

(115)

JP: The first thing she'd do [if she had a job] is find a place of her own ... I think she'd like to be more independent of us.

SH: What would you feel?

JP: I'd want her to try it. Whatever she wanted to try ... everyone likes their children to be independent.

(Mrs Joan Peters, mother of Elaine Peters, Abbeyview)

Mrs Peters is not, however, wholly right. Not everyone does want their children to be independent. Just as the support and encouragement of parents can facilitate a smooth transition to adult status, so the emotional demands of parents can place obstacles in the path of a son or daughter:

(116)

RJ: If Audrey leaves home and gets married, will you think of her as adult then?

VB: We'll break our hearts. Well, she's still a child. We'll break our hearts. Audrey thinks I'm hard, but Audrey don't realise ...//... Oh, I don't know. I would like to see her, well, I know she will eventually get married, I suppose. Well, perhaps she won't. You don't know ...//... But, er, we will miss her very much.

(Mr Victor Ballinger, Abbeyview)

On the whole, however, our impression is that the Ballingers are the exception. Even they recognised at many points during the interviews that their wish to keep Audrey – an only child and treasured – at home required justification or defence. It was not that they did not want their daughter to be independent: they wanted to delay matters as much as possible, to control Audrey in order to protect her. And they did not want to be lonely. It is important to the majority of parents that their children should 'grow up'. This is, after all, a central element of the job of parenthood; the successful production of mature and independent men and women who can take their place in the world, to the public credit of their parents. Increasingly, parents are also looking forward to a period 'after the kids have grown up', when they can spend money on themselves and do things which the demands of their children have hitherto prevented them from doing. In these respects, therefore, mothers and fathers have a vested interest in their offsprings' successful assumption of adult status.

And they are, of course, not the only ones with a vested interest. The young people concerned are also (most of them) actively striving to achieve full adult status. *Not* becoming adult is, literally, almost unthinkable. One may be able to avoid some of the responsibilities implied in adulthood – and a few of the young men we interviewed, in particular, were managing to do so successfully[7] – but there is the attraction of independence, if it can be achieved. Here it is perhaps important to note the distinction between attempting to *evade* or *postpone* adulthood and being *prevented* from becoming an adult. There is a world of difference between 'won't' and 'can't'. Most of the young women and men to whom we spoke – and this is once again an impressionistic judgement – had not, however, given the matter much thought. Becoming an adult is, in this sense, something which in contemporary Britain is almost inevitable for young people by their early twenties.[8]

Which is not to say that the deprivation entailed by long-term unemployment has *no* consequences for the passage into adulthood or the nature of the subsequent experience of adult life. A number of the quotations above – for example (98), (101), (105), (112) and (115) – explicitly suggest otherwise. We shall discuss this issue in more detail in the next section.

Adulthood and unemployment: some evidence

The overall thrust of this chapter should by now be clear: despite the many problems resulting from their unemployment, and the arguments of authors such as Willis notwithstanding, the young people who we interviewed were still, to all intents and purposes, passing from youth to adulthood. Unemployment does, however, have its impact:

(117)
SH: Do you see yourself as an adult?
GW: It depends. If I've played up, I feel a real idiot [he has a history of

behaviour which he recognises himself as unreasonable]. Otherwise I feel in between.

SH: What makes an adult?

GW: A job, a home, the responsibility of something to work for, to take care of.

(Geoffrey Wallis, age 24, Abbeyview)

(118)

SH: What makes a person an adult?

EW: I don't know. I always thought when you started to work and be independent. And you knew then what life was about. You've got to stand on your own two feet. But they don't have a chance to do that nowadays, because there's no work for them. I wouldn't say he's independent today. When you have twenty pounds a week you're dependent on who's keeping you, aren't you?

(Mrs Elsie Wallis, Abbeyview)

(119)

SH: What would make Malcolm [Rees] grow up?

GL: Responsibility. I think work is a responsibility, as you have to get up for work, you have to be there at a certain time and do X amount of hours. That gives you a sense of responsibility.

(Mrs Gwyneth Lynch, High Oak)

(120)

My mother worked in a club all her life. She said, 'Oh he'll grow up with the men. He'll get more responsible because he's with men, not with young boys.' And [when he was working part-time] he did.

(Mrs Cynthia Alexander, High Oak)

(121)

SH: Has unemployment had any effect on Andrew?

PJ: Yes, I think it's stopped him from growing up, in a way. He hasn't developed the responsibility he would have by now if he'd been in a job, being answerable to someone else other than us ... I think he's still a bit immature, more so than if he'd been working.

(Mrs Peggy Jones, Ty-Gwyn)

(122)

SH: Do you see Samantha [Smith] as a child or an adult?

Mrs H: Not as a child. I do see her as an adult in a lot of things, but there again being unemployed doesn't give them much incentive to act as an adult. I don't mean rudely or nastily.

SH: In what way?

Mrs H: ...//... They're able to take more on their minds [if they are in employment] because they've got no worries or anything. Being unemployed makes her afraid to do anything because she can't foresee the future.

(Mrs Horner, Ty-Gwyn)

These extracts suggest at least five ways in which unemployment impinges upon the fragile adulthood of some of the young people who we interviewed. In the first place, the absence of a reasonable income is an obstacle – albeit one which many people disregard – to the assumption of responsibilities such as an independent home or a relationship. Similarly, employment provides the basis for the exercise of a greater degree of independence – not only financial, but also in terms of personal confidence and social enablement – than is possible in the absence of a job.

Independence and responsibility are themes which we have already explored. The third point has also been mentioned earlier: the company of adults – as colleagues and superiors – provides a context within which adult behaviour can be learnt and an adult identity reinforced and validated. Workmates are not like parents: they have a different set of expectations, more tolerant of some things, less of others. The relationship is qualitatively different and, outside of apprenticeships and youth training schemes, it is typically a relationship between fellow adults. Neither the peer group nor the family can provide a replacement for this kind of interaction. Related to this is the argument, put forward by Mrs Lynch (119) and Mrs Jones (121) that employment provides an external discipline, distinct from the constraints imposed by parents or other family members. Learning to accept that discipline is perceived as an important part of 'growing up'. The kind of behaviour which that discipline produces – getting up on time, for example – is itself 'grown up'. Thus the experience of employment both demands and encourages behaviour which is socially defined as adult.

As an aside, it may be worth mentioning here that issues such as 'maturity' and 'responsibility' are also of importance to employers when they are recruiting labour. As part of their quest for the acceptable, self-motivating worker – someone who is 'reliable' – many managers place great stress on maturity. For men, they are particularly interested in 'the married man with two kids and a car', somebody who is disciplined by the weight of his commitments and *has* to come to work everyday (Blackburn and Mann 1979: 105; Jenkins 1986: 60–1, 67–8; Nichols and Beynon 1977: 97). In another context, one of the present authors has noted the importance of the acquisition of domestic commitments and consumer orientations in habituating (particularly male) workers to the constraints and drudgery of wage labour (Jenkins 1983: 133), something which Wallace has also discussed (Wallace 1987: 222–7). The transition to adulthood and the demands and disciplines of the labour market and employment should therefore be conceptualised as reciprocally and intimately bound up with each other, part of the complicated process of social production and reproduction which constitutes the on-going history of civil society in a capitalist democracy such as Britain.

Finally, unemployment is a social state which, at least in part, is characterised by insecurity and uncertainty. The long-term may often be something which is best not thought about: foreseeing the future becomes even more difficult than under 'normal' circumstances. Planning may, for some people, be impossible. The result is conservatism, the minimisation of risks; waiting for something to happen instead of initiating events and making decisions. It is a passive rather than an active engagement with the world.

To say this is a cue for another aside. So far, employment has been discussed in unambiguously positive terms, as something which encourages independence, breeds confidence and provides sufficient material resources to allow the proper exhibition of 'responsible' behaviour. It should not, however, be forgotten that many jobs – particularly the kinds of jobs which are open to working-class young people – are undermining, boring, possibly actually unpleasant, frequently insecure and typically badly paid. Health and safety at work may often be neglected. Some jobs encourage dependency, sap one's confidence and permit only a financially impoverished existence. For many young people the right to work is, in fact, the right to submit to conditions such as these.

To return to our argument, the above conclusions are, it might be said, to some degree in broad agreement with Paul Willis's view of long-term unemployment as a limbo between youth and adulthood. They do, however, require considerable qualification. First, it is clear to us that unemployment, in these respects, does not affect all unemployed young people to the same degree. Only a minority are likely to be severely undermined or held up in their transition to adult status. While none of the young unemployed are likely to find their lives completely untouched, their vulnerability in this respect is related to a range of factors, from individual psychology to the economic resources available to their families. The social and psychological consequences of unemployment vary – for young people and adults – for a variety of reasons and in a variety of ways (Allen *et al.* 1986; Fineman 1987; Fryer and Ullah 1987). Just as there is no 'standard' sequence of personal responses to unemployment, neither is unemployment likely in itself to have determinate consequences for life-course transitions.

The second substantial qualification to these findings is that, regardless of their ubiquity or severity, the effects of unemployment only touch upon part of the transition to adulthood. There is, as we have seen, a range of criteria which are involved in the construction of an adult social identity. There is also a range of contexts in which a sufficient degree of 'adult behaviour' can be accomplished. Some of these criteria and contexts are not employment-derived. For many young people, there are enough appropriate niches available within which to make a successful public claim to some degree of responsibility and independence – qualities which are at the core of the notion of adult behaviour. Significant others – parents, friends, other adults – are, what is more, implicated in the young person's performance as adult; their supporting roles provide that performance with solidity and credibility.

In support of the argument that many facets of adulthood are not necessarily related to unemployment, a comparison of our interview material from Abbeyview, High Oak and Ty-Gwyn reveals very similar patterns. The overwhelming majority of the young interviewees from each area saw themselves as adult or on the threshold of adulthood, although their parents were a little less convinced. This is one respect in which differences in local unemployment levels and communal experiences of unemployment did not appear to effect the views of our respondents.

Inasmuch as adulthood – whatever else it may be – is a legally defined status, closely related to citizenship, there is an important core component of adulthood which is neither performative nor dependent upon material resources. As such it is, for the vast bulk of the population, an inescapable consequence of 'coming of age'. This is the final important point to be made: Willis's conception of adulthood is performance-oriented: partly social (motherhood, independent living) and partly economic (the wage, market capacity as a consumer), although these are of course closely related. This is, however, a substantively insufficient and theoretically unsophisticated model of adulthood. To return to Linton's distinction between status and role, Willis is concentrating upon the role dimension of adult identity, and only on part of that. It is the failure to distinguish the legally constituted rights and duties defining adult status – which, taken together, may be conceptualised as a portfolio of enablement and obligation – from the capacity, whether economically based or whatever, to actualise the potential bound up in that status, which allows Willis to diagnose the suspension of adulthood for the young unemployed.

However, to close this section, Willis is correct about one thing. While some aspects of adulthood are relatively securely rooted in law and the administration of the state, the rest – the performative dimensions – are practical accomplishments. As such they are, like all performances, vulnerable to interruption and subversion. Our argument in this sense is that, while we consider it to be a distortion to suggest that long-term unemployment can prevent young people from becoming adult, it does undoubtedly affect the quality of their lives as adults and their ability to achieve all of the dimensions of 'complete' adulthood. They are adults, but they are unfulfilled and impoverished adults, unrealised and ambiguous:

(123)
SH: Do you treat Anthony [Lonsdale, age 20] as a child or an adult?
CL: Well, I try to treat him as an adult.
SH: How do you see him?
CL: I think I see him as an adult. He can be very sensible. When he's got something to say I try to listen to him ... Sometimes I'm very protective towards him.
SH: What would make him an adult?

CL: He can be very sensible. He can be a bit of both at times. Sometimes he can be very irresponsible.

SH: When he's in a group?

CL: No, I think in himself.

SH: Would it be different if he had a job?

CL: I think so. I think Anthony, on some occasions, lacks confidence. I think a job would, you know, give him that much more confidence in himself.

SH: Did the YTS [Youth Training Scheme] give him confidence?

CL: No, not really. He wasn't doing anything. He wasn't achieving anything. You could see there was going to be no end result to it. What youngster of 18 or 19 wants to be cleaning out toilets? It's dreadful.

(Mrs Christine Lonsdale, Ty-Gwyn)

Coming of age unemployed

In this chapter we have examined some of the arguments concerning the impact of long-term unemployment upon the transition to adulthood in modern Britain. We have also presented evidence from our research in Swansea and Port Talbot which bears upon those arguments. We have rejected the notion that long-term unemployment somehow actually prevents young women and men from becoming adults, for four reasons.

First, adulthood, before it is anything else, is a status legally and administratively defined by the state; it is bound up, in a weaker or stronger sense, with notions of citizenship and full membership in the polity. Jural and political adulthood in modern Britain is not dependent upon employment status. With limited exceptions, none of the thresholds of adulthood are gender-specific: they are universally bestowed aspects of citizenship, involving and invoking both rights and responsibilities. They are not all, however, automatically acquired: the right to vote in local and national elections, for example, depends in practice upon the individual's inclusion on the electoral register. Nor do they all converge at one time in a sharply defined change of legal status. There is, instead, an incremental and gradual inclusion into official adulthood, culminating for most people in Britain at the age of 18 with the right to vote and the right to marry without parental consent.

Second, social security benefits, while not as symbolically powerful or as economically substantial as a 'proper wage', allow young men and women more independence from their parents than they enjoyed whilst at school. Benefit is a resource of their own, the management of which allows them the opportunity to exhibit – or not – a degree of adult independence and responsibility. Claiming benefit is, in itself, an adult transaction between the individual and the state. Within the family of origin, benefit payments permit the giving in of 'lodge' money. Even though it might only be a small amount, and even though it may be returned to them in one guise or another, this is another adult transaction, an important indicator of the assumption of responsibility for oneself, recognised as such by both parents and their daughters and sons.

Third, the young people who we looked at proceed into adulthood at least in part because their parents help them to do so. In all sorts of ways, mothers and fathers – particularly mothers – assist in this process: cajoling, bullying, supporting, constructively neglecting, pushing, whatever it takes. People have *got* to grow up. Most parents *want* their children to become adults. It is, in fact, a public testimony to their own success as parents in 'bringing them up'.

Finally, of course, it is not only parents who have a great deal invested in this process of growing up. Most young people *want* (eventually) to grow up. It is 'only natural'. The majority of young people, experiencing the complicated cocktail of social, psychological and physiological maturation which makes up the transition from youth to adulthood, have little option anyway. The possibility of evading adulthood is not even considered. Within the bounds of socially defined 'normality', adulthood is more or less inevitable. While being on the dole may disrupt that normality, it does not destroy it for most people.

To sum up, while long-term unemployment does undoubtedly have specific effects upon young people's lives during their transition to adulthood, there seem to be no grounds for suggesting that it actually prevents them from becoming adults. Independent living and/or marriage and sexual partnership are but two facets of adulthood. It is the *right* to each, not their presence at any particular instance, which is most important. Willis's argument, therefore, as discussed at length above, is founded on much too narrow a conception of adulthood, on the one hand, and a misunderstanding of the distinction between adult rights and responsibilities in general and the actualisation of those possibilities by particular individuals, on the other. Many social identities – and adulthood is one – do not require the fulfilment or activation of all of their constituent elements in order that the status be satisfactorily acquired or the role filled. Some of these elements may be central, some less so and some peripheral (Nadel 1957: 31–5). Viewed from this perspective adulthood in British society is a robust, if inexactly defined, identity which, while certain aspects of it are likely to be threatened or curtailed by unemployment and economic hardship, cannot be undermined by circumstances which do not damage or destroy its central components.

To talk about topics such as citizenship and responsibility is to move our discussion into the realms of politics and political consciousness. One of the more important issues in this respect is the understanding which people have of unemployment and its causes. This is the central theme of the following chapter.

| 6 |

EXPLAINING UNEMPLOYMENT

We have discussed the effects of the long-term unemployment of young adults upon their family relationships, upon their courtship and marriage patterns and upon their assumption of adult status. It is clear to us, however, that unemployment does not have 'objective' or determinate effects (although it may be easier sometimes to write about it as if it does). Unemployment is a socially constructed state of being and experience. Its effects, whatever they may be, are produced by people, employed and unemployed, standing in hierarchically structured institutional and informal social relationships to each other, in the course of their daily practice and interaction. The allocation and distribution of scarce resources, both material and non-material (i.e. status, prestige, etc.), lie at the heart of these practices.

This being so, then, an important aspect of this process is the construction of a discourse or discourses about unemployment. Talk about unemployment and the unemployed is part of the process whereby the social state of unemployment – along with the unemployed, both as a category and as individual subjects – is constituted.[1] What is more, talk about unemployment, in particular attempts to explain or account for it at both the general and particular levels, is likely to have political significance inasmuch as unemployment is a subject with a distinctive resonance for politicians and parties.

Explanations and understandings of unemployment are also significant within families and in other social relationships. How a father, for example, interprets his daughter's unemployment is likely to influence the way in which he responds to it. Conversely, his understanding of her worklessness may also, in part, be a function of the history of the relationship between them. Similarly, the response which an individual will make to becoming and being unemployed is likely to be contingent upon a host of factors rooted in past and present circumstances. It will to some extent depend upon – and, reciprocally, contribute to – his or her understanding of why unemployment happens in general, why it has happened to them and why at that particular time. In order, therefore, to understand as fully as possible the manner in which families 'take the strain' when one of their younger members is unemployed in the long term, we must look at the different explanations and understandings of unemployment offered by the individuals concerned. Before doing so, however, it may be worth discussing briefly some of the assumptions underlying our account and some of the theoretical issues which it raises.

Understanding, explanation and attitudes

Perhaps the first question to be asked is, to what degree can we be sure that our interview questions actually reveal what people 'really' think? This, of course, is a question which is relevant to our whole study, not merely this chapter, and the answer, unfortunately, is that we cannot be certain. We can never be certain; it is, strictly speaking, impossible to know what is going on in somebody else's mind. This is the classic philosophical problem of 'other minds' (Carruthers 1986).

What we can, however, do is observe the practices of other people, both speech and other practices. In particular, one must listen to what people say, what they *tell* you that they think. Things such as consistency within their discourse and a degree of 'fit' between what they say and the surrounding cultural and social context, are indicative that one may take interviewees 'at face value' or 'at their word'. These expressions are instructive; they reveal the routine nature of this problem for all social actors in day-to-day interaction. There is always the possibility of falsehood and bad faith. In the absence of indicators to the contrary, the researcher, like everyone else, simply has to work on the assumption that one's knowledge of other people's beliefs and intentions, on the basis of their words and deeds – in the interview situation, largely their words – is reliable.

There is, however, consistency and consistency. It is reasonable to expect some kind of consistency from actors; such an expectation is, indeed, one of the bases of routine social interaction. None the less, many of us will profess different views on a particular subject, depending on the context, without either deceit or pretence. It is a truism of ethnomethodology and other schools of interactional sociology that meaning is situational. As such, there is little more to be said about it here. From the point of view of this chapter, a more interesting question is whether one set of attitudes 'held' by a person must be consistent with the rest of their attitudes. In other words, once you know what somebody's views are on one issue, in so far as it is possible to know that, can you predict their views on other issues? This is an important question if we are to try to relate our respondents' views about unemployment to the wider political context.

Apropos of this kind of question, Anthony Heath (1986) has differentiated between four different kinds of attitudinal consistency.

Logical and *technical* consistency are, generally speaking, concerned with the absence of contradiction either within a set of attitudes (i.e. attitudes about a broadly defined subject) or in the relationship between desired goals and proposed methods for their achievement. *Normative* consistency refers to agreement or concordance between desired goals and *ideological* consistency to the relationship between discrete sets of attitudes, goals and norms within an overall world-view. Moving from logical to ideological consistency, 'so the level of concordance in people's attitudes predictably declines' (*ibid*.: 14). This is also a move from the less to the more abstract. However, looking at material from the 1985 British Social Attitudes survey, Heath suggests that while ideological consistency is not to be found in the national sample as a whole, there are – as one might expect in a pluralist, liberal democracy – a number of ideological packages of attitudes which can be identified, albeit loosely. One can, therefore, reasonably expect to find some consistency in the attitudes held by people; at the same time, particularly with respect to the normative and the ideological, one should not be surprised by either the weakness or the absence of consistency.

Stewart and Blackburn have approached similar questions in their discussion of the nature of the 'consent' which individuals give to the systems of structured social inequality in which they live and under which they suffer disadvantage (Stewart and Blackburn 1975). Rejecting an explanation based on voluntarism and choice, they suggest that 'feelings of satisfaction can co-exist with strong negative evaluations of position in the social structure, and that these negative evaluations need not threaten the stability of the structure' (*ibid*.: 482). This is partly because judgements of satisfaction or dissatisfaction are generally made within narrow, specific contexts and need not, therefore, extend to the wider pattern of social institutions and arrangements, and partly because some degree of constraint on individual action is seen as inevitable and does not, as a consequence, illicit moral disapproval. In this latter sense, disadvantage is simply taken-for-granted as axiomatic: 'satisfaction need not measure pleasure, but merely marginal differences in a context of anticipated deprivation, (*ibid*.: 505). Once again, this is an argument for not regarding a degree of attitudinal inconsistency as anything other than to be expected.

Related issues surface in Coxon and Jones's sophisticated study of social cognition and stratification (Coxon and Jones 1978, 1979; Coxon, Davies and Jones 1986). Among the relevant points is the ambiguity and dissensus which exists about evaluations of occupational prestige and the place of occupations within the class structure. While their research subjects did agree, as a whole, in their identification of the ends of the hierarchy – the top and bottom – there was no such consistency concerning the middle reaches of the class system. Of similar interest is the discovery that, in category sorting exercises for the researchers, 'some people, for example, claimed that social class had no place in their thinking and then proceeded to use it liberally' (Coxon and Jones 1979: 189). Here, perhaps, is a particularly common political and cognitive inconsistency. Finally, and it is a comparable point to Stewart and Blackburn's argument, the closer to the bottom of the hierarchies of class, status and power an individual is, the shorter the scale of those hierarchies is perceived to be (conversely, the closer to the top a person is, the greater the perceived social and economic distance between top and bottom). One's perception of the class structure is, therefore, closely linked to one's position within it.

There are, of course, many other pieces of research or theoretical discussion which might be to the point here. For example, many contributors to the debate about class-based 'images of society' suggest that there is a close connection between occupational community, locality and shared perceptions of society and inequality (Bulmer 1975). This perspective has, however, been criticised by Howard Davis (1979) as relying upon an oversimple sociology of knowledge. Instead, he stresses that the experience of the social world is, for many people, fragmentary; their images of that social world are correspondingly fractured and inconsistent.

Another theoretical tradition to which one might, in a longer discussion, want to relate these issues is the analysis of the cultural reproduction and legitimisation of class society developed by authors such as Bourdieu (1977, 1984; Bourdieu and Passeron 1977), MacLeod (1987) and Willis (1977). At the risk of oversimplifying these arguments, the basic notion – in sharp contrast, for example, to the mechanical overdetermination which drives the models of writers such as Althusser (1971: 127–86) – is that while actors do have access to a cultural framework which allows them, in part, to understand and perceive their own class-based disadvantage and domination, other elements of that framework, such as notions about gender or ethnicity, serve to negate or neutralise those understandings. Hence, according to these authors, the working class's apparent acquiescence in, and contribution towards, its own subjugation. This is another kind of political and cultural inconsistency.

The final issue is the relationship between what people say and what they do. It is a commonplace observation that the two are often contradictory; it has also been noted by social scientists (e.g. Holy and Stuchlik 1983). The example from Coxon and Jones's research, cited above, is merely one of many. The strength of participant observation is precisely that it allows the relationship between discourse and other practices to come out into the open, something which interviewing – of the kind which we have done – does not easily permit. However, to return to our opening remarks, discourse is a practice, and one which contributes in a major way to the constitution of social reality. It is therefore legitimate and important to pay attention to what people say.

This section may have seemed to some readers something of an irrelevant excursion away from the main thread of our analysis. If so, we hope to have

modified that view by the end of this chapter. For our purposes, we have
made three basic points which will underpin the discussion which follows.
First, the views which people hold about issues such as inequality, class and
politics are, to some extent, derived from their social position and experience; equally, however, they are likely to exhibit a (possibly considerable)
degree of inconsistency or contradiction. Second, the relationship between
the attitudes which people appear to hold and their behaviour is not
straightforward. The one cannot necessarily be read off from the other.
Third, while we acknowledge the impossibility of discovering what people
'really' think, we also recognise the role of discourse in the on-going
production of social life. Talk about unemployment is an important aspect
of the generation and experience of unemployment as a stigmatised
category of social being.

The allocation of responsibility

Inconsistency and contradiction do not imply incoherence. Culture and
discourse are social phenomena; there is pattern and continuity to be found
as the necessary basis for communication and shared understandings. In the
literature which looks at how young people in capitalist societies,
particularly unemployed young people, understand their situation, one of
the recurring themes or patterns has been the importance of an ideology of
individualism in their discourse.

As Steven Lukes has observed, individualism is a notion to which many
different meanings attach, depending on time, place and social context
(Lukes 1973).[2] In this particular context, we shall simply use it to mean, 'a
way of looking at the world which explains and interprets events and
circumstances mainly in terms of the decisions, actions and attitudes of the
individuals involved' (Jenkins 1982: 88). The combination of individualism
with, on the one hand, a daily experience of inequality and relative
powerlessness, and, on the other, a localist frame of reference which reflects
limited geographic mobility and social networks, limits the possibilities of
working-class political action and is an important buttress for the status quo
of the class system (Jenkins 1983: 131–2). Individuals are typically blamed –
by themselves and by other people – for their own misfortunes and held
responsible for their own lot in life; where responsibility is allocated
elsewhere, it falls generally upon vague stereotypes, the distant 'them'
which is the other side of the local 'us', or highly visible, but remote,
'personalities'.

This kind of interpretation has been taken up by other studies of young
people. Coffield and his colleagues, for example, have highlighted the
centrality of individualism – and, correspondingly, self-blame – in the
thinking of the young unemployed in the North-East of England (Coffield
1986: 83–4). Ian Watson, writing of unemployed young women and men in

Australia, attaches central importance to an ideology of individualism as the organising framework of 'human nature' within which solutions to life's difficulties are sought and as a major obstruction to the development of working-class collectivism in politics and industrial relations (Watson 1985). In an American context, Jay MacLeod argues that one of the factors producing the self-limitation of working-class 'levelled aspirations' is the embracing of an individualistic 'achievement ideology' in a context of poverty and disadvantage (MacLeod 1989). Even the oppositional group in his study, The Hallway Hangers, while rejecting the education-based path of achievement and mobility, view their social world in a resolutely individualistic fashion: life is, in part, what *you* make of it, even though that for them may not involve going to college. Phillip Brown's study of the education of 'ordinary kids' in Swansea provides comparable evidence of the commitment of young people to values which emphasise individual effort and achievement (Brown 1987).

One of the most interesting analyses of these kinds of issues can be found in Derek Walsgrove's study of unemployed youth in Kidderminster (Walsgrove 1987). As economic and social failures – in their own eyes and in the eyes of other people – they are stigmatised. In response to this, and in an attempt to maintain a 'normal' identity, these young men and women 'police themselves' in terms of their behaviour, their maintenance of an orientation to working in the future and the preservation of their self-respect. Such is the power of competitive individualism as the internalised yardstick of self-evaluation.

None of this should, however, be particularly surprising. Individualism is one of the dominant themes of Western European culture: from the media, from education, from politicians, from our peers, from advertising and the market, the message is the same. Notions about the responsibilities and freedoms of the individual are the foundation stones of modern capitalism and liberal democracy. What would have been truly odd – even in South Wales, with its long-standing (although now, one fears, doomed) traditions of trade unionism and collectivism – is an absence of individualistic explanations for unemployment.

There is another reason why individualism is so influential. At the risk of appearing naïve or crudely positivist, individualism is commonsensically true. What we mean by this is that human beings exist as physically discrete individuals. Nor are these individuals either automata or governed in their behaviour by instinct. Although the nature of choice is problematic and the capacity to exercise it limited and unevenly distributed, we none the less routinely experience that capacity, both in ourselves and in our dealings with other people. Hence the taken-for-grantedness of the individualistic understanding of the world. Individualism, therefore, should not be understood as some kind of false knowledge, preventing us from seeing the way things 'really' are. It may, *on its own*, offer a limited or inadequate view of the world, and it may have social and political consquences which we regard as undesirable; these however, are different arguments.

The social importance of individualism as the explanatory framework within which things such as economic decline and unemployment are understood can be shown by referring to data from the 1983 British Social Attitudes survey, fieldwork for which was carried out in the months before the general election of June of that year (Harrison 1984: 58–9, 68–71). The sample was asked to prioritise, from a list of alternatives, the causes of Britain's economic difficulties. Apart from 'decline in world trade' and 'energy costs', which topped the table, the most frequently identified causes – ranging in their popularity from 69 to 60 per cent of respondents – were the reluctance of British workers to adopt new working practices, the government's lack of effort in creating jobs, bad management and people not working hard enough. All of these can be readily reduced to statements about people, about individuals; the priority of the explanations referring to energy cost and trade can, what is more, be related, at least in part, to pre-election publicity on behalf of the government.

Which is not, however, to suggest that the matter is wholly straightforward. In the survey responses cited above, one can perhaps discern strands of explanation other than the individualistic. And the research to which we have referred, with the exceptions of MacLeod and Watson, tends to take the ideology of individualism somewhat for granted, as something rather more simple than it probably is. In this chapter, we will take some steps towards unpicking the nature and logic of the individualism of our respondents.

First, however, it remains to outline explicitly the basic position from which our discussion will proceed: in a system in which material and symbolic rewards are distributed with massive inequity, the ubiquity of an individualistic way of looking at the world undermines the self-image and sense of personal value of many working-class people. Their disadvantage is understood, by themselves and by others, as a failure, a consequence of personal inadequacy. Inasmuch as this happens, the system of social relationships and its inequities is further legitimated. This is among the most severe of the 'hidden injuries of class':

> The terms of individual freedom are so defined that in demonstrating special merit, a man or a woman is no closer to validating the dignity of the self ... everyone in this society, rich and poor, plumber and professor, is subject to a scheme of values that tells him he must validate the self in order to win others' respect and his own ... [For workers there are] three general results of such assertion: the search for respect is thwarted; the individual feels personally responsible for the failure; the whole attempt accustoms him to think that to have individual respect you must have social inequality.
>
> (Sennett and Cobb 1977: 74–5)

Responsibility and respect, as used by Sennett and Cobb in this quotation, are words which we came across in looking at the nature of adulthood. They are clearly important notions locating the discourse of adult identity within the larger discourse of individualism. In the section which follows we will look at the way in which that individualism finds expression (or not) in explanations of unemployment.

Explaining unemployment

Looking at the interview material which is concerned with the perceptions of our unemployed respondents and their parents of the reasons for their own or their child's unemployment, a number of lines of differentiation emerge. The most obvious is the distinction between those explanations which blame (in some sense) the young person concerned, and those which offer other reasons:

(124)
Well, I know they say blame the government and all that. They are to blame in one way 'cause they brought the axe down too quick. 'Cause they didn't prepare ... They slashed everything. All those people on the dole, they didn't think first before they've done it. Especially for the youngsters. They're coming out of school ... Their dole money. They've nowhere to go but the streets. That's why we've got so much trouble. The government's to blame ... What did they do for our children? They've got nowhere to go in the nights ... I've brought up four of them, two of them boys. I never had a knock on my door to say they were in trouble. I was lucky ... But these poor children coming up. They go out with a gang of boys, on the dole. What are they going to do? ... I'm sorry for the parents who've got them, 'cause they've nothing to look forward to. Nothing to occupy themselves.

The speaker in (124) is Mrs Rosemary Hughes from Abbeyview, whose 22-year-old daughter, Rebecca, is a single parent living at home. Compare this with the views of Mrs Jean Hildreth from Ty-Gwyn, whose daughter Kelly is 21:

(125)
SH: What are Kelly's prospects?
JH: As a matter of fact, when Kelly came out of school we made her sit down and write to every firm in Swansea. In the end she had a choice of three jobs. I think a lot depends on how determined you are to work. Jobs are about if you chase them and I keep chasing them all the time. And if you don't mind what you do I think that comes into it ... to do menial jobs. I think a job is a job, but the attitude today is 'I can get as much money on the dole.'

Mrs Hildreth's opinions are more individualistic in their tenor than those of Mrs Hughes. They still represent, however, a relatively mild version of individualism. Consider the quotation below, from Paula Jones of Abbeyview, aged 21:

(126)
RJ: Why, do you think, is there so much unemployment nationally?
PJ: Basically, job cuts, I think.
RJ: And locally?
PJ: I think a lot of them in Port Talbot personally prefer bed and
    breakfast. They get everything paid for them ... I mean, there's lots
    of boys who don't want to work, they can go to bed and breakfast,
    get their lodgings paid ... I know a lot of family *men* who don't like
    working, who do prefer to be on the dole, and they've proved that.

Paula Jones's individualism – coming as it does from somebody who had finally found work, starting the week after the interview took place – is uncompromising. Elsewhere in the interview she made the same harsh judgement of her younger sister and brother, both unemployed. People are unemployed, according to Paula, because they haven't tried hard *enough*. She did, and eventually she got a job. There is a similar stress upon *effort* in the comments of Swansea school kids – 'ordinary kids' – about education and jobs, recorded by Phillip Brown (1987: 163–8).

Paula's views in (126), inasmuch as they are concerned with explanations of unemployment nationally and locally, take us a little away from the point at issue. When looking at the explanation for a particular young woman or man's unemployment offered by themselves or their parents, there is a continuum from the abstract and structural, concerned with 'the system', to the concrete and immediately individualistic, concerned with named and known people. The explanations offered by Mrs Hughes and Mrs Hildreth fall well short of either end of that continuum. At one end references are made to inflation or the conditions of world trade, at the other the absence in the particular young person of qualities such as hard work, persistence or flexibility may be bemoaned. As can be seen from Table 6.1, however, explanations for individual unemployment are not evenly distributed along that continuum, nor is the pattern of explanation offered by our respondents the same in each area which we looked at.

All of the usual qualifications about the small size of the samples apply to Table 6.1; there are none the less a number of interesting conclusions which one can draw from it. Perhaps the most obvious is that explanations which allocate blame or responsibility to the individual young man or woman concerned – around half the responses – are the single most popular category of explanation. In this sense, although 'structural' explanations referring to political and economic factors are by no means insignificant,

Table 6.1 Explanations of the unemployment of individual young people, by area (percentages in brackets)

	Individual's fault or responsibility		Political or economic factors		Mixture of these reasons		Don't know or 'no comment'		Total	
Abbeyview										
Young										
people	6	(29)	11	(52)		–	4	(19)	21	(100)
Parents	3	(18)	10	(59)	3	(18)	1	(6)	17	(100)
High Oak										
Young										
people	15	(65)	2	(9)		–	6	(26)	23	(100)
Parents	13	(48)	8	(30)	3	(11)	3	(11)	27	(100)
Ty-Gwyn										
Young										
people	15	(79)	1	(5)		–	3	(16)	19	(100)
Parents	15	(75)	2	(10)	2	(10)	1	(5)	20	(100)
TOTAL										
Young										
people	36	(57)	14	(22)		–	13	(21)	63	(100)
Parents	31	(48)	20	(31)	8	(12)	5	(8)	64	(100)

Note: These figures refer to the explanations provided by unemployed young people for why they themselves were unemployed, on the one hand, and parents' explanations of why their sons/daughters were unemployed, on the other.

individualistic explanations provide the major theme in our interview material (as, indeed, one might have expected).

It is important to moderate this view, however, by drawing attention to the data from Abbeyview: here, the reverse is true, individualistic explanations are very much in the minority. This difference between Abbeyview and the other areas is of considerable importance. It is a further illustration of the local specificity of the experience of unemployment. In Port Talbot, unemployment is a fairly public problem, suffered by many people. In the eyes of the community – and, to a large degree, in truth – unemployment is due to, or began with, the redundancies at the steel works. And that was the result of decisions made by the British Steel Corporation and, less immediately, of government policy and conditions in world steel markets. In High Oak or Ty-Gwyn, however, there is less unemployment, it is more privately experienced and there is no easily identifiable event or series of events with which to explain the situation. The explanations of unemployment offered in these areas are different precisely because the *experience* and communal impact of unemployment is different.

There are also important differences to note with respect to the young people, on the one hand, and their parents, on the other. In particular, the sons and daughters are – paradoxically perhaps – more likely than their parents to view themselves as responsible or to blame for their own unemployment. This is less easy to interpret. Taken in the context of their greater propensity to answer 'don't know', it may be reasonable to suggest that their youth and their experience of schooling renders them less confident in their judgements; it may simply be less complicated to blame oneself. It may even be seen as what is expected by the world at large. More speculatively, these young people may be driven to provide individualistic explanations of their own worklessness in an implicit and paradoxical recognition of the bleakness of the contemporary labour-market situation, particularly as it affects young workers. The stark fact that there are not enough jobs – and are not going to be enough jobs in the future – may be too much to bear when you are the victim. At least an individualistic explanation allows for the prospect of individual change and possible improvement. It is an assertion that one still has some influence over one's life and its outcomes. These answers may also be a reflection, albeit once again a paradoxical one, of the optimism of youth, an expression of hope and confidence in one's own powers.

It may, however, be their experience of success and failure in the labour market which colours their answers. Many of the young people concerned have been told too often – in the Job Centre, in an interview or on reading a newspaper advertisement – why they haven't got the job or why they are not eligible to apply for it. They are either unsuitable or unacceptable: too young, the wrong qualifications or too few qualifications, not enough experience, or whatever. It is a message which is reinforced by the rhetorical emphasis on training in government employment programmes. In this sense, they *know* why they are unemployed: *personally* speaking, they do not fit the bill. It is in part the experience of assessment and rejection which is reflected in these answers – regardless of whether or not they accept the assessments of their inadequacy as accurate – and which distinguishes their explanations from those offered by their parents.

We also asked our interviewees why they thought unemployment was so high generally, that is locally and nationally. The responses to this question are summarised in Table 6.2; this material is less easy to categorise or interpret than the material relating to individual employment.

Before attempting to interpret this material, we must first explain the distinction between the personal and the impersonal which we have used to categorise those answers which refer to economic or political factors. Something of the flavour of this distinction can be had by returning to the testimony of Mrs Hughes (124) and Mrs Hildreth (125). Mrs Hughes explained unemployment in personal terms '*They*' are to blame ... *they* brought the axe down ... *they* slashed everything ... *they* didn't think first ...'). Mrs Hildreth, while adopting an individualistic perspective on her daughter's unemployment in (125), spoke impersonally about the reasons for unemployment in general:

Table 6.2 Explanations of high levels of unemployment in general, by area (percentages in brackets)

	Economic or political factors (personal)		Economic or political factors (impersonal)		Other individualistic explanations		Don't know or 'no comment'		Other		Total	
Abbeyview													
Young people	10	(48)	1	(5)	1	(5)	9	(43)	–		21	(100)
Parents	12	(71)	4	(24)	1	(6)	–		–		17	(100)
High Oak													
Young people	2	(9)	8	(35)	5	(22)	7	(30)	1	(4)	23	(100)
Parents	7	(26)	11	(41)	2	(7)	6	(22)	1	(4)	27	(100)
Ty-Gwyn													
Young people	3	(16)	7	(37)	4	(21)	5	(26)	–		19	(100)
Parents	5	(25)	11	(55)	2	(10)	2	(10)	–		20	(100)
TOTAL													
Young people	15	(24)	16	(25)	10	(16)	21	(33)	1	(2)	63	(100)
Parents	24	(37)	26	(41)	5	(9)	8	(12)	1	(2)	64	(100)

(127)
... *it's* world recession. That attributes a lot to *it* ...//... I think *it's* a change like when industries started ...//... I think change is coming and *it's* gradually been accepted now ... *it's* technology [emphasis added].

Two further quotations, drawn from answers to the question, 'Why do you think there is so much unemployment nationally and locally?', will help to clarify this distinction between personal and impersonal modes of explanation:

(128)
Well, I should say it's the government, definitely. I mean, she's slashing everything down. She's all for America ...//... With Maggie Thatcher, *she* never knew what it was to be without ...//... and *he* [Norman Tebbitt] was the one who had the cheek to say 'Get off your arse and look for jobs'.

(Mrs Margaret Jones, Abbeyview, original emphasis)

(129)
GG: It's the general trend at the moment ... World recessions, a lack of resources everywhere, people can't employ so many people ... As to the complicated reasons, I don't know ... There's a lack of government money in support.
PG: World recession and the monetarism policy of the government ...

Added to the change in industrial patterns. More machines and less hands needed.

(Mrs Georgina and Mr Paul Griffiths, Ty-Gwyn)

It is interesting to compare these views on unemployment in general with what Mrs Jones and Mrs Griffiths had to say about the unemployment of their own children:

(130)
RJ: Why are your daughters unemployed?
MJ: There's bugger all around, man. I mean Paula have been in London looking ...//...
RJ: You don't think it's their fault?
MJ: No, you can't blame the kids at all. I blame the government. No-one else but the government. She's selling off everything ...//... Land-Rovers, how many jobs gone from that?

In sharp contrast, Mr and Mrs Griffiths stress the individual choices made by one of their sons and are severe in placing personal blame at the door of their other son:

(131)
RJ: Why, do you think, is Peter unemployed?
GG: Through choice, really. He's decided to take this year out and do a few voluntary jobs and so on ...//...
PG: We don't really look on him as unemployed. It's a matter of him doing his training and something will come along.

(132)
RJ: What are the reasons for Matthew's unemployment?
GG: Basically, a lack of skills and maybe it's connected with his attitude, to do with looking for work ... And, of course, there are not as many jobs as there were ...//...
PG: [He's] got a history, which started with dyslexia, which has all sorts of impacts on life, and an inability to cope with exams or cope with discipline ... He's had plenty of opportunities, but he's never buttoned down to the job.

The comparison of Mr and Mrs Griffiths with Mrs Jones is interesting. In the case of the Griffithses, unemployment in general is understood largely in abstract and impersonal terms while the unemployment of Matthew and Peter is explained in individualistic language, albeit that the situation of each son is understood very differently. Mrs Jones, however, while explaining her daughter's unemployment in terms of the economy and of politics, does so in terms which are highly personalised. The one set of explanations is almost the mirror image of the other.

This pattern is repeated when one compares the results from the three areas in Tables 6.1 and 6.2. Put in simple terms, while individual employment was typically ascribed to the force of external circumstances in Abbeyview, the general unemployment situation, and the economic and political factors believed to have caused it, were talked about in very individualistic language. It was a personal thing; Mrs Thatcher, in particular, was the personification of what people saw to be the problem:

(133)
Well, I think this government is wrong ... She's closing the works down and buying from abroad. Look at our oil now. We could have made that in a circle, distributed it around and given people work, couldn't we? Instead of selling it.

(Mrs Elsie Wallis, Abbeyview)

(134)
SH: What are the reasons for unemployment?
VD: Honest opinion?
SH: Yes
VD: Margaret Thatcher, to be honest with you. Two words, Margaret Thatcher.

(Mrs Violet Davies, Abbeyview)

(135)
It's what we've got up in London. The Prime Minister's causing it all. She's hitting Wales more than anything else. I don't know why she's doing it. It doesn't make sense.

(Mr Alexander Field, Abbeyview)

If nothing else, these responses are an eloquent testimony to Mrs Thatcher's public domination of parlimentary politics and the Conservative Party since 1979.

In High Oak and Ty-Gwyn, in contrast to Abbeyview, individual unemployment is typically explained in individualistic terms while the economic and political factors causing high unemployment locally and nationally are talked about impersonally.

(136)
It's an accumulation of a lot of things. Automation is definitely one reason. For the boys and the men, they're shutting down the basic industries like the steel company. It's less for girls because there's supermarkets starting up. The basic industries are being, sort of chopped up and the shops and stores are taking on the younger girls.

That's why there are more boys unemployed ... Japanese imports. God
knows what. It's not just one thing, but half a dozen.

(Mr Michael Lynch, High Oak)

(137)

It's got to do with government policy. It's got to do with world
recession and I do think the provinces suffer more than the central part
around the home counties ... I think the north country is as bad as
South Wales.

(Mr Alun Anderson, Ty-Gwyn)

How are we to explain this difference between Abbeyview and the other two
areas? It is not necessarily the case that the distinction is simply one between
anti- and pro-Conservative (or -government) views, as can be seen from
(137). The distinction is, we suspect, at least in part, actually an indication
of the power of the individualistic world-view. In Abbeyview, where the
accumulation of personal and collective experience is likely to make
individualistic explanations of individual unemployment relatively
implausible to most people, the unemployment situation in general, in its
economic and political context, tends to be explained personally and
individualistically: it's 'their' (or 'her') fault.

In High Oak or Ty-Gwyn, however, explanations of individual
unemployment are more likely to reflect the fact that, despite the existence
of high overall levels of unemployment, most young people from these
areas continue to obtain employment. To be unemployed is a more isolated
and a more deviant state of being than in Abbeyview. The questions 'Why
me?' or 'Why my daughter/son?' are, therefore, both pertinent and
immediate and, as such, demand answers. Why can Jack or Jill, next door,
find a job but not me, or not our Philip or Angela? What is the difference
between those that do get jobs and those few who do not? Questions such as
these plumb the depths of personal uncertainty and the experience of
failure. And it is, after all, as individuals that failure (and, of course,
success) is subjectively experienced. In Abbeyview the individuality of that
experience remains; it is, however, modified by the experience of shared
diversity, the ready availability of a set of alternative explanations and the
relative absence of stigma attaching to unemployment.

The experience of unemployment may also have something to do with the
differences which we have noted between the personal and the impersonal
modes of understanding economic and political factors. Abbeyview, a run-
down community, traumatised by the steel redundancies in 1980 has –
certainly in the eyes of many of our respondents – been attacked and
undermined. It has not simply been at the mercy of vague economic forces
or general state policy; rather it was the object of *particular* attention from
'the powers that be'. This sense of collective injury is linked to the estate's
history as a 'company town': at least 65 per cent of the families in the

Abbeyview sample, for example, had male heads who either worked or had worked for BSC. That, and its physical location, isolated from the rest of Port Talbot, serve to reinforce a local identity. Ty-Gwyn and High Oak, inasmuch as they suffer collectively at all, have only done so along with everyone else. Nor are they particularly cohesive or well-bounded social entities. Hence, perhaps, the impersonal understanding of unemployment in general evinced by many of our respondents from these areas and the personal feelings of threat and injury which we recorded in Abbeyview.

Finally, although we have earlier suggested that the distinction between Port Talbot and west Swansea is not simply one of left- and right-wing politics, it is undeniably likely that there is also much of this in it. More precisely, Abbeyview's history and the relationship of its community to the steelworks is rooted in a collectivisitic trade-union tradition, the experience of working together and the memory of industrial action, particularly the national steel strike in 1980. In Abbeyview in particular, therefore, there is also a collectivist ideology co-existing with the dominant framework of individualism. We do not wish to overstate this case or present a romanticised picture of a solid working-class community, united in politics and life-style. That is very far from the case. If such a picture was ever accurate, that solidarity does not appear to have survived the impact of mass unemployment. Despite this, however, collectivism remains an important aspect of the world-view of people in Abbeyview.

Thus far we have been discussing how the varieties of expression of individualism are rooted in differing experiences. In this sense, individualism should be seen not as a monolithic and determinate set of rules or norms, but rather as an interpretive framework which derives its power and resilience from its very vagueness or generality. Individualism is, in our understanding, a loosely and implicitly defined body of generative principles, concerned with the kinds of issues which can with levity be described as 'the meaning of life', and which find their expression in the improvisatory context of changing circumstances (Bourdieu 1977; Cicourel 1973).

The identification of both individualism and collectivism in the interview material from Abbeyview, in particular, highlights one of the contradictions or inconsistencies which may exist in people's world-views. There is another kind of contradiction in the material from Ty-Gwyn and High Oak – and something very similar has been noted in other research (Breakwell 1985: 496) – in so far as personal unemployment is explained in individualistic terms while unemployment in general is seen as a failure of the system. Something similar is also present in a few of the interviews from Abbeyview; Paula Jones, in (126), is a good example.

This may not in fact be much of a contradiction. Certainly, we have little evidence that either young people or their parents actually perceive or experience it as a contradiction. The fact that our interviewees were asked to provide explanations for both general and individual unemployment has, of course, a bearing on this issue. It is not that the questions 'led' the respondents in any obvious sense; it is more that the interview questions produced statements about two different orders of social phenomena, one abstract and remote, the other concrete and immediate, which are not necessarily considered together in day-to-day discourse. In a nutshell, they were different questions about different topics. There is, therefore, no necessity that a contradiction between these explanations should be experienced in that same everyday discourse. In addition, the nature of the research interview, in which these questions were followed in fairly quick succession by questions concerned with other topics, make it unlikely that inconsistencies which are (later) identified by the researcher going through a transcript will be apparent to the person being interviewed during the interview.

To sum up this section, we have argued that the dominant framework within which the unemployment of young people is understood is an individualist ideology of personal agency and responsibility. However, due to the differing economic histories and social situations of the three areas involved, this individualism finds different expressions in each. In Abbeyview it is the powerful – particularly Mrs Thatcher – who are held responsible as individuals; in High Oak and Ty-Gwyn that responsibility is largely allocated to the young women and men themselves. We have also identified a degree of inconsistency between explanations of individual unemployment and explanations of unemployment in general. In line with our discussion in the previous section, we do not regard this as anything other than routine or to be expected. In the section which follows, we will attempt to draw some conclusions about the implications for family relationships and political behaviour of the way in which unemployment is understood and talked about.

Families, politics and unemployment

We have distinguished between the strictly individualistic explanations of personal unemployment (the majority) and those which refer to political and economic factors. It is now time to unpack the category of individualistic explanations and distinguish between the allocation or acceptance of a degree of personal *responsibility*, on the one hand, and the attribution of individual *blame*, on the other.

This distinction is important if we are to understand the situation within families. It is possible to acknowledge or allocate personal responsibility without necessarily invoking a rhetoric of moral failure and recrimination. 'Lack of qualifications' is a common explanation of individual unemployment; in High Oak, for example, of the thirteen individualistic explanations offered by parents (see Table 6.1), seven were of this kind. However, lack of qualifications is often seen as not the fault of the young person concerned:

(138)
SH: Why is Simon [Terrance, aged 18 years] unemployed?
RT: Well, one thing could be he's got no qualifications which they are
   now looking for. They've got such a pick now of unemployed people
   with a lot of qualifications, you know.
SH: Why didn't he get them?
RT: He always tried hard. He's clever with his hands, not otherwise.
   He's no good at putting it down on paper.
SH: And a job?
RT: No, he's looked. He's really looked.

(Mr Roger Terrance, High Oak)

With respect to education, parents think (correctly) that there is a
connection between low formal educational achievement and unemployment.[3] Their explanation of unemployment becomes entangled, therefore,
with their explanation(s) of poor educational achievement. And there are
many of these available, most of which do not devolve blame onto the
student's shoulders: poor schools or teachers, progressive education,
variations in 'natural' ability or talent ('clever with his hands, not
otherwise'), disruption due to moving around, specific problems (such as
dyslexia) or lack of effort. Only the last of these is explicitly critical or
blammatory.
   Additional individualistic explanations of unemployment which do not
involve blame include 'no experience', 'wrong age' and – nebulous but
doubtless, in some cases, completely accurate – 'bad luck'. The importance
of perceived effort in obviating blame has already been mentioned. Brown,
in his study of education and employment in Swansea (1987) suggests that
'making an effort' and offering reasonable conformity to school discipline
constitute a claim to respectability within working-class canons of life-style
and culture. Similarly, in our discussion of family conflict in Chapters 2 and
3, we have discussed the role of being seen to do things, of being seen
making an effort (to look for work, to do housework, or whatever), in the
symbolic economy of family relationships. In the absence of other
negotiable assests – whether symbolic or strictly material – a degree of
visible effort is, perhaps, the only offering which the unemployed young
person can make.
   The line between blame and its absence is not always easy to plot,
however. An individualistic explanation remains an individualistic
explanation; the potential for accusation and recrimination is always there.
We know from earlier chapters that family conflict varies from area to area,
with reported conflict becoming more severe as we move from Abbeyview
to High Oak to Ty-Gwyn. In this chapter, we have seen that there is a
preponderance of individualistic explanations for personal unemployment
in High Oak and Ty-Gwyn.

It is possible to unpack our interview material a little further and look at the relationship between family conflict and the way in which a daughter or son's unemployment is explained or talked about by their parents, and how this varies by area. Looking only at those parents who said that their offspring's unemployment was something for which the son or daughter was individually responsible or to blame, none of the relevant Abbeyview parents, 38 per cent of the High Oak parents and 53 per cent of the Ty-Gwyn parents also reported severe family conflict. However, of those parents who thought their child's unemployment was caused by political or economic factors, only 10 per cent from Abbeyview, 12 per cent from High Oak and none from Ty-Gwyn reported severe family conflict. These findings should be seen in the light of the small number of Abbeyview parents offering individualistic explanations and the even smaller number of Ty-Gwyn parents who referred to political and economic factors when talking about the reasons for their daughter or son's unemployment (see Table 6.1 for further details).

The interpretation of these results is, however, not straightforward. In the first place, it seems clear, as suggested in Chapter 2, that where the young person's unemployment is explained by reference to political and economic factors, rather than individualistically, there is less severe conflict between parents and children. It is also clear that, as in so many other respects, High Oak is something of a halfway house between Abbeyview (relatively low levels of conflict; predominantly political and economic explanations of unemployment) and Ty-Gwyn (relatively high levels of conflict; predominantly individualistic explanations). Similarly, these figures suggest that the interaction between family conflict and discourse about unemployment is more intense in Ty-Gwyn, for example, than in High Oak. What is not, however, clear is the *nature* of the relationship between the ways in which unemployment is talked about or explained and conflict within the family. There are two possibilities. First, it could be that conflictual relationships between parent and child lead to the young person being, at best, held partly responsible or, at worse, actually blamed for their unemployment. Hence in this version of events it is family conflict which produces or encourages the adoption of individualistic explanations. Alternately, the reverse might be true: an individualistic understanding of a son or daughter's unemployment, involving blame and accusation, may create or exacerbate conflict.

We do not think the situation is likely to be as simple as either of these possibilities, nor do we see them as crude alternatives. It is, rather, more likely to be the case that each is, to some extent, true and that both processes are occurring within families at the same time but to different degrees, depending on the context. This seems to us to be the most likely explanation for the fact that the relationship between individualistic parental explanations of a child's unemployment and severe generational conflict is, for example, stronger in Ty-Gwyn than in High Oak. The situation should not be interpreted solely within the narrow confines of relationships inside the family. There is a global difference between the experience and meaning of unemployment in Abbeyview, in High Oak and Ty-Gwyn. Both family conflict (or its absence) and explanatory models of inaction and subjection are bound up in the weft and warp of those experiences and meanings.

We have already alluded to political differences between the areas which we studied. There are a number of angles from which we can approach this topic using our material. Viewed with a relatively naïve eye – our own common sense as residents of West Glamorgan – Abbeyview is a solidly working class, solidly trade unionist and solidly Labour area, while Ty-Gwyn is likely to be the opposite. High Oak is rather more difficult to categorise, a bastion of working-class conservatism. In South Wales this tends to imply voting Labour, but there will be some – possibly many – people in a place like High Oak who consistently vote Conservative.

So much for common sense and broad generalisation. What does our material suggest about the relationship between being unemployed, or having a child unemployed, and political views and behaviour? These are difficult issues; bearing in mind the problematic relationship between discourse – what people say – and other aspects of their lives and behaviour, we can only be tentative in our conclusions. The following suggestions can, however, be offered with some degree of confidence.

First, looking at their views of the future, the unemployed young men and women were, in general, more optimistic about their prospects than their parents. Second, another strong thread of opinion in the data suggests that the prospects for individuals were seen as much better than the prospects for young people in general. These findings, which do not vary significantly by area, are in broad agreement with the earlier material which indicates that young people are more likely to offer individualistic explanations for their unemployment than are their parents. In addition to the rose-tinted spectacles of youth, their relative optimism and their individualism may be a perverse reflection of the severity of the economic climate and employment situation in South Wales. The worse things appear to be, the more important it is to hang on to some hope of individual improvement and the prospect of change, despite one's pessimism about the overall labour-market situation. Realism suggests, perhaps, that a change for the better in one's own life is all that can be hoped for; such a hope is probably the best strategy for coping with the dispiriting experience of unemployment.

Attitudes to the Youth Training Scheme (YTS) are also worth looking at as a barometer of political opinion. There was a common distinction in the comments of both parents and young people between *general* views, which referred to fairly abstract notions of justice and injustice, and *specific* comments about the experience of particular schemes. For example, some sons and daughters disapproved of YTS on principle but could recount worthwhile experiences of this or that scheme. Others believed YTS to be a valuable programme but had themselves had bad experiences on the ground.

The Community Programme and YTS[4] were frequently referred to as part and parcel of the same package of 'government schemes'. Attitudes to YTS, however, were generally more hostile. In particular, the level of payment – the youth training allowance – came in for strong criticism. There is, however, more to it than money: notions of morality and fairness, similar to those documented by Allatt and Yeandle (1986) and McRae (1987b: 124–5), are implicit in much of the interview material concerned with these topics. The most common description of YTS, by both parents and young people, was 'slave labour'. This, however, was a view tempered by other considerations; the following quotations illustrate well the ambiguity which was felt about employment schemes by many of the people we interviewed:

(139)
Well, the one in BP ... They were very nice to her [Audrey Ballinger, age 20]. She gained, well, she gained a lot of, well, she was doing typing and experience ... I don't agree myself. I've got to be honest, I'll tell you to your face, the jobs ... She was going for £25 per week. The lady sitting by the side of her was having £95 a week and she was doing the same work. And that makes me ... even on the both schemes ... it's scab labour, like we say.

(Mrs Ann Ballinger, Abbeyview)

(140)
EW: I think they're exploited, the young ones. They do the same amount of work as the older ones. And when they've done the scheme, they're put back on the dole.
SH: But would it help Geoffrey?
EW: Yes, definitely, it would give him something to do in the day, give him a purpose in life, wouldn't it?

(Mrs Elsie Wallis, Abbeyview)

(141)
It was good for him [Hugh Reynolds, age 20]. He'd just left school and he quite enjoyed it. He would have liked to have learnt something, but he found that they more or less made him a tea-boy. He would like to have learnt ... I agree with all of these schemes, it does keep them off the road, but it doesn't promise them anything at the end of it. They get the same as being on the dole and they feel they're being used. It's slave labour.

(Mrs Diana Reynolds, High Oak)

The testimony of these mothers captures the essence of the popular critique of YTS and other employment schemes: not only is it poorly-paid slave labour, it is also undermining the jobs and wages of other workers (scab labour); very often nothing is taught and nothing is learnt; finally, there is, at the end of the day, no job in it for the young person anyway, it is simply an interlude between spells on the dole. On the other hand, however, there are also positive aspects which parents and young people recognise: it may be enjoyable; some youngsters do acquire training and useful experience; it can help to provide a purpose in life and keep young people off the streets; some trainees do find employment as a result. From the point of view of both young people and their parents it certainly provides an opportunity for 'making an effort', which, as we have seen, is so important in the management of family relationships.

Views about other state agencies, such as the Careers Service, the Job Centre and the DHSS, were also a mixture of criticism and a recognition of their usefulness (or at least necessity). The general spectrum of our respondents' views about state employment schemes and agencies did not show any significant variation by area, an indication perhaps of a consistency of experience; consistent ambiguity, but consistent none the less.

This ambiguity, which appears to be the defining feature of our interviewees' views about the state and unemployment, is of some political significance. On the one hand, there is dismay at the exploitative and ineffective nature of state intervention; on the other, we found the recognition that it is better than nothing and may, in the case of specific schemes, have positive values. In the middle there emerges a pragmatic acceptance of the situation and a determination to try to make the best of things for one's own daughters and sons. The young women and men themselves, as in McRae's study (McRae 1987b: 131–7), are more interested in getting on, or at least coping, than they are in political resistance or struggle. Whatever else they may be, they are not revolting: discontented, unhappy and impoverished perhaps, but not politically dangerous.

Our material and our impressions relating to the political dimensions of unemployment for our respondents are in general accord with Stewart and Blackburn's view of social inequality, which we discussed earlier (Stewart and Blackburn 1975). Judgements of satisfaction or dissatisfaction are typically made within narrow limits and need not extend to the wider social structure, which is generally taken-for-granted as the status quo. A degree of constraint or limitation on one's actions is only to be expected as 'the way things are'. A recent discussion of the political quiescence of the unemployed by Marshall and his colleagues says something similar (Marshall *et al.* 1988). They argue that the preference of the unemployed for individualistic solutions to their problems – rather than, say, political organisation as a pressure group – is largely a pragmatic, if resigned, acceptance of 'the painful lesson that they must expect to fend for themselves' (*ibid.*: 224). This is not something which they positively *choose*; within a bureaucratised and indifferent political and economic system, orientated towards and predicated upon notions of individual achievement, they in fact have no choice.

In this chapter we have attempted to make some sense of the social construction of unemployment in the views and discourse of young women and men and their parents. Although individualism is the dominant framework of this discourse, it varies in its expression from place to place, depending on local history and circumstance; it co-exists uneasily in Abbeyview with a collectivist world-view derived from trade unionism. Within families, there is an association between individualistic explanations of a daughter or son's unemployment and parent–child conflict. The more personal unemployment is explained with reference to political and economic factors, the less likely it is that the young man or woman will be blamed for their unemployment. Within the explanatory frameworks or world-views which we have identified, there is, however, a degree of inconsistency or contradiction which is itself a reflection of the fragmentation and heterogeneity of social experience. It is not only between areas that differences exist; it is also within areas, although to a lesser degree. At the level of politics, a combination of individualism, ambiguity, a pragmatic acceptance of the role of the state in intervening through employment schemes and limited frames of reference which take the status quo for granted, tends to result in solutions to unemployment being sought at the individual level: it is oneself or one's children who come first.

The primacy of self-interest should not be a particularly surprising finding, nor should it be taken to mean that *only* self-interest – narrowly defined – is at work. There are political differences between the three areas, and a variety of political positions from left to right were clear in the testimony of our respondents. However, the experience of having a son or daughter unemployed, or of being an unemployed young adult, does not seem to make much difference to one's politics. It may sharpen views on the left, or moderate hard-nosed conservatism, but not much more. It is almost as if unemployment has become a non-political problem.

We shall return to a discussion of unemployment as a political issue in the final chapter. In this chapter and those which precede it, we have drawn upon our material as a whole to advance arguments and illustrate themes arising from our study. This has necessitated a somewhat disembodied approach to the people who we interviewed. In Chapter 7 we will attempt to rectify this shortcoming by presenting some case-studies of unemployed young women and men and their families.

| 7 |

CASE STUDIES

So far we have drawn upon our interview material in a piecemeal fashion, to identify themes in the data and illustrate our arguments. In this chapter we will present more rounded portraits of particular families, in order to put a little flesh on the bones of those themes and arguments. Our choice of cases has been decided in part by our concentration upon certain topics: the contrasts between the experience of unemployment in Abbeyview, High Oak and Ty-Gwyn, the management of conflict within families, the importance of individual differences and the process of becoming adult. We could have chosen other topics, but these are the ones which seem to us to be central to our concerns. The issues of individualism and gender differences with respect to the experience of unemployment, family relationships and the transition to adulthood, while not explicit objects of our attention, should be regarded as implicit themes running through the case studies. In addition to the material presented in this chapter, the reader should also consult the Appendix, where we provide summary details of each family we interviewed. That material is particularly useful for giving a sense of the sharp differences between Abbeyview, High Oak and Ty-Gwyn.

Our selection of cases to discuss has, then, been partly determined by their suitability in terms of the subjects upon which we have chosen to focus. They have also been selected by reference to other criteria, however: the number of people interviewed (for one family member does not make a case study), the liveliness and intrinsic interest of what they have to say (a personal judgement admittedly, but who wants to read a dull case study?), the volubility of particular informants and the assessment that, while not in any hard sense representative, the material is not particularly unrepresentative of the area or the situation either. As a consequence of taking liveliness and talkativeness into account, some of the material used in the case studies will already have been used elsewhere. We have attempted to keep this repetition to a minimum. Some minor details have been changed in what follows in order to safeguard the anonymity of our respondents. So much for the criteria and rationality of selection and construction; now for the case studies themselves.

Abbeyview, High Oak and Ty-Gwyn

When we interviewed Geoffrey Wallis in January 1986, he was 24 years old. The youngest of three children, and the only one still at home, he lived with his mother, Elsie Wallis, in a small but tidy council house in Abbeyview. His father was retired from the steelworks, where he had worked as a furnaceman, his mother worked part-time as a home help. Since leaving the local comprehensive school without any qualifications at the age of 16, he had tried his hand at a variety of things: a three months' work preparation course in the Skill Centre, a few months working in a do-it-yourself suppliers and, eventually, a job as an apprentice in British Steel:

(142)
My brother, my father, my sister were all working there. I put my name down when I left school. They were taking people on at the furnace. Eighty pound a week it was when I started. Then more. It was my first proper job.

Ten months later, at the age of 18, he was made redundant. Since then, apart from some 'hobbles' (working while claiming benefit) and 2 months in 1985 when he was employed for a contractor doing maintenance work in the steelworks, he had been unemployed. In January 1986 he was 'on the sick', 'suffering with my nerves'. He has also had problems with gallstones.

(143)
I don't ever go out of the house. I was on medication. Some days I feel really active and there's nothing out there. You don't want to go over to the club. You want to do something that isn't leisure. It gets you depressed.

Relationships with his parents were, he felt, not too bad. His mother coped well; his father, despite 'a terrible temper', did not blame Geoffrey for his unemployment often. Usually he accepted it as 'the times'. Geoffrey had broken up the previous May with his girlfriend of three and a half years standing, but he didn't think it had been anything to do with unemployment. Since then he had been knocking around with a group of mates, male and female: girls who were friends, rather than girlfriends. Asked about his prospects in 5 years time, he couldn't say: 'Hope it's more than I'm doing now'.

His mother worried about him; Geoffrey was the last child at home, and while she enjoyed his company, it wasn't a good thing. She would like him to get away and see something of life beyond Port Talbot. Unless he did this, she did not think that he would have any chance of improving his situation. All of Geoffrey's mates were unemployed, and although they went out and put their names down at the Job Centre nothing ever came up. Mrs

Wallis blamed the government and Mrs Thatcher for unemployment (see quote (133) in the previous chapter). She blamed Geoffrey's unemployment, at least in part, on his illness. There was some conflict at home between father and son – they were both hot-headed – and she played the part of peacemaker. Geoffrey, she said, was good with his money.

As for Mr Wallis, he refused to be interviewed. He didn't believe in surveys, they didn't *do* anything. Any working-man knew what it was like to be unemployed. He'd been unemployed when he was young. And if he did talk to us, he would only get het up. Which leaves the last word to Geoffrey's mother:

(144)
I break my heart for him, mind. Because he's the one now who's been with us the longest ...//... We've seen more of Geoffrey while he's unemployed. We've seen it happening.

Moving across Swansea Bay, Helen Roderick from High Oak was interviewed in November 1985. She was a month away from her twenty-third birthday. Tall, attractive and well-dressed, Helen lived with her parents in a post-war council house. Much like the Wallis's, the house was tidy and smart. Her father worked as a carpenter, her mother as a part-time lunch supervisor in a primary school nearby. Another child, her eldest sister, an occupational therapist, had married and left home to live in Essex; her other sister, Dawn, aged 26, lived at home and worked in Port Talbot. Helen herself, apart from a six-month YTS scheme, had only had two temporary shop assistants' jobs since leaving school at 16 with no quali-fications. At the time of the interview she had been unemployed for nearly 2 years.

She thought that she was unemployed because she had no qualifications: 'Even if they don't suit the job, the qualified ones gets it.' She never had enough money for clothes or going out and occasionally borrowed off her mother or Dawn, although she always tried to pay it back. She went out every night with her boyfriend, generally to the cinema or for a drink. Sometimes they stayed at his house (he owned his own house in Ty-Gwyn). As for friends, 'There's only me and one left. The rest are married ...//... Even if I didn't have a boyfriend I wouldn't see the others, because they're married.' She didn't see the neighbours much, spending most of her time during the day either doing housework, knitting or watching television.

Family relationships were not too bad: her mother never pressurised her, she didn't see that much of her father ('I'm not here long in the evenings when he comes home, because I go out'), and although Dawn did get at her once in a while to get a job, she had also been unemployed in the past (for 2 years) and had some sympathy for Helen's plight. Every 3 weeks or so she went out 'with the girls'.

Helen's parents explained her unemployment by reference to her lack of qualifications – as her father said, 'I'm not blaming her entirely. I think the school deteriorated from the time when the scholarships were going out' – and bad luck. In terms of her prospects, where Helen thought they were 'not very good', her parents and Dawn appeared a little more optimistic:

(145)
She's quite a capable girl. She's far from lazy. She'll have a go at anything. If there are any opportunities going, I think she'll stand a fair chance.

(Mr Robert Roderick)

(146)
We're hoping all the time. She could do [get a job] ... Maybe. We look each night in the Post.

(Mrs Rosemary Roderick)

(147)
It can't get any worse. I hope it will get better ...//... She might be lucky ...//... It's been such a long time. They've looked in the paper. Helen's written off. Nothing's come of it. A lot of it is who you know.

(Dawn Roderick)

The appeal to luck, on the one hand, and 'who you know', on the other, as the avenues out of Helen's present position, is an interesting combination of fatalism and individualism. It is also, of course, not wholly inaccurate. Such a view certainly manages to reconcile a recognition of the difficulties involved in finding employment with the hope that a change may still be possible.

Helen's situation may, of course, have been in part a consequence of being a woman. It might have been seen by her family as less important that she should find work. The interview material does not, however, support such an interpretation: 'I'd like to see her married if that's what she wants to do' (Mr Roderick). There did not seem to be any push to get either daughter out of the house and married, nor was it seen as unimportant for women to work. If anything, the reverse was the case.

In Ty-Gwyn, Steve Anderson, an only child, was 22 when we interviewed him in July 1986. The Anderson house was, in terms of its furnishings and decor, the most 'middle-class' of the homes which we visited. A brick built semi-detached house in a quiet road in Ty-Gwyn, it was the epitome of solidity and immaculate respectability. Steve appeared to welcome the interview as an entertaining interlude in an otherwise tedious day. His father was employed in local government, having previously worked, prior to redundancy, in the petroleum industry, part of that time being spent in the Middle East. Mrs Anderson worked for the Civil Service in Swansea. Since gaining a law degree in 1985, Steve had spent two-and-a-half months working in a record shop in London. Since December 1985 he had been at home, unemployed: 'I've been unable to cope since I left college.' Much of his time was spent in his bedroom, working on electronic music or writing science fiction. His intention was to return to London to become a success in the world of entertainment. He had turned his back on the law, and perhaps on 'straight' employment of any kind:

(148)
It's largely my own ... well, I don't use the word 'fault'. I could have stayed in London and got another job. Jobs aren't difficult to get up there, of one sort or another. As I told you yesterday, I don't particularly want to spend the next forty years as economic fodder, if you like, for somebody else's business.

His parents, unlike many of the parents from Ty-Gwyn to whom we spoke, were reasonably tolerant of his life-style and ambitions:

(149)
I think it's purely because he truly doesn't know what he wants to do. The thought of going in for the Civil Service, banking, working nine to five for the next 40 years, absolutely appalls him ...//... He thinks his music is a way of getting to people, getting messages over ...//... I can't see it coming to anything ... but then he always surprises us.
(Mrs Hilda Anderson)

(150)
[He's unemployed] Because he wants to be ... he wants to do something else. He has this project ...//... The trouble is, with Steve that I agree with everything he says and does, but Steve doesn't realise that whatever he does requires application. He needs to work at it.
(Mr Alun Anderson)

Clearly Mr and Mrs Anderson are keen to understand Steve's outlook and position. It is interesting to note in this context that when asked about the reasons for unemployment in general, Mr and Mrs Anderson talked about government policy and economic factors. None the less, it is possible to detect an undercurrent of criticism and anxiety in Mr Anderson's words, above (150). And, since his return from London, Steve had experienced some conflict with his parents:

(151)
Particularly now and again then their worry has really come to the surface. Things seem a lot easier now. There have been rows. Not many. Three or four since Christmas. There was one particularly nasty one, where I stormed out and the rest of it.

Reading between the lines of the interview with his parents, there was also some conflict between them about how Steve was to be understood and treated. His mother was inclined to be less hard on him than his father. What they were all agreed upon, however, was the uncertainty about Steve's future and the difficulty he was finding in growing up. As Mrs Anderson said, 'He's got a bit of a Peter Pan in him'. It was accepted that it was unlikely that he would remain in Swansea.

Steve Anderson is, in many respects, unusual in the context of this study. It would have been easy, at this stage, to offer a case study of more severe family conflict in Ty-Gwyn (and, indeed, we shall do so later). However, the Andersons do serve admirably to illustrate the differences between Ty-Gwyn and the other areas with respect to the locally available structure of possibilities and opportunities. These differences are graphically brought out by the further details of the samples which are offered in the Appendix. If an individualistic explanation is offered for Steve Anderson's being on the dole, as compared to the account offered by Mrs Wallis for Geoffrey's unemployment, than that must be in large part because their situations are totally different. Steve Anderson *could* be employed *if he wanted to be*, of that there seems little doubt; Geoffrey Wallis *wants* to be employed but *can't* find anything. For Helen Roderick, there are some possibilities of employment but they are either highly competitive (there is no shortage of applicants for shop assistants' jobs), part-time (in which case she is probably better off on benefit) or unacceptable (cleaning jobs, for example).

And this is the point of the comparison of the three areas through these case-studies. Ideologies or explanatory frameworks – of individualism, collectivism or whatever – are important and undoubtedly contribute to the way in which the situations of these young people are understood by their families and by themselves. But alongside this we must set the fact that their situations are very different. Ideology and values are not sufficient explanations. Nor is it simply a question of the *external* structure of opportunity being markedly different in each area. This also, of course, makes a difference *within* families: the Andersons are financially better off than the Rodericks, who are, in turn, better off than the Wallises. Steve Anderson does not in any real sense *need* to work: taking some time out to 'get his act together' is an indulgence which he and his parents can afford. The contrast with Geoffrey Wallis, suffering from depression after years of unemployment, could not be more stark.

Scenarios of family conflict

During the course of a research project of this kind, it is often difficult to stand back and be 'objective'. One encounters situations and people who touch one's feelings: sympathy, anger, unhappiness, the affection engen-

dered as individuals keep in touch over a period of time, these can all come
in to play. This was particularly so in those families where there was
conflict.

The Preece family is one such. Living in one of the newest houses in High
Oak, Simon Preece, who was 18, had been on the dole for 6 months when
we interviewed him in February 1985, having previously spent a year on a
Construction Industry Training Board YTS scheme. His parents are di-
vorced, and his father, a bricklayer, is remarried and lives not far from Port
Talbot. His mother is also remarried and her husband is called Preece too.
He 'works away' on the oil rigs, in order to make a sufficient wage. Mrs
Preece, with five children at home (Simon is the eldest), has to go out to
work. She is employed as a domestic in the University for 32 weeks a year.
The house is clean, tidy and comfortable, but bears the signs of a struggle to
keep it that way.

Simon and his mother clearly love each other. Simon's father is also
concerned about his son and, as parents, despite their divorce, they try to
work together in supporting Simon; Mrs Preece, however, bears the brunt
of his problems. His unhappiness at being unemployed, her worry about
him, and the general domestic and financial strain which she has largely to
shoulder alone, come together in confrontation and anger:

(152)
We argue all the time, like ... it's being stuck in the house, like. I'm just
under her feet. I'm in a miserable mood, she's in a miserable mood ...
Sometimes she rings my father and he comes over and gets me and I go
and stay there for a week. It gives her a break.

(Simon Preece)

(153)
We only had one row. It ended up with him getting so upset that he
nearly burst into tears and he went into the garden to pull himself
together ... And I thought, never again, it isn't worth it ... it isn't the
money. I don't want him to get into such a rut so that he won't have the
guts to go for an interview.

(Mrs Preece)

(154)
She phones me up now and then. He don't let go steam, but she's very
disappointed. When he got his report [from the YTS scheme], she
thought he was going to be kept on. She's more upset than anything
else, because she really thought he had done enough.

(Mr Preece)

And so they persevered. For Mrs Preece, however, there were only further
black clouds on the horizon. In the summer of 1985, her daughter and her
husband's twin sons by his first marriage were all due to leave school. She

stood to lose three lots of Child Benefit plus her daughter's maintenance contribution from Simon's father (although, as in Simon's case, she recognised that Mr Preece would probably continue to pay what he could): 'God, I hope I don't end up with five on the dole and I've got to get up for work ... I'm going to be very resentful, aren't I?'

Mrs Preece and Simon, despite their financial and other problems, have a source of support in family solidarity and affection that has even managed to survive a divorce. The next case we will look at, the Reynolds family, who lived a couple of minutes walk away in High Oak, are not so lucky, although their economic situation is not so tight.

The Reynolds household is more obviously prosperous than the Preece's: the furniture newer and more stylish, the paint and wallpaper fresher. Mr Reynolds is a clerk in a local factory, his wife is a ward sister in a hospital nearby. Since leaving school in 1981 with two O-levels and four CSEs, Hugh Reynolds, who was 20 when we interviewed him in February, 1985, had been in a variety of jobs and on one YTS scheme. He had been unemployed since September, when he was sacked for bad timekeeping from a job as a sales assistant which he had got through his father, who 'knew someone'. Hugh has one younger sister.

Family relationships, according to Hugh (it was all he would say directly on the subject), were 'not too good'. On talking to his mother, and subsequently interviewing her formally, a fuller picture emerged. Mr Reynolds, although cordial enough during one brief meeting, was never available for interview: 'he thinks it's Big Brother watching him. He doesn't see the point, he wants to know what good it will do'.

There appeared to be a number of axes of conflict in the Reynolds family, some involving Hugh directly, some indirectly. At the risk of presenting a partial view, we are forced to rely on his mother's testimony, culled from a number of sections of the interview and from less formal conversation:

(155)
Hugh's not very good with his money, sometimes he'll blow all of his money at once ... There are moments like that, I say to him, 'Good God, Hugh, what did you do with your money?' ...//... He must owe me £200 altogether. Before Christmas he was paying me a fiver [in lodge money] but since then he's been giving me ten, to pay it off, or so he thinks ...//... The trouble with Hugh and his dad is they've never been able to have a real conversation. He's [Mr Reynolds] always been away playing rugby. There's a lot of tension between me and my husband anyway ... But I do try to side with Hugh, its maternal instincts, you protect your kids ...//... Hugh has been marvellous lately, tension has been building up. My husband hasn't got time for us. Over the last two years I've been digging my heels in, I'm refusing to be a door mat. It can't go on, something's got to give ...//... He

takes more than £40 a week pocket money and only gives me £150 every month for the housekeeping ... And he says *he* allowed *me* to go back to work! The atmosphere in the house is fine until I hear that key in the door.

There had been a particularly bad domestic scene the previous weekend – Mrs Reynolds had stormed out of the house and stayed out until late evening – which may explain some of the confessional character of the interview. And there were other sources of worry. Mrs Reynolds has problems with her daughter, 'who's at that age' and resented the family rows. Hugh's father was pushing him to go out and get a job. Hugh himself was unhappy about his relationship with his, very middle-class, girlfriend:

(156)
It's a strain. Money-wise. Not being able to afford things I want, or take her where she wants to go ... She tends to want to pay a lot, which is embarrassing for me. I just feel ashamed. And she tends to get uptight if I refuse ...//... Her mother and father knowing I'm unemployed. That's also been a strain. You can imagine ... A girl brings a boy home and he's not working. There's no real future.

Questions of the future aside, in the present there was, for the Reynolds family, a tangle of conflict: between parents, between parents and children, and between brother and sister. Hugh's unemployment was only one thread in this tangle, although it did nothing to improve the situation and provided a peg upon which to sometimes hang other problems. As Hugh said about his problems with his father, 'It's not because I'm unemployed. It's just family history.' Leaving home was the only solution he could see, either to join the Navy (he had applied at the time of the interview) or to move into a place of his own (and he did not think he could afford that).

We argued in Chapters 2 and 3 that unemployment in itself does not often actually *cause* family conflict; it contributes, rather, to existing tensions or difficulties. This would certainly appear to be true, to differing degrees, for the Preece and Reynolds families. In the next situation we shall look at, however, it appears that the unemployment of a son has undermined a previously harmonious household.

Timothy Owens lived in a semi-detached house in Ty-Gwyn; there was an extension built on the back and they had just had hardwood double-glazing fitted. The eldest of three boys, he was 18 when we interviewed him in June 1986. His father, Wynford, was a sales representative; his mother, Ceridwen, worked part-time in an old people's home. Timothy left comprehensive school in 1984 with one O-level and seven CSEs. Until August 1985, he had been on a YTS scheme, with a small training agency in Swansea. There was no job at the end of it, however, and he had been unemployed since. Unemployment was clearly not what his parents had reckoned on. It was not his lack of earning power that was worrying them, however. As Mrs Owens said:

(157)
The thing that really gets me down is that he hasn't got a job. As I said to him, if he wanted to try for a lower-paid job, a stop-gap while he's looking for something else, I would take less off him ...//... It's made me very depressed. Sometimes I wonder if he's ever going to get a job at all. I know it's an awful thing to say ...//... I've shed many a tear over it. It's got me down so much. I never thought I would get so depressed over such a thing.

Mr Owens was also upset about Timothy's unemployment. It was, he thought, partly Timothy's fault because he was not go-getting enough. Conflict, when it came, was about a variety of things: pressure on Timothy to look for a job, the use of the phone and heating during the day by Timothy and his mates, Timothy's taking for granted of lifts into town from his father.

All of these things hinge around 'making an effort' or the use of resources without a contribution. We got the strong impression, from Timothy and his parents, that their relationship had previously been relatively free from conflict. Now the rows, when they came, were explicitly about unemployment:

(158)
SH: Are there any rows about his unemployment?
Mrs Owens: Oh, yes ... usually when he gets into that phase when he's not going to look for anything, we try to gee him up a bit ...//... Sometimes you say things when you're in a temper.

(159)
SH: What sort of things do you have rows about?
Timothy: Money, mostly.
SH: Is that mostly because you're unemployed?
Timothy: Yes. If I was working, I wouldn't be in the house mainly. As I'm in the house all the time, everyone's penned up together.

(160)
SH: Has he ever threatened to leave home?
Mr Owens: [laughing]: I don't think so. I've threatened to throw him out.
SH: What about?
Mr Owens: Jobs.

SH: And would you?
Mr Owens: Not really

Mr Owens might not really have meant it. None the less, the atmosphere in the house was uncomfortable. During part of the interview with Timothy, Mr Owens was present, upbraiding him publicly and harshly for his lack of thought and consideration (this rebuke is quote (39) in Chapter 3). Issues like the use of the phone or the heating did not, however, seem to be about *money*. As we suggest in Chapters 2 and 3, what is at issue is the exchange of signals – 'making an effort' – within the symbolic economy of family relationships. Timothy's unemployment was like a bone which they were continuously gnawing away at or fighting over. Nor, short of his finding employment, did they seem able to find a way round the problem. Mrs Owens did her best to act as a buffer between father and son; that, however, could only be done at the expense of worsening her own anxiety.

There is a limit to what can be done with case studies such as these. In themselves they only scratch the surface of the interview material which we have available for each family. However, they do serve to illustrate a number of points about family conflict and unemployment. Conflict is generally exacerbated rather than caused by unemployment. Money matters a great deal, but it is often within a symbolic economy of relationships and exchanges that this importance resides (although the harsh facts of subsistence are also important in many families). Finally, the role of mothers in managing both family conflict and the problems of unemployment is absolutely central.

Problems of the kinds which we have been looking at in this section may be severe enough within families where one son or daughter is unemployed in the long-term. What, however, of the case where two young people from the same family are in that situation? We shall discuss two such cases next.

Brothers and sisters

The Jones house in one of the side streets of Abbeyview was one of the most obviously poor houses which we visited. The furniture, the decoration, even the dog, looked old and battered. Everybody smoked and most people talked all at once. But it is a warm house in which the visitor is made welcome. The hubbub is a comfortable hubbub. The father had been confined to bed since February when the interviews took place in September 1986, and was in receipt of sickness benefit. Mrs Jones was not employed. Three of the children were in school; the other three were all unemployed. Paula, the eldest at 21, was due to start work the following week on a Community Programme scheme. She was moving in with her boyfriend soon. Her younger sister, Helen, who had just turned 20, was moving out into lodgings the week after:

(161)

The unemployment for this family's terrible. Well, I'm moving now Monday to a different address. I'm going up to Station Road. I'm moving up to by there. Bed, breakfast and laundry. Get out and buy my dinner, or my mother'll make me a dinner.

Her mother was not at all happy about the girls leaving. It did, however, make economic sense and they would still be 'where I can see them'. They would still be popping in and out; Helen would be at home every day. And Paula's boyfriend? Mrs Jones was unequivocal in her praise: 'Oh, he's fantastic. Oh, he's a lovely boy.'

In many respects the two elder daughters have much in common. Both attended the local comprehensive school, but left without any qualifications. Both regard their time at school as having been useful, but only within limits:

(162)

Paula: You learn a lot from school ...//... To read, you learn to read in school. To write. History, which can be useful. Geography. Maths ... maths can be very useful. So can English ... but job-wise, looking for work, I don't think so. Education-wise, yes. Work? ... no.

(163)

Helen: Well, you get a proper education, don't 'oo? For a job and all that. I liked school, but sometimes I couldn't be bothered. It got me down a bit.

Since leaving school in 1981 Paula has been on a YTS scheme as a nursery assistant for a year, was a voluntary worker at the local youth club, tried to find a job in London for a while but hated it, and was a temporary clerical worker for the Inland Revenue. At the time of the interview she had been on the dole for 18 months. Helen left school at Easter, 1983. From September 1983, for a year, she worked on a YTS scheme for the Council's parks and gardens section. Since then she had been ill and hadn't worked, although, like Paula before her, she is working as a volunteer in the youth club: 'It's all right. It's something to do with the night, is passes the time for me.'

Here the similarities between the two sisters end; they may, indeed, be more apparent than real. Paula is an outgoing, even a noisy, young woman; full of life and vitality, the interview was carried along on a wave of her enthusiasm and opinion. With Helen, while she was not difficult to interview, it was a more careful process; she struck one as shy, if not withdrawn. This contrast is underlined by comparing their private lives outside the family.

Since she broke off with her fiancé, two years earlier, Helen had not 'really' been out with any young men, although she was, if anything, the more conventionally attractive of the two. She had some male friends – 'mates' – and she went out every two or three weeks with her girlfriends, all of whom were working. Apart from this, however, her leisure time was taken up with solitary pursuits such as swimming and running, or pool, table-tennis and badminton down at the Youth Centre. Paula's life was completely different. She did not hang around much with her female mates: 'They're all mothers ... They've just become mothers.' Her entire social life was wrapped up with Eurof (pronounced Eye-rof), her boyfriend. If they did not go out, they stayed in, in the comfort and domesticity of his own house:

(164)
I can't afford to go out and have a good time now. But I'm lucky, I got Eurof. Who does, sort of pay, and say, well don't worry, you know we're together and I'll pay, sort of thing ... And I don't like that all the time, I like to pay my own way as well ... But I can't afford it. So I say, let's stay in 'cause I can't afford it. Perhaps he can, but I don't know.

It might be that Helen's illness was the source of some of her diffidence and withdrawal. During her time on the YTS she suffered an accident while lifting something heavy. She has since had two operations. At the time of the interview she was still having problems in the wake of the last operation. Paula, however, has had her share of medical problems as well. A miscarried pregnancy a few months earlier had been a major trauma, although by the time we saw her she felt that she was beginning to get over it.

So we have two sisters, close together in age and similar in other respects. However, in at least three important aspects, from the perspective of this study, they are very different indeed. First, there is the effect which they feel that unemployment has had on them:

(165)
Paula: I've quietened down since I've been out of work ...//... I used to be very rowdy, noisy sort of person. Very outgoing, but being out of work sort of pulled me back.

(166)
Helen: It's very depressing. Oh yes, terrible depression ...//... Terrible. I'm round the house, I don't know what to do. Trying to find something to do and it's already been done, and stuff like that. When I go out to the garden I just dig anywhere, do anything ... Cut the grass when it's raining ... That depressed, I'll do anything.

So although being on the dole for so long has had its effect on Paula, it
seems to have hit Helen harder. 'Quietening down' is one thing, 'feeling
depressed' another. We also asked them how they saw themselves – as
young people or adults:

(167)
Paula: Um, recently more of an adult. If you had asked me a couple of
months ago, I would have said basically a young person. Whereas
since Christmas, since after losing ... since first falling for the baby,
it sort of matures you ...//... since then I've looked on myself as an
adult ...//...
RJ: What makes the difference?
Paula: You feel you're more mature in yourself, and you mustn't, you
sort of think to yourself, well, you must be more lady-like, when
you're out, sort of thing, you know? ...//... When you're sort of an
adult, you're sort of laid back, very quiet, sort of thing. ...//...
RJ: And do you think having a child would make a difference?
Paula: Yes, you feel ... You'll have your own independence then,
wouldn't you? You feel, great, I got my own money. More
independence, saving, a bank account. Makes you feel more ...
great, you know?

(168)
Helen: A young person, I should say.
RJ: What makes an adult?
Helen: Oh, I don't know really ... Growing up. Going out, enjoying
themselves. Making themselves into an adult, like.
RJ: Do you think being on the dole affects that?
Helen: I think it does ...//... I don't know, but I think it does affect
becoming an adult anyway. It's just ... You're a young person when
you're on the dole. You just can't grow up quick enough when
you're on the dole. I found that out myself ...//... You just don't
grow up so quick when you're on the dole.

Here is further evidence that adulthood is a multifaceted social identity.
While unemployment may disrupt or impede the transition to adulthood, it
does not in itself prevent it happening. There are many important criteria of
adulthood: behaviour, reproductive capacity, self-image and maturity,
having a bank account. All of these are part of 'making yourself an adult'.
Paula feels she has become an adult, Helen does not. While Helen may feel
that her unemployment is a brake upon her movement into adulthood, for
Paula it was pregnancy not employment which made the difference.

The final difference between the sisters which we wish to highlight here
relates to their ambitions for the future: while Paula wanted a job,

preferably in the field of caring, Helen's major goal, although she wanted a 'really steady job' for a couple of years, was to settle down and start a family.

Notions about starting a family and the importance of her pregnancy as a key event in Paula's life-course – the threshold, to her, of her adulthood – suggests that there might be some interaction here between gender and the notion of adulthood. In Chapter 5 we argued strongly that our material relating to models or criteria of adulthood – notions such as responsibility, independence and so on – was relatively undifferentiated by gender. These criteria apply as much to young women as to young men. We also suggested in Chapter 5, however, that young men find it easier than young women to escape the responsibilities of adulthood (they generally embrace the *rights* enthusiastically). If this is so, it is probably because women are forced to face the culturally-defined responsibilities of their adulthood, in the shape of the potential of their own fertility, earlier and in a way that men are not. If it is true that women 'grow up' before men, and that more men than women never grow up at all, we suspect that one does not have to look much further for the reason.

The other thing which Paula and Helen's case study serves to illustrate is the importance of self-definition and, crucially, the defintions of others, in the achievement of adulthood. It is not only what Paula thinks about herself which matters, it is also how she behaves in order to foster an impression in the eyes of other people, so that they also will define her as an adult. It is not only sociologists who understand the art of impression management!

In choosing Paula and Helen, we deliberately chose two very different personalities who, although in many respects (relationships with their families, employment histories, educational background) very similar, are apparently set on divergent paths precisely because they are so different in personal terms as individuals. The two brothers we are going to look at now, Matthew and Peter Griffiths, are also different personalities. What is of most interest to us, however, is the gulf which separates them in terms of their relationships with their parents. Whereas the emphasis in our brief discussion of Paula and Helen Jones was upon deprivation, unemployment and adulthood, the theme of our excursion into the lives of the Griffiths family will be conflict and the fragility of family relationships.

The Griffiths brothers lived in a quiet cul-de-sac in Ty-Gwyn. Mrs Georgina Griffiths is a primary school teacher, her husband Paul, a small businessman. Although there were two cars in the drive, they had both seen better days. A teacher's salary is not huge and business often precarious. By their own lights, the Griffiths family never had enough money. What they did have, however, was the certainty of their faith: mother, father and two of the three sons, Peter and Luke, are enthusiastic born-again Christians, heavily involved in the life of a local evangelical congregation. Their religious fervour is a source of both solidarity and schism within the family.

Matthew, the oldest son, and not a Christian, was 21 when we interviewed him in May 1985. After a troubled experience of school, marred by conflict (it was a Christian private grammar school and he was one of the few non-evangelicals attending) and poor academic performance due to dyslexia, Matthew left secondary education in 1980 with three CSEs. In the five years which followed, he worked at a variety of jobs, with only a couple of short periods of unemployment. His last job had been as a van driver; he was sacked from that in September 1984 for poor timekeeping and muddling up deliveries and had been unemployed since, a period of 8 months. This had been his first experience of unemployment in the long-term.

Peter was interviewed on his nineteenth birthday. He had attended the same grammar school as Matthew, leaving at 16 with six O-levels; 2 years at a local comprehensive school had further kitted him out with three A-levels. Apart from a month spent as a warehouseman – only a temporary job at Christmas time – he had been unemployed since leaving school the previous year. Unlike Matthew, who basically just wanted a job to earn money, Peter's ambition was to go into social work. At the time of the interview he was doing voluntary work as a part of the church's programme of community activities; he intended eventually to go to college to obtain a formal social work qualification.

Of the two brothers, it could be said that, apart from his current spell on the dole, Matthew had the better employment record, in terms of consistency of employment and 'effort'. This was certainly not how his parents saw matters, however (see quotations (131) and (132) in Chapter 6); while Peter was 'taking some time out' as part of his preparation for a career, Matthew was seen as having an attitudinal problem, he wasn't prepared to 'knuckle down' and make a go of employment.

The differences in the parental evaluations of the two brothers' unemployment must be viewed within the broader context of parent–child relationships as a whole and of relationships between siblings within the family:

(169)

Mr Griffiths: [Unemployment is] lost in its size of impact because it's only a very small segment of a character problem which we see in Matthew ...//... The shortcomings in Matthew have been brought to the suface by him not having any money and having to borrow from Peter ...//... Luke [the youngest son] not having had difficult teenage years, has the view of Matthew as being someone who just can't cope and does all the wrong things. It gets him down ... But he is critical sometimes.

(170)

Mrs Griffiths: Paul reacts more strongly than I do, really. We do worry, particularly about Matthew getting and keeping a job. It does obviously affect the relationship ... it puts pressure on our finances as well as his ...//... And the feeling of someone hanging around not doing anything that seems worthwhile during the day.

(171)
Matthew: The secret is to get up early and go out and stay out all day ... And if I can avoid it I stay out for tea ...//... He [Peter] never goes out. Peter never goes anywhere if it involves spending money.

(172)
Peter: 'I think he's [Matthew] unemployed because of himself. Often he hasn't ... not getting to the job on time, and doing it sloppy, have caused him to be unemployed. He's had lots of jobs, and he could still have them now, well not all of them, if he'd been more careful with them. But at the same time I don't think his prospects are very good.

What emerged from the long interviews with Matthew, Peter and their parents, and from a number of less formal conversations, was a picture of a family which, with the lonely exception of Matthew, was tightly bound together by a shared sense of Christian purpose and a consensus about morality and right behaviour. It wasn't Matthew's unemployment which was the problem – although it was, indeed, *a* problem – it was everything about him, his life-style. Peter, however, effectively unemployed by choice, lived the right kind of life and he wasn't seen as a problem.

In fairness to Mr and Mrs Griffiths, it was possible to sympathise with their point of view. Matthew contributed nothing to the family's budget and regularly borrowed money, which he could not always repay, from his mother or from Peter; Peter did not borrow and paid in £5 a week 'keep', in addition to money which he gave to the church. Peter neither smoked nor drank; Matthew smoked, drank and – by his own admission – regularly arrived home stoned out of his brain (dope was another pleasure he had difficulty affording). Peter did some housework, Matthew nothing. Peter discussed with his parents how he was managing his money; for Matthew that was a subject he had learnt it was better to avoid. While Peter looked clean and tidy (in the local sense of 'respectable', as much as anything else), Matthew did his best to look like any one of the myriad surfie-cum-beach-bums who hang round Mumbles and the nearer Gower beaches.

It was tempting – certainly we found it so – to see Matthew as a lovable rascal, struggling to express himself within the straight-jacket of a narrow, conformist family environment. It was tempting because there was a deal of truth in it. He was also, however, a trial and a tribulation for his parents and a major source of worry, as we hope the paragraph above reveals. What is interesting to us is the fact that, in the context of the differences between

Matthew and Peter – the exclusion of one and the inclusion of the other –
the unemployment of each was seen in a totally different light. Matthew's
was a problem, a negative thing, Peter's quite the reverse, a positive opportunity, despite the fact that Matthew was actively looking for employment
while Peter was not.

Nor is this solely our diagnosis. The family recognised that Matthew was
the problem, from their point of view, not his unemployment. Matthew
acknowledged this too:

(173)
Matthew: They don't like it [his unemployment] ...//... I'm the odd
   one out ...//... it [unemployment] does come in. Usually dad. He
   gives me a lot of stick ... Not actual rows. We do have some, but not
   over unemployment ... But unemployment does get used.

(174)
Mr Griffiths: Again, it wouldn't be the kernel of why he was getting a
   row. It would be a side issue ... irresponsibility, bad habits ...
   Unemployment wouldn't be the ... It may have been because he lost
   the job.

It is also tempting to wonder whether or not the 'real' core of the problem
was Matthew's refusal to embrace Christianity. That may be how Matthew
saw it himself sometimes. We are not certain, however, that complex
situations of family conflict such as this have easily identifiable cores or
single causes. They are more likely to be a complex combination of factors,
rooted in a history of personal relationships over a long period of time.
Matthew's father certainly saw it as a wider problem than one of religion:

(175)
It would be wonderful if he would embrace the faith, but it's not that.
It's the lack of balance, order and responsibility. He does suffer by
comparison with the other two ... There's no reason why he should
...//... Matthew is more than ever dependent because of his lack of
stability. If he continues the way he is, he's going to be more dependent,
with a wife and kids and the cornerstone of that relationship is going to
be unstable. And there's only so much we can bear.

With this quotation we come back to the central issues with which this
book has been concerned. The family was taking the strain of Matthew's
predicament, and conflict was being contained and managed. Unemployment, while not the source of the conflict, did nothing to improve matters.
Relationships were bad, but they could have been worse (Mrs Griffiths, in
particular, functioned as the mediator and defuser of conflict). Matthew

had threatened to leave home several times; so far he had always been headed off. Despite the financial burden of his presence, his parents did not want him to go. They feared for him and the mess he might get himself into. Among the central issues about which Mr and Mrs Griffiths worried with respect to Matthew were responsibility, maturity and independence: in a word, adulthood. As far as they were concerned, Peter, although he was younger and also unemployed, was already exhibiting the right kind of characteristics. He had grown up; at 19 he was already an adult.

This brief case study of the Griffiths family is a timely reminder that living in a middle-class area such as Ty-Gwyn does not guarantee economic security. While their financial predicament was nothing like as desperate as that of the Jones family from Abbeyview, these things are, of course, relative. Mrs Griffiths was certainly more *worried* about her situation than was Mrs Jones. Money and its handling was certainly more of an issue for the Griffiths boys than it was for the Jones girls.

Finally, the two cases in this section also throw a little more light on the nature of individualism. Within the Jones family, Paula was the only one who explained the unemployment of her siblings or neighbours as due to their own unwillingness to work (see quotation (126) in the previous chapter). However, her views in this respect did not appear to disrupt her relationships with them; she might have thought that they were bone idle, but this did not necessarily mean that she thought ill of them. Within the Griffiths family, while individualism was the dominant world-view, the choice made by Peter not to work was approved while Matthew's involuntary unemployment was seen as his fault and reflective of a weak character. If nothing else, these examples are a reminder, first, that individualism may find its expression in many different ways and, second, that one cannot easily predict behaviour from attitudes or values.

In this chapter, we have used case studies to both provide more substantial glimpses of some of the families which we looked at and to illustrate certain key themes within our argument: the complexities of conflict management, the importance of the particular lives of individuals as well as the patterns which can be perceived in the samples taken as a whole, the transition to adulthood, the complex role of individualism as an explanatory framework and the significance of gender. In the final chapter we shall expand upon these themes and sum up our conclusions.

8

TAKING THE STRAIN

In our opening chapter we itemised six topics in which we were interested: the effect of long-term youth unemployment upon, respectively, family relationships, the transition to adulthood and courtship and marriage, the role of gender in structuring those effects, the differences in the experience and meaning of unemployment from one locality to another and, finally, the impact of long-term youth unemployment upon the political positions adopted by young people and their parents. In Chapters 2 to 7 we have examined these topics using our interview material from families in Port Talbot and Swansea. We shall now briefly review our findings and arguments with respect to each topic in turn.

To turn first to family relationships, we argued that they were, indeed, disrupted and threatened by the long-term unemployment of daughters and sons. In a range of situations and to varying degrees, there can be little doubt of that. However, there were few cases where unemployment in itself actually *caused* severe family conflict where previously there was none. The effects of unemployment, such as they are, must therefore be understood in the context of the nature and quality of pre-existing relationships between family members. In some families with unemployed young adult members there does not appear to be conflict of a major kind (or, indeed, conflict at all); in other families, the tension and struggle are tangible as soon as one walks in the door. There is a continuum of situations in between.

We can offer, with appropriate diffidence, given the highly specific focus of this study, some general observations about families and interpersonal conflict. Most immediately, we cannot, on the basis of our research, defend a view of family conflict as necessarily deviant, abnormal or pathological. It is, rather, a 'normal' part of the fabric of family life and human social experience. This is not to suggest that a human propensity for conflict is somehow innate (it may be, but we cannot imagine how that can ever be known, one way or another), nor are we turning a blind eye to the physical and mental suffering of many parents and children or a deaf ear to their cries. What we are saying is that within families there are bound to be genuine clashes of interest, of generation and of personality. In many such situations, depending on how they are managed by the people concerned, a degree of open conflict is likely to contribute to the resolution of those differences. In many other such situations, schism and fission will result.

This is all part of the on-going and changing pattern of family relationships, as much a part of that pattern as affection, succour and security. Neither aspect of family life is inevitable, however, nor are they necessarily contradictory. Families may be a mixture of both – conflict and affection, oppression and security – all at the same time. It seems to us, therefore, to make little sense to put normative notions of 'traditional family life' on a pedestal as the core values of society. Nor, however, can we support a view of the family as necessarily anti-social or psychologically disabling. Family life, viewed broadly, is neither good nor bad. It is simply what goes on in the business of finding partners and rearing children, and that is a very broad – and fluid – spectrum of possibilities indeed.

In the management of family conflict, as in the provision of support and succour, women – particularly mothers – play a pivotal role. This is so in a variety of situations, of which unemployment is only one. If anyone – apart, of course, from themselves – is taking the strain of the long-term unemployment of the young women and young men we interviewed, it is their mothers. They are the managers, mediators and negotiators at the heart of the symbolic economy of family relationships. Among the media of exchange are money, domestic labour and the appearance of 'effort'. The values and identities which are affirmed or produced in the daily round of transactions include responsibility, independence and equality of status in the world of adults (or, in the extreme opposite case, the reverse of these). Money, of course, is important because it ensures physical subsistence and the nature of one's life-style; it also has other uses, however, as a medium for symbolic exchanges, and these should not be forgotten.

The transition to adulthood was our second focus of interest. A number of commentators, Paul Willis most notably, have argued that one of the most serious consequences of long-term youth unemployment is the exclusion, in the social equivalent of a state of suspended animation, of young people from adulthood. We did not find any convincing evidence to support this argument. Quite the reverse: *despite* their unemployment, the overwhelming majority of the young people we interviewed were continuing to claim their adulthood. Being unemployed in the long-term may make the transition to adulthood more problematic; it may also affect the nature of one's claim to adult status, but these are different arguments.

Adulthood in a modern industrial society such as Great Britain is a multifaceted and imprecise status. Among the most important criteria of adulthood are, on the one hand, a battery of legally or administratively bestowed rights and duties (many of which are bound up with citizenship), and, on the other, a repertoire of interactional competences which serve to identify 'adult behaviour'. Employment is only one aspect of adulthood and the 'right to work' is not unconditional; it is a permissive or enabling right attached to adulthood. Just as one cannot be *made* to work (although this freedom is under threat), one cannot *demand* employment either. Willis's argument fails, we suggest, because it is, on the one side, based on too narrow a model of adulthood and, on the other, does not distinguish the rights and responsibilities of adulthood from the capacity to exercise them. What is more, while unemployment may weaken that capacity with respect to some of those rights and responsibilities, it leaves many others untouched.

The other important sense in which the young unemployed continue their move into adulthood depends on themselves, on their families and on other people. Young women and men *want* – most of them – to become women and men (often earlier than the rest of us are prepared to accept or recognise). By the time their daughters and sons have reached their late teens and early twenties, most parents also want them to grow up. If for no other reason, this is because having one's children grow up successfully, taking their place in the world as independent adults, is the public apotheosis of successful parenting. Many parents also actively look forward to 'when the kids grow up' so that they can restore some space for themselves – as a couple or as individuals – to their lives. Finally, the social world of significant others also expects people from this point in their lives onward to behave as adults and treats them accordingly, or treats them accordingly in the absence of evidence to the contrary. There is thus a considerable psychological and social head of steam which pushes and pulls young people into adulthood, unemployment notwithstanding.

One of the most important practices which is implicated in the transition to adulthood is the complex of custom, ritual and law bound up with courtship and marriage. This, too, shows signs of disruption, in part as a consequence of levels of male unemployment which are higher than levels of female unemployment. Established conventions about 'the man paying' are under threat, as are entrenched notions about when, or even if, couples should marry. There appears to have been a shift in the balance of power in the courtship and marriage market in the favour of young women.

We have no doubt that some of the major changes in courtship and marriage practices and patterns which have taken place in the last decade – and which continue as we write – bear the teeth marks, as it were, of unemployment. It is, however, equally clear that these changes are to do with much more than unemployment. With their roots in the 'sexual revolution' of the 1960s and in the women's movement, they reflect and are a consequence of a range of factors too numerous to discuss here. With the impact of the AIDS epidemic perhaps at last beginning to make itself felt in mores and behaviour, it is impossible to predict the direction which change might next take. It seems unlikely, however, that the unemployment of young people will have anything other than a minor contribution to make to that direction.

The fourth topic was the role of gender categories in structuring the effects of the long-term unemployment of young people upon families, the transition to adulthood and courtship and marriage. Within the family, we found that young women and men were treated in fairly similar ways, in both cases bordering on the indulgent. Gender was significant inasmuch as the freedom from domestic labour – in Diana Leonard's terms the 'spoiling' – of these young women and men was underwritten by the mother's sole responsibility for household work. The apparent gender equality of young women within the family can thus only be understood in the context of a wider, generational pattern of gender inequalities. The young woman's relative freedom within the household is likely to be shortlived, vanishing with marriage and the move into an independent household.

The transition to adulthood was, in some respects, surprisingly unstructured by gender. The major formal and informal criteria of adult status are not gender dependent. Where there is a difference is in the apparent ability of some males to put 'full' adulthood off or, and this is probably a better way of putting it, in their scope for irresponsibility. Whereas women's adulthood is more heavily weighted towards socially defined *responsibilities* – in particular for children – men seem more likely to enjoy the *rights* attached to adult status. This situation is probably encouraged by unemployment, although such a conclusion must remain more of an impression than a defensible finding.

Looking at courtship and marriage, we have already said that there have been major changes with respect to gender roles in this area. Some of these are related to disproportionate levels of male and female unemployment. The gender equality of social security payments for single young adults also has implications in this area of their lives, as we discussed in Chapter 4. However, as we argued above, we do not think that the connection between, on the one hand, the long-term unemployment of young women and young men and, on the other, widespread changes in courtship behaviour and marriage patterns, is particularly strong. In so far as there is a connection, however, it is structured by conventional gender categories.

One of the most striking threads of continuity in our interview material, with respect to a wide range of topics, is the clarity with which differences emerged between Abbeyview, High Oak and Ty-Gwyn. In all sorts of contexts, Abbeyview and Ty-Gwyn were polar ends of a continuum, with High Oak occupying a middle position between them. The experience of being unemployed in each area appeared to be quite different, with implications for family relations, the transition to adulthood, courtship and marriage and political perspectives. These differences are related to area-specific economic and demographic profiles, local opportunity structures, contrasts of social milieu and divergent communal histories, both recent and more distant. There is no such thing as *the* experience of unemployment, only locally-specific experiences; the effects of unemployment are not determinate and predictable, they depend heavily on context.

Having said this, however, within those local patterns of experience there is considerable diversity. In this sense, localities represent clustered cores of individual lives; there is a continuum from Ty-Gwyn to High Oak to Abbeyview, and there is some overlap and continuity, both at the level of the experience of individuals and at the level of overall pattern. In emphasising the difference between localities, it is important to also remember these other levels of analysis.

Finally, there is the issue of the impact of long-term unemployment upon the political attitudes and positions of young people and their parents. This is a difficult question and we do not pretend to have done more than scratch the surface of the issues which it raises. There are, none the less, some interesting things to be said. We looked, for example, at the role of individualism in the explanations offered for unemployment – both personal unemployment and unemployment as a general problem – and concluded that as an explanatory framework individualism is sufficiently vague to be put to a variety of uses, with a variety of effects. Having said this, there was a connection between individualistic explanations of a son's or daughter's unemployment and severity of family conflict. However, in contrast to some writers about young people and their views of the world (including, it must be admitted, the earlier work of one of the present authors), we wish to emphasise the fluidity and situational diversity of individualistic understandings of the social world. Individualism is not a monolithic ideology, nor is it wicked false knowledge serving the interests of capital. Life is a little more complicated than that. We still have some way to go in terms of research and analysis before we can begin to pretend to a comprehensive understanding of the meaning and implications of individualism as a cultural framework.

With respect to attitudes to state interventions such as employment schemes (the Youth Training Scheme or the Community Programme), our respondents exhibited considerable ambiguity. On the one hand, they were an affront to moral notions of fairness: 'slave labour' was a common description. On the other, however, it was recognised that they could have their uses. Either way, they were there and hard to escape, so pragmatism determined that the most sensible thing to do was to try to get the best out of them for oneself or one's daughter or son.

Perhaps the most important thing which we can say in this respect is to point to the degree to which the issue of unemployment has become virtually depoliticised. People do have ideas of why unemployment happens and many of these ideas are harshly critical of the present Conservative government. We did not, however, come across any evidence that people's political preferences, where they were clear, had been changed by their own unemployment or the unemployment of their children. Once again, this is an impression rather than a 'hard' finding; it is, however, a strong impression. Our informants could and did offer solutions to the youth unemployment problem: changing the retirement age, preventing married women from working, or whatever. What they did not do was advocate even mild political activity, let alone anything radical or revolutionary. This should not surprise us: what they wanted was jobs for their children or for themselves, not a new kind of society.

In closing, we can offer two more general observations about the political impact (or the lack of it) of the long-term unemployment of young adults. First, the experience of unemployment is complex and fragmentary, structured by family circumstances, gender, economic constraints, cultural differentiation, locality, age and educational background, to mention only some of the factors involved. All of these contribute to the privatisation or compartmentalisation of the experience of unemployment. Since there is, as a consequence, only a common experience of unemployment in a limited sense, the unemployed are not likely to mobilise politically. This atomisation is reinforced by the competitiveness of the labour market: jobs are given to individual workers, one at a time. For every attribute or experience which the unemployed share as a category, there are many other attributes or experiences, divisive and distinguishing, which serve to prevent their coalescence as a meaningful social group.

Second, the other reason why the employment problems of the under-25s have never become a major political problem – and this is probably true for unemployment more generally – is that the young unemployed and their families are getting by. They are taking the strain, refusing to surrender their adulthood, refusing to abandon their future. In homes up and down the country young women and young men, their mothers and fathers (particularly their mothers), their brothers and sisters, are doing the best that they can to cope. It is not easy, relationships suffer, the pressure is not evenly distributed, for some the pressure is too much, but, overall, the line holds. The problem is contained, managed and limited, because there is nothing else that these people can do. They are not in a position to solve the problem, other than in the most immediate and individual way. If they are lucky they or their son or daughter will find work. That is the best which can be hoped for. And it is all most of them want.

The result of these minor epics of domestic heroism and perseverance is that unemployment remains, to appropriate C. Wright Mills's famous words, very much more a personal trouble than a public issue. Nobody actually starves (the welfare state still sees to that) and the rest takes care of itself. Except in those situations where unemployment is compounded by other problems, such as racism and police harassment, the unemployed are not going to take to the streets, whether in hunger marches or bread riots.

Unemployed people are, by and large, not a nuisance to the rest of society. Inasmuch as the young unemployed and their families struggle to keep their end up, succeeding – even if only in part – in preventing things from becoming too bad, they make their own modest if unintended contribution to the creation of a political climate in which unemployment remains a problem incapable of prodding the rest of the electorate, those who are working, into raising their eyes above the sides of the trough. Precisely because the parents we spoke to cared so much about the plight of their daughters and sons, the rest of us, it seems, feel justified in ignoring it.

POSTSCRIPT

We began this research in the spring of 1985. Since then many things have changed. Most important from our point of view has been the slow but none the less steady decline in the unemployment figures. Even allowing for the contribution of statistical definitional changes to that decline, there seems little doubt that unemployment is dropping. This is clearly a good thing and to be welcomed. It does not, however, mean that the problems we have documented in this book – the real, everyday problems of many young men and women and their families – are less urgent or that they have gone away.

In the first place, long-term unemployment remains disproportionately concentrated in the 18- to 25-year-old category. In the second, unemployment is not evenly distributed geographically. The advertising slogan for the Training Commission's launch of its new adult training initiative – on television screens and hoardings as we write (July 1988) – offers to train the workers without the jobs for the jobs without the workers. A laudable enough goal. However, many of the jobs without the workers are at the other end of the country from the workers without the jobs. So, unless this situation is rectified, something which successive employment and training programmes have failed to do, substantial areas of severe and stubborn long-term unemployment will remain. Finally, the new initiative itself, Employment Training, is likely to create further problems. The Community Programme, so important a source of reasonably paid and personally rewarding part-time employment for the long-term unemployed is to disappear in September 1988. Trainees in the Employment Training programme will receive £10 a week over and above their benefit entitlement, considerably less for single people than a Community Programme job could offer. This will exacerbate the economic hardship suffered by long-term unemployed young adults and their families. As we have seen, this is likely to increase the strain on mothers, in particular. We have no doubt that most will, as before, take that strain. Nor, however, do we have any doubt that they will pay the price for doing so. Out of sight and sound of the media, the public and politicians, their struggle will continue.

APPENDIX
THE SAMPLES: ABBEYVIEW,
HIGH OAK AND TY-GWYN

Throughout the book we have used the interview material in an *ad hoc* and piecemeal fashion, with the exception of the case studies in Chapter 7. Our intention in this appendix is to provide brief pen-portraits of the families and individuals with which we were concerned during the research, in order to provide the interested reader with the minimum background information against which to set the de-contextualised quotations of the main text. All of the personal names are pseudonyms; those names which have been italicised are of people who were actually interviewed. Some minor details have been altered to render the camouflage more effective. In a small number of cases we have included young people under 18 years who had been unemployed for more than 6 months, or young people who, although they had not been unemployed for 6 months or more at the time of the interview, had been unemployed in the long-term in the past. This was largely to allow us to build up large enough sample groups.

We also have a second purpose in presenting this material. Even the most cursory flip through the following pages should make the reader appreciate the major differences between the three areas. In this sense, this appendix is an adjunct to the comparison of the areas in Chapter 1 and the case studies in Chapter 7.

A number of points should be made or remade here. First, Abbeyview is dominated by a single employer, BSC. Second, of the ten young people we interviewed who had been on the dole for more than two years at the time of interview, six came from Abbeyview. Third, approximately half of our respondents came from households where male 'breadwinners' were either absent through death or marital breakdown, or were dependent on benefits or pensions of one kind or another. Once again, those households come disproportionately from Abbeyview.

In the following, we use a number of abbreviations:

BSC   British Steel Company, Port Talbot
CP   Community Programme
FE   Further Education
YTS   Youth Training Scheme

Abbeyview

Karen Anderson, 18 years.
Living at home with an elder brother and sister, both working, and a school-age sister. Father unemployed (previously a pipe-fitter's mate at BSC); mother chronically ill. Karen had worked for 12 months on a YTS scheme. She had been unemployed for 18 months at the time of the interview.

Audrey Ballinger, 21 years.
An only child, living with her parents, *Victor* and *Ann Ballinger*. Father made redundant from BSC 5 years ago; mother working part-time as a hospital domestic. Audrey has had three short-term jobs and been on a course at FE college between spells of unemployment. She was working on a CP scheme at the time of the interview.

Michelle Bowen, 19 years.
Living in lodgings, having left home 2 years ago. Her elder brother, unemployed, and sister, working, had also left home. Parents divorced. Father working, mother not working. Michelle had worked for 3 months on a YTS scheme. She had been unemployed for 3 years at the time of interview.

Neville Clifford, 21 years.
Living at home with his parents and elder brother, working. Another brother was working away. Father retired on an invalidity pension 10 years ago, now chronically ill; mother not working. Neville had worked briefly on three YTS and CP schemes. Apart from these he had been unemployed for 5 years at the time of the interview.

Philip Evans, 21 years.
Living in a privately rented house on the fringe of Abbeyview with his girlfriend *Amanda Coughlin* and her baby. Father employed as a crane driver at BSC. Mother not working. Philip had worked on and off at BSC as a lorry driver since he had left school. He had been unemployed for 2 months at the time of the interview.

Thomas Field, 23 years.
Living with his father, *Alexander Field* and his girlfriend *Wilma Dennis*, Thomas was the youngest of seven children. All had left home and were married. One of his two brothers was unemployed. Father, a crane driver at BSC took early retirement 5 years ago; mother dead. Wilma worked part-time at an old people's home. Thomas had worked on a YTS scheme for 12 months. He had worked on temporary labouring jobs between spells of unemployment. He had been unemployed for 6 months at the time of the interview.

David Francis, 19 years.
Living at home with his mother, *Pearl Francis*, father, a younger brother on a YTS scheme and a school-age sister, David had previously shared a flat with friends for a year. Father retired on an invalidity pension, mother not working. David had worked for short spells on three YTS schemes. He had been unemployed for 9 months at the time of the interview.

Caroline Howells, 23 years.
Living at home with her parents, Caroline was the youngest of five children. All left home, three were married, two of her three brothers were unemployed. Father had retired from BSC 5 years ago; mother a pensioner, Caroline had a BA from Hatfield Polytechnic. She had returned home and had been unemployed for 7 months at the time of the interview.

Rebecca Hughes, 23 years.
Living at home with her mother, *Rosemary Hughes*, her father, her 8-month-old daughter and her younger sister, who was working. Two older brothers had married, left home and were working. Father, a process worker at a local factory, mother not working. Rebecca had worked for 12 months on three YTS schemes. She had held several temporary jobs, interspersed with spells of unemployment. She had not worked since the baby was born.

Paula and *Helen Jones*, 21 and 20 years.
Living at home with mother, *Margaret Jones*, father, and younger brother, (unemployed) and three school-age siblings. Father, a pipe-fitter for BSC, on sickness benefit for 7 months, mother not working. Paula had worked for 12 months on a YTS scheme. She had had a temporary job and done voluntary work. She had been unemployed for 18 months at the time of the interview and had just taken a part-time CP job at the time of the interview. Helen had worked for 12 months on a YTS scheme. She had been unemployed for 2 years.

Gary Johnson, 20 years.
Living with his girlfriend and 2-month-old baby, Gary is the eldest of eight children. A younger brother was on a CP scheme, a younger sister unemployed; the remaining siblings are of school age or under. Father, *Mr Johnson*, a fitter, retired on an invalidity pension from the BSC 6 years ago, mother not working. Gary had been unemployed for 4 years at the time of the interview.

Elizabeth and *Mark King*, both 19 years.
Recently married and living with Elizabeth's mother and stepfather, *Glenda* and *Adrian Miller*; two school-age stepsisters and a baby stepbrother,

Elizabeth was several months pregnant and they were waiting for a council house. Stepfather, a rigger erector at BSC, had retired on an invalidity pension 7 years ago. Mother not working. Elizabeth had worked for 2 years on two YTS schemes. She had worked, for 12 months, part time in an old people's home. She had been unemployed for 12 months at the time of the interview. Mark had worked for 12 months on a YTS scheme and been kept on as a garage mechanic. He had been unemployed for 6 months at the time of the interview.

Ciaran McCann, 20 years.
Living in lodgings, he had recently left home where his mother, *Ruth McCann*, father and two school-age siblings lived. Father, employed as a fitter's mate at BSC, mother a part-time dinner lady. Ciaran had worked for 9 months on a YTS scheme. He had been unemployed for $3\frac{1}{2}$ years at the time of the interview.

Elaine Peters, 19 years.
Living at home with her parents, *Joan* and *Ralph Peters*, and younger brother on a YTS scheme. Father employed as a plant operator at BSC; mother a part-time dinner lady. Elaine had worked on a YTS scheme for one month. She had been unemployed for 3 years at the time of the interview.

Gwyn and *Richard Thomas*, 22 and 21 years.
Living at home with their parents, *Maureen* and *William Thomas*, a younger brother who works for a BSC contractor and a school-age brother. Father a self-employed businessman recently bankrupt; mother not working. Gwyn had worked as an apprentice panel-beater for $3\frac{1}{2}$ years. After a temporary job he had been unemployed for 3 years at the time of the interview. Richard had worked for 3 months on a YTS scheme. He then worked with his father making fibre glass canoes. He had been unemployed for 3 months at the time of the interview.

Geoffrey Wallis, 24 years.
Living at home with his mother, *Elsie Wallis*, and father. Two older siblings had left home, married and were working. Father, a furnaceman at BSC, had retired on an invalidity pension 8 years ago, mother a home-help. Geoffrey had a temporary job in a DIY shop and then took an apprenticeship at BSC. After 10 months he was made redundant. After 5 years unemployment he had a temporary job with a contractor at BSC. He had been on sickness benefit for five months at the time of the interview.

Andrea Watkins, 20 years.
Living at home – a private owner-occupied house on the fringe of the

council estate – with parents and two school-age siblings. Father unemployed for 4 months, mother not working. Andrea had left school at 17 and worked for 12 months on a YTS scheme. After 6 months' unemployment she spent 4 months working in an electronics factory. She then worked part-time for 5 months in a nightclub in the north of England. She had been unemployed for 5 months at the time of the interview.

High Oak

Theresa Ace, 19 years.
Living in bed-and-breakfast accommodation. Theresa had recently left home where her mother, *Pauline Ace*, elder sister *Kelly Ace* (employed), and school-aged brother lived. Parents divorced. Father a telephone engineer, mother not working. Theresa left FE college at 18. She had been unemployed for 7 months at the time of the interview.

Jonathan Alexander, 20 years.
Living at home with his parents, *Cynthia* and *Thomas Alexander*, and two school-age sisters. Two stepbrothers were married and working in northern England. Father retired from Remploy on an invalidity pension; mother not working. Jonathan had worked part-time in a bar for 18 months. He had worked for 3 months in a bar in the North. He had been unemployed for 6 months at the time of the interview.

Elinor Anstey, 17 years.
Living at home with her parents. An older brother had left home, married and was working. Father employed as a garage mechanic after 3 years unemployment; mother working part-time in a pub. Elinor had worked for 12 months on a YTS scheme. She had been unemployed for six months at the time of the interview.

Philip Broughton, 21 years and *Katherine Mansell*, 19 years.
Living at home with Philip's stepfather and Katherine's father, *Fred Mansell*. Parents divorced. Father a marine engineer, employed. Philip left school at 17 and went to FE college for a year. He had been unemployed for 3 years at the time of the interview. Katherine had been to FE college for a year. She had had one short job and had been unemployed for 12 months at the time of the interview.

Joanna Furness, 19 years.
Living at home with her parents, *Gwyn* and *Hugh Furness*, but on the point of moving into a private flat with her boyfriend. She was the youngest of six children. The other children were married and had left home. One of her brothers was unemployed. Father, a steel-fixer, retired 9 years ago; mother

retired from part-time shop work. Joanna had worked for a year in a florists. At the time of the interview she was studying for O-levels at FE college part-time, while registered unemployed.

Rachel Furness, 19 years.
Living at home with her divorced mother and an older sister who was employed. Her mother was not employed. Rachel had worked for 18 months on three hairdressing YTS schemes. She had been unemployed for 18 months at the time of the interview.

Richard Haig, 23 years.
Living at home with his mother, *Glenys Haig* and his younger sister who was employed. His three older siblings had left home, one sister was at university; another sister, *Lucy Haig*, and a brother were both married and employed. Parents divorced. Father, a welder, employed, mother not employed. Richard had worked for 2 years on YTS and CP schemes. He had worked part-time in a hotel on and off for 3 years. He had also worked for 6 months on a kibbutz. At the time of the interview he had been unemployed for 12 months and was just starting a CP scheme.

James Jackson, 20 years.
Living with his long-term foster parents on a lodging allowance. His older brother had left home, married and was now unemployed. Foster father a retired school caretaker; foster mother a pensioner. James had gone into the army but had left after 6 months. He had since worked on various YTS and CP schemes. He had been unemployed for 6 months at the time of interview.

Gary Jenkins, 20 years.
Living at home with his parents, *Carol* and *Frank Jenkins*, and two school-age sisters. Father, a self-employed salesman; mother not employed. Gary had worked for a year in a computer firm which went bankrupt. At the time of the interview he had been attending FE college part-time for 6 months and was taking an exam for the RAF. He had been registered unemployed for 12 months.

Francis Lewis, 25 years.
Living at home with her mother, *Mary Lewis*, and stepfather, *Jim Sullivan*. Francis had married 6 months earlier and she and her husband, who was employed, were hoping to buy a house. Francis was the youngest of 7 children. All of her siblings had left home and had married. Her four brothers were employed. Stepfather a retired painter and decorator; mother a pensioner. Francis had worked for the same retail firm for nearly 9 years, since leaving school. She had left the job when she married and had been unemployed for 6 months at the time of the interview.

Katherine Mansell, 19 years: see *Philip Broughton* (above).

Rhiannon Miles, 20 years.
Living at home with her parents and 7 months pregnant. She was the youngest of six children. One brother was single and living in a flat. The other siblings were married. Her two brothers were employed. Father a retired carpenter and merchant seaman; mother not employed. Rhiannon had worked for 6 months on a YTS scheme. She had been unemployed for 3 years at the time of the interview.

Trisha Phillips, 17 years.
Living at home with her mother. Her father was dead. Trisha was the youngest of four children. All her siblings were married. Her only brother was unemployed. Mother not working. Trisha had been unemployed for 10 months at the time of the interview.

Dean Powell, 18 years.
Living at home with his parents, *Cliff* and *Louise Powell*, his sister *Jeanette Powell* (working on a YTS scheme) and a school-age sister. Father employed as a chef on British Rail, mother employed part-time as a school cleaner. Dean had worked for 12 months on YTS schemes and had been unemployed for 12 months at the time of the interview.

Simon Preece, 18 years.
Living at home with his mother, *Doreen Preece*, stepfather, two siblings and two step-siblings, all at school. His father, *David Preece*, employed as a bricklayer, lived 10 miles away; stepfather employed, mother employed as a domestic at university part-time. Simon worked for 12 months on a YTS scheme. He had been unemployed for 6 months at the time of the interview.

Melanie Reilly, 18 years.
Living at home with her parents but expecting to move into a council flat. Her two elder sisters were married. Father retired, mother retired. Melanie had worked for 3 months on a YTS scheme and had had a part-time job for 2 months. She had been unemployed for 5 months at the time of the interview.

Malcolm Rees, 20 years.
Living at home with his mother, *Gwyneth Lynch*, and stepfather, *Michael Lynch*. He had lived away from home for short periods. His elder brother, *Jim Rees* was married and employed. His elder sister was divorced and unemployed. Father unemployed. Stepfather employed as a forklift operator; mother employed as a care assistant. Malcolm had had three short jobs for a year after leaving school. He had been unemployed for 12 months at the time of the interview.

Hugh Reynolds, 20 years.
Living at home with his mother, *Diana Reynolds*, father and a school-age sister. Father employed as a clerk; mother a nurse and employed. Hugh worked for 6 months on a YTS scheme. He then worked for $2\frac{1}{2}$ years in three jobs. He had been unemployed for 6 months at the time of the interview.

Helen Roderick, 22 years.
Living at home with her parents, *Rosemary* and *Robert Roderick*, and an older sister, *Dawn Roderick*, who was employed. A third sister was married and living away. Father a carpenter and employed; mother employed part-time as a dinner lady. Helen had worked for 6 months on a YTS scheme. She had had two short-term temporary jobs. She had been unemployed for 2 years at the time of the interview.

Peter Squires, 19 years.
Living at home with his father, *Gareth Squires*, who had very recently remarried. His mother was dead. His four older sisters had left home and three were married. Father employed as a stores controller; stepmother working in a florists. Since leaving school Peter had had a series of short jobs interspersed with periods of unemployment. He had been unemployed for 4 months at the time of this interview.

Alan Sweetman, 17 years.
Living at home with his mother, *Joyce Sweetman*, and father and two school-age sisters. Father, a pipe-fitter's mate, had retired on an invalidity pension 10 years ago; mother not working. Alan had worked for 12 months on a YTS scheme. He had been unemployed for 8 months at the time of the interview.

Simon Terrance, 18 years.
Living at home with his parents, *Margaret* and *Roger Terrance*, and an elder brother who was employed. Father, a self-employed builder, working; mother employed as a shop assistant. Simon had worked for 12 months on a YTS scheme. After 6 months unemployment he had had one temporary job. He had been unemployed for 6 months at the time of the interview.

Caroline Young, 17 years.
Living at home with her parents, *Mrs Young* and *George Young*, elder sister, *Mandy Young*, employed, and school-age brother. Two elder sisters had married and left home. Father, a building labourer, unemployed; mother not employed. Caroline had worked on a YTS scheme for 6 months and then had had a job for 6 months. She had been unemployed for 7 months at the time of the interview but had applied to join the Army.

Ty-Gwyn

Steve Anderson, 22 years.
An only child, living at home with his parents, *Hilda* and *Alun Anderson*.
Father used to work in the oil industry, made redundant 4 years ago, now
working as a court usher, mother a civil servant. Steve had a law degree and
had been living at home and unemployed for 7 months at the time of
the interview.

Chris Bishop, 18 years.
Living at home with his mother, *Hilary Bishop*, an older sister on a YTS
scheme and a school-age sister. His parents were divorced. Mother not
working. Chris had worked for 4 months on a YTS scheme. He had been
unemployed for 18 months at the time of the interview.

Arthur Evans, 18 years.
Living at home with his parents, *Clive* and *Megan Evans*, and a school-age
brother. Father the principal of a Further Education College, mother a
primary school teacher. At the time of the interview Arthur was attending
FE college part-time to complete his A-levels. He had been registered as
unemployed for 4 months.

Sean Evans, 21 years.
Living at home with his mother, *Ruth Evans*; father; younger brother
(unemployed); and school-age sister. Father a skilled factory worker;
mother local authority home help. Kevin had worked for 2 years on three
YTS schemes. He had had two temporary jobs. At the time of the interview
he had just started on a CP scheme after being unemployed for 12 months.

Diana Fullerton, 17 years.
Living in a bedsitter, having left home, where her mother, *Sarah Fullerton*,
and a school-age brother lived, 4 months earlier. Her father was working
abroad. Father an oil engineer, mother a civil servant. Diana had left FE
college 16 months ago where she was studying for O-levels; she had been
unemployed since.

Matthew and *Peter Griffiths*, 21 and 19 years.
Living at home with their parents, *Georgina* and *Paul Griffiths*, and a
school-age brother. Father a small businessman, mother a teacher. Matthew
had had seven jobs interspersed with short periods of unemployment. He
had been unemployed for 8 months at the time of the interview. Peter had
left school at 18 with three A-levels. He had worked for 1 month and did
part-time voluntary work for the church which he attended. He had been
unemployed for 3 months at the time of the interview.

Kelly Hildreth, 21 years.
Living at home with her mother, *Jean Hildreth*, and father. An elder sister was married. A younger sister had left home and was working part-time. Father a retired builder now working for an estate agent; mother a part-time shop assistant. Kelly had left school at 18 with clerical qualifications. She had worked as a library assistant for 2 years. She set up and ran a small business with her boyfriend *Jason Keith* for about 12 months. She had been registered unemployed for 10 months at the time of the interview.

Andrew Jones, 18 years.
Living at home with his parents, *Frank* and *Peggy Jones*, and a school-age brother. Father employed as a fitter; mother not working. Andrew had left school at 18 with four A-levels. Having been turned down as a pilot in the RAF he had applied to the police. He had been unemployed for 8 months at the time of the interview.

John Locke, 18 years.
Living at home with his parents, an elder sister (a student nurse) and a school-age brother. Father a self-employed plasterer, working; mother a part-time auxiliary nurse, working. John had worked for 12 months on a YTS scheme. He had been unemployed for 10 months at the time of the interview.

Anthony Lonsdale, 20 years.
Living at home with his mother, *Christine Lonsdale*, and an older sister, working. Father an engineer working in Saudi Arabia, after having been made redundant 4 years earlier; mother now employed. Anthony had spent 4 months in the Army. He had worked for 12 months on two YTS schemes. He had worked for a roofing contractor for 12 months. He had had two spells of unemployment and worked for 12 months on a CP scheme. He had been unemployed for 9 months at the time of the interview.

Charles and *Kenneth Mason*, 20 years and 18 years.
Living at home with their mother, *Mrs Mason*. Their father had died 2 years earlier. Father had been an electrician; mother a nurse, working full-time. Charles had completed a 3 year electrician's apprenticeship in the Fire Service. He had had one job in a garage for 2 months and had been unemployed for 6 months at the time of the interview. Kenneth had worked for 2 months on a YTS scheme and had been unemployed for 10 months at the time of the interview.

Timothy Owens, 18 years.
Living with his parents, *Ceridwen* and *Wynford Owens*, and two school-age brothers. Father a sales representative, working; mother working part-time

as a care assistant in an old people's home. Timothy had worked for 12 months on a YTS scheme and had been unemployed for 10 months at the time of the interview.

Richard Pugh, 20 years.
Living at home with his father and an elder brother, employed. The eldest brother had left home and was employed. Parents divorced. Father a signwriter, working; mother not working. Richard had worked for 5 months on a YTS scheme. He had left home and worked for a tunnelling contractor near Liverpool for 9 months. After 12 months unemployment he had spent 12 months on a CP scheme. He had been unemployed for one month at the time of the interview.

Gwyn Roberts, 20 years.
Living at home with his parents, *Anthea* and *Ivor Roberts*. An older stepbrother had left home and was employed. Only Mr and Mrs Roberts and Gwyn's girlfriend, *Wilma Mortimer*, were interviewed. Gwyn was always out when we called, surfing. Father an insurance agent, working; mother a secretary, working full-time. Gwyn spent 12 months at FE college. At the time of the interview he was working on a CP scheme after having been unemployed for 3 years.

Samantha Smith, 24 years.
Living at home with her mother, *Mrs Horner*, stepfather and two stepbrothers, one of school age, one a baby. Two older brothers were living away, married and working, one younger step sister was living away and married. Stepfather, a marine engineer, unemployed for three years; mother not working. Samantha had left school at 17. She had worked for 9 months on a YTS-type scheme. She had trained as a nurse in Essex for 15 months. After 12 months unemployment she worked for 12 months in a children's home and a home for mentally handicapped people. She had had a temporary job for 4 months in an old people's home. She had been unemployed for 18 months at the time of the interview.

Frances Stevens, 19 years.
Living at home with her father and stepmother. Father, stepmother and mother all working full-time. Frances left school at 18 and had been unemployed for 12 months at the time of the interview.

Shiree Vivian, 20 years.
Living at home with her parents. An older brother, a graduate, had left home and was working. Father a postman, working; mother a salesperson, working full-time. Shiree had spent 12 months at FE college. She had worked for 18 months on two YTS type schemes. She had been on an adult

education course following 6 months unemployment. At the time of the interview she had just taken a part-time cashier's job after 9 months unemployment.

Jason Wilding, 20 years.
Living at home with his father, stepmother, *Sheila Wilding*, an elder stepsister, working, and a younger school-age stepsister. A stepbrother of the same age had left home and was unemployed. An older stepsister had left home, married and was working. Father, an insurance underwriter, working; stepmother working part-time in a florists. Jason had left FE college at 18 with 4 A-levels. He had worked for 12 months on a YTS-type scheme. He had worked for 2 months as a salesperson. At the time of the interview he had just started working on a CP scheme after being unemployed for 2 years.

NOTES

1. Introduction

1. *Employment Gazette*, vol. 95, No. 9 (September 1987), p. 529.
2. *Unemployment Unit Statistical Supplement*, June/July 1987, p. 4.
3. *Employment Gazette*, *op.cit.*, p. 539.
4. *Ibid.*, p. 527.
5. The other two strands of the 'new blood' research activity were a comparative study of changes in recruitment practices as a consequence of the recession in the East Midlands and South Wales, undertaken in collaboration with the Work and Employment Research Group, Loughborough University and, in collaboration with Phil Harding, a critical study of the literature relating to the 'hidden economy'.
6. These figures derive from the quarterly *Labour Market Report, Wales* (Cardiff, Manpower Services Commission Office for Wales).

2. Family Relationships

1. This is, we realise, a definition of the nuclear family which some readers will find unsatisfactory. Goode, for example, defines the nuclear family as 'a unit comprised of husband, wife and their children' (Goode 1964: 45). Harris, in his discussion of the nuclear family, appears to recognise that the presence of both parents is not strictly necessary for such a group to exist (Harris 1983: 34). In the same passage, however, he implies that the presence of the mother is. While biological constraints presuppose the existence of *a* mother at some stage, we would not wish to exclude, for example, families where the (biological) mother is absent – whether a stepmother or other female carer is present or not – from the category of 'nuclear family'. Nor would we wish to make what may be unwarranted presumptions about the 'primordial' nature of the mother–child relationship, as, for example, in the work of Fox, who argues that this is 'the most fundamental and basic of all social bonds' (Fox 1967: 27). For these reasons, we prefer to work with a definition of the nuclear family which does not presuppose the presence of two parents and which treats either parent – and parenthood here is defined *socially* rather than *biologically* – as in principle equally and sufficiently competent for the purposes of parenthood in a modern industrial society.

3. Getting By

1. Comprehensive and detailed accounts of the absolute deprivations of poverty and unemployment can be found in the work of Peter Townsend (1979). Evidence about the impact of unemployment and poverty on health can be found in the Black Report (Townsend and Davidson 1982) and the Health Education Council's update of its findings (Whitehead 1987).
2. It may, of course, be the case – and here our old friend Oedipus rears his head again – that maternal affection for children, especially sons, may undermine relationships between the father and mother.

4. Courtship and Marriage

1. In this respect, the present study should be seen as the latest in a line of substantial sociological research reports documenting social life and change in Swansea and its surrounding area: Brennan, Cooney and Pollins's survey of social change in south-west Wales in the 1940s and early 1950s (Brennan, Cooney and Pollins 1954), Rosser and Harris's work on social change and the family (Rosser and Harris 1965), Bell's study of middle-class families and mobility (Bell 1968), the Blaendulais Centre's survey of the role of Christianity in south-west Wales (Jones 1969), Leonard's work on courtship and marriage in the late 1960s (Leonard 1980), Sewel's study of pit closure in the early 1970s (Sewel 1975), the work of the Redundancy and Unemployment Research Group on the 1979 redundancies at the BSC works at Port Talbot (Harris *et al.* 1987) and, most recently, Brown's research into education and youth unemployment (Brown 1987).
2. The gradual disintegration of female peer groups as a consequence of courtship has been remarked upon in a number of studies (e.g. Griffin 1985: 60–2; Lees 1986: 76–8; Leonard 1980: 79–81). Other research, however, has suggested that this does not necessarily occur: Beuret and Makings (1987: 68–9) and Coffield *et al.* (1986: 171–3).
3. For contrasting views on women and public drinking, see the work of Hey (1986), on the one hand, and Hunt and Slatterlee (1987), on the other.
4. The commercial and cultural reconstruction of leisure venues – in particular, the changing face of the public house (witness the rise of 'fun pubs', 'real ale pubs', 'disco pubs' and 'theme pubs', not to mention the ubiquity of the wine bar) – is a subject worthy of more serious sociological attention than it has hitherto attracted.
5. This, of course, begs the question of what the conventional balance between work and leisure might be, and how many people experience it; it is more likely to be the case that there are a *number* of more or less conventional patterns available.
6. We suspect that regional/cultural factors are important in determining the nature of female peer groups, hence perhaps the contrasting pictures presented by different researchers whose material is drawn from different places (see also note 2, Ch. 4, above).

5. Into Adulthood

1. This should not be read as suggesting that biology – the physiological changes attendant upon the onset of reproductive maturity and bodily ageing – is irrelevant. Far from it. From our point of view, however, it is what cultures *do* with these 'givens' which is of interest.

2. For a further discussion, in which the situations of the young long-term unemployed and young people with a mental handicap are contrasted in order to delineate the contours of adulthood in contemporary Britain, see Jenkins (1989).
3. See Aschenbrenner 1975; Anderson 1976; Hannerz 1969; Liebow 1967; Rainwater 1971; Stack 1974.
4. Drawing upon a distinction originally proposed by Jenkins (1983: 81) between *planned* and *precipitate* paths into marriage and/or parenthood, the latter involving unplanned pregnancy, it is possible to differentiate between conscious (planned) *responses* to the problems posed by unemployment, and the (precipitate) *consequences* of a situation in which alternatives are few and only 'choosable' in terms of differing degrees of undesirability, if indeed they are chosen at all (Wallace 1987: 163-9; Youth Review Team 1985: 110-14).
5. Put in this way, the possibility is raised of conceptualising youth as a social class, in Weberian terms.
6. On the distinction between analytical and folk models – and the relationship between them, in terms of epistemology – see Jenkins (1982: 13-14; 1987: 154-5). In this sense, folk or popular models include those generated by the state or within formal organisations.
7. The issue of gender and the differential transition to adulthood is complicated, combining as it does questions of psychological, physiological and social maturation. Women certainly mature physically earlier on the whole (Oakley 1972, 1987). Commonplace observation suggests that they might also mature earlier in the psychological sense.
8. Adulthood is not inevitable for all, however (see Jenkins 1989).

6.   Explaining Unemployment

1. Much the same could, of course, also be said about the notions of adulthood, as discussed in Chapter 5, and conflict, discussed in Chapter 2.
2. For further discussion of the meanings of individualism, see Abercrombie, Hill and Turner (1986: 1-85), Hayek (1949: 1-32), MacPherson (1962) and Pocock (1972), although there are, of course, many other authors who could – and should – be recommended also.
3. This should not, however, be taken to mean that the relationship between educational achievement and labour-market outcomes is particularly straightforward (Jenkins 1988).
4. The distinction between YTS and the Community Programme (CP), at the time when the research was undertaken, was essentially between on- or off-the-job training schemes of up to a year's duration for 16 to 17-year-olds (YTS), and part-time job-creation projects for long-term unemployed adults (CP).

BIBLIOGRAPHY

Abercrombie, N., Hill, S. and Turner, B. S. (1986). *Sovereign Individuals of Capitalism*. London, Allen & Unwin.

Allatt, P. and Yeandle, S. (1986). 'It's not fair, is it?: youth unemployment, family relations and the social contract', in S. Allen *et al.* (eds.), *The Experience of Unemployment*. London, Macmillan.

Allen, S., Waton, A., Purcell, K. and Wood, S. (eds.) (1986). *The Experience of Unemployment*. London, Macmillan.

Althusser, L. (1971). *Lenin and Philosophy and Other Essays*. London, New Left Books.

Anderson, E. (1976). *A Place on the Corner*. Chicago, University of Chicago Press.

Ariès, P. (1973). *Centuries of Childhood*. Harmondsworth, Penguin.

Aschenbrenner, J. (1975). *Lifelines: Black Families in Chicago*. New York, Holt, Rhinehart and Winston.

Ashton, D. N., Maguire, M. J. and Garland, V. (1982). 'Youth in the labour-market', *Research Paper No. 34*. London, Department of Employment.

Ashton, D. N., Maguire, M. J. with Bowden, D. *et al.* (1986). 'Young adults in the labour market', *Research Paper No. 55*. London, Department of Employment.

Banks, M. H. and Jackson, P. R. (1982). 'Unemployment and risk of minor psychiatric disorder in young people: cross-sectional and longitudinal evidence', *Psychological Medicine*. 12: 789–98.

Barrett, M. and McIntosh, M. (1982). *The Anti-social Family*. London, Verso.

Bates, I., Clarke, J., Cohen, P., Finn, D., Moore, R. and Willis, P. (1984). *Schooling for the Dole? The New Vocationalism*. London, Macmillan.

Bell, C. (1968). *Middle Class Families*. London, Routledge & Kegan Paul.

Berger, P. and Luckman, T. (1967). *The Social Construction of Reality*. London, Allen Lane.

Beuret, K. and Makings, L. (1987). ' "I've got used to being independent now": women and courtship in a recession', in P. Allatt *et al.* (eds.), *Women and the Life Cycle*. London, Macmillan.

Beynon, H. (1984): *Working for Ford*, 2nd edn, Harmondsworth, Pelican.

Blackburn, R. M. and Mann, M. (1979). *The Working Class in the Labour Market*. London, Macmillan.

Blau, P. (1964). *Exchange and Power in Social Life*. New York, Wiley.

Bostyn, A-M. and Wight, D. (1987). 'Inside a community: values associated with money and time', in S. Fineman (ed.), *Unemployment: Personal and Social Consequences*. London, Tavistock.

Bourdieu, P. (1977). *Outline of a Theory of Practice*. Cambridge, Cambridge University Press.

(1984). *Distinction: A Social Critique of the Judgement of Taste*. London, Routledge & Kegan Paul.

Bourdieu, P. and Passeron, J-C. (1977). *Reproduction in Education, Society and Culture*. London, Sage.

Bowlby, J. (1953). *Child Care and the Growth of Love*. Harmondsworth, Penguin.

Brah, A. (1986). 'Unemployment and Racism: Asian Youth on the Dole', in S. Allen *et al.* (eds.), *The Experience of Unemployment*. London, Macmillan.

Brake, M. (1980). *The Sociology of Youth Culture and Youth Subcultures*. London, Routledge & Kegan Paul.

Branthwaite, A. and Garcia, S. (1985). 'Depression in the young unemployed and those on Youth Opportunities Schemes', *British Journal of Medical Psychology* 58: 67–74.

Breakwell, G. M. (1985). 'Young people in and out of work', in B. Roberts, R. Finnegan and D. Gallie (eds.), *New Approaches to Economic Life*. Manchester, Manchester University Press.

Brennan, T. and Cooney, E. W. (1950). *The Social Pattern: A Handbook of Social Statistics in South West Wales*. Swansea, Department of Research in Social Studies, University College of Swansea.

Brennan, T., Cooney, E. W. and Pollins, H. (1954). *Social Change in South-West Wales*. London, Watts.

Brown, P. (1987). *Schooling Ordinary Kids: Inequality, Unemployment and the New Vocationalism*. London, Tavistock.

Bulmer, M. (ed.) (1975). *Working-class Images of Society*. London, Routledge & Kegan Paul.

Byrne, D. and Pond, C. (1987–8). 'Out of school and out of pocket – removing the dole from 16 and 17 year olds', *Low Pay Review* 32: 3–11.

Campbell, B. (1984). *The Road to Wigan Pier Revisited*, London, Virago.

Carruthers, P. (1986). *Introducing Persons*. London, Croom Helm.

Cashmore, E. and Troyna, B. (eds.) (1982). *Black Youth in Crisis*. London, Allen & Unwin.

Champion, A. G., Green, A. E., Owen, D. W., Ellin, D. J. and Coombes, M. G. (1987). *Changing Places: Britain's Demographic, Economic and Social Complexion*. London, Edward Arnold.

Cicourel, A. V. (1964). *Method and Measurement in Sociology*. New York, Free Press.

(1973), *Cognitive Sociology*, Harmondsworth, Penguin.

Clark, D. Y. (1987). 'Families facing redundancy', in S. Fineman (ed.), *Unemployment*. London, Tavistock.

Cockburn, C. (1987). *Two Track Training: Sex Inequalities and the YTS*. London, Macmillan.

Coffield, F. (1987). 'From the celebration to the marginalisation of youth' in G. Cohen (ed.), *Social Change and the Life Course*. London, Tavistock.

Coffield, F., Borrill, C. and Marshall, S. (1986). *Growing Up at the Margins*. Milton Keynes, Open University Press.

Cohen, G. (1987). 'Introduction: the economy, the family and life-course', in G. Cohen (ed.), *Social Change and the Life Course*, London, Tavistock.

Collins, R. (1975). *Conflict Sociology*. New York, Academic Press.

Connell R. W. (1983). *Which Way Is Up? Essays on Sex, Class and Culture*. Sydney, Allen & Unwin.

(1987). *Gender and Power: Society, the Person and Sexual Politics*. Cambridge, Polity Press.

Coxon, A. P. M. and Jones, C. L. (1978). *The Images of Occupational Prestige*. London, Macmillan.

(1979). *Class and Hierarchy*. London. Macmillan.

Coxon, A. P. M., Davies, P. M. and Jones, C. L. (1986). *Images of Social Stratification*. London, Sage.

Cross, M. and Smith, D. I. (eds.) (1987). *Black Youth and YTS: Opportunity or Inequality?* Leicester, National Youth Bureau.

Davis, H. H. (1979). *Beyond Class Images*. London, Croom Helm.

Deem, R, (1986). *All Work and No Play?* Milton Keynes, Open University Press.

Dex, S. (1982). 'Black and white school-leavers: the first five years of work', *Research Paper No.33*. London, Department of Employment.

(1985). *The Sexual Division of Work*. Brighton, Wheatsheaf.

Donzelot, J. (1980). *The Policing of Families*. London, Hutchinson.

Douglas, M. and Isherwood, B. (1979). *The World of Goods*. London, Allen Lane.

Dunnell, K. (1979). *Family Formation, 1976*. London, HMSO.

Eggleston, J. (ed.) (1982). *Work Experience in Secondary Schools*. London, Routledge & Kegan Paul.

Eisenstadt, S. N. (1956). *From Generation to Generation: Age Groups and Social Structure*. New York, Free Press.

Ekeh, P. (1974). *Social Exchange Theory*. London, Heinemann.

Erikson, E. H. (1968). *Identity: Youth and Crisis*. London, Faber.

Fagin, L. and Little, M. (1984). *The Forsaken Families*. Harmondsworth, Pelican.

Fiddy, R. (ed.) (1983). *In Place of Work: Policy and Provision for the Young Unemployed*. Brighton, Falmer.

Finch, J. and Groves, D. (eds.) (1983). *A Labour of Love: Women, Work and Caring*. London, Routledge & Kegan Paul.

Fineman, S, (ed.) (1987). *Unemployment: Personal and Social Consequences*. London, Tavistock.

Finn, D. (1987). *Training without Jobs: New Deals and Broken Promises*. London, Macmillan.

Fletcher, R. (1973). *The Family and Marriage in Britain*. Harmondsworth, Pelican.

Fothergill, S. and Gudgin, G. (1982). *Unequal Growth*. London, Heinemann.

Fox, R. (1967). *Kinship and Marriage*. Harmondsworth, Pelican.

Frith, S. (1984). *The Sociology of Youth*. Ormskirk, Causeway.

Fryer, D. and Ullah, P. (eds.) (1987). *Unemployed People: Social and Psychological Perspectives*. Milton Keynes, Open University Press.

Gavron, H. (1966). *The Captive Wife: Conflicts of Housebound Mothers*. London, Routledge & Kegan Paul.

Giddens, A. (1976). *New Rules of Sociological Method*. London, Hutchinson.

(1979). *Central Problems in Social Theory*. London, Macmillan.

(1984). *The Constitution of Society*. Cambridge, Polity Press.

Gleeson, D. (ed.) (1983). *Youth Training and the Search for Work*. London, Routledge & Kegan Paul.

Goode, W. J. (1963). *World Revolution and Family Patterns*. New York, Collier-Macmillan.

(1964). *The Family*. Englewood Cliffs, Prentice-Hall.

Griffin, C. (1985). *Typical Girls? Young Women from School to the Job Market*. London, Routledge & Kegan Paul.

Hakim, C. (1979). 'Occupational segregation', *Research Paper No. 9*. London, Department of Employment.

Hannerz, U. (1969). *Soulside*. New York, Columbia University Press.

Harris, C. C. (1983). *The Family and Industrial Society*. London, Allen & Unwin.

(1987). 'The individual and society: a processual approach', in A. Bryman *et al.* (eds.) *Rethinking the Life Cycle*. London, Macmillan.

Harris, C. C. and the Redundancy and Unemployment Research Group (1987). *Redundancy and Recession in South Wales*. Oxford, Basil Blackwell.

Harrison, A. (1984). 'Economic policy and expectations', in R. Jowell and C. Airey (eds.), *British Social Attitudes: The 1984 Report*. Aldershot, Gower.

Hartley. J. (1987). 'Managerial unemployment: the wife's perspective and role', in S. Fineman (ed.) *Unemployment*. London, Tavistock.

Hartley, J. and Fryer, D. (1984) 'The psychology of unemployment: a critical appraisal', in G. Stephenson and J. Davis (eds.), *Progress in Applied Social Psychology,* Vol. 2. Chichester, Wiley.

Hayek, F. (1949). *Individualism and Economic Order*. London, Routledge & Kegan Paul.

Heath, A. (1986) 'Do people have consistent attitudes?' in R. Jowell, S. Witherspoon and L. Brook (eds.), *British Social Attitudes: The 1986 Report*. Aldershot, Gower.

Hebdige, D. (1979). *Subculture: The Meaning of Style*. London, Methuen.

Henwood, F. and Miles, I. (1987). 'The experience of unemployment and the sexual division of labour', in D. Fryer and P. Ullah (eds.), *Unemployed People*. Milton Keynes, Open University Press.

Henwood, M., Rimmer, L. and Wicks, M. (1987). *Inside the Family: Changing Roles of Men and Women*. London, Family Policies Study Centre.

Hey, V. (1986). *Patriarchy and Pub Culture*. London, Tavistock.

Hogan, D. P. and Astone, N. M. (1986). 'The transition into adulthood', *Annual Review of Sociology* 12: 109–30.

Holy, L. and Stuchlik, M. (1983). *Actions, Norms and Representations*. Cambridge, Cambridge University Press.

Hudson, B. (1984), 'Femininity and adolescence', in A. McRobbie and M. Nava, (eds.), *Gender and Generation*. London, Macmillan.

Hunt, G. and Slatterlee, S. (1987). 'Darts, drinking and the pub: the culture of female drinking', *Sociological Review* 35: 575–601.

Jackson, J. A. (ed.) (1972). *Roles*. Cambridge, Cambridge University Press.

Jackson, P. R., Stafford, E. M., Banks, M. H. and Warr, P. B. (1983). 'Unemployment and psychological distress in young people: the moderating role of employment commitment', *Journal of Applied Psychology* 68: 525–35.

Jackson, P. R. and Walsh, S. (1987). 'Unemployment and the family', in D. Fryer and P. Ullah (eds.), *Unemployed People*. Milton Keynes, Open University Press.

Jahoda, M. (1982). *Employment and Unemployment: A Social-Psychological Analysis*. Cambridge, Cambridge University Press.

Jahoda, M., Lazarsfeld, P. F. and Zeisel, H. (1972). *Marienthal: The Sociography of an Unemployed Community*. London, Tavistock.

James, A. (1986). 'Learning to belong: the boundaries of adolescence', in A. P. Cohen (ed.), *Symbolising Boundaries: Identity and Diversity in British Cultures*. Manchester, Manchester University Press.

Jenkins, R. (1982). *Hightown Rules: Growing Up in a Belfast Housing Estate*. Leicester, National Youth Bureau.

(1983). *Lads, Citizens and Ordinary Kids: Working-class Youth Life-styles in Belfast*. London, Routledge & Kegan Paul.

(1986). *Racism and Recruitment: Managers, Organisations and Equal Opportunity in the Labour Market*. Cambridge, Cambridge University Press.

(1987). 'Doing research into discrimination', in G. C. Wenger (ed.), *The Research Relationship*. London, Allen & Unwin.

(1988). 'Intervening against "racial" disadvantage: educational policy and labour-market outcomes in the United Kingdom', *Comparative Education Review* 32: 1-19.

(1989). 'Dimensions of adulthood in Britain: long-term unemployment and mental handicap', in P. Spencer (ed.), *Anthropology and the Riddle of the Sphinx: Youth, Maturation and Ageing*. London, Routledge.

Jenkins, R. and Hutson, S. (1986). 'Young people, unemployment and the family', *School of Social Studies Occasional Paper No.14*. Swansea, University College of Swansea.

Jones, G. (1987). 'Leaving the parental home: an analysis of early housing careers', *Journal of Social Policy* 16: 49-74.

Jones, V. (ed.), (1969). *The Church in a Mobile Society*. Swansea, Christopher Davies.

Keesing, R. M. (1975). *Kin Groups and Social Structure*. New York, Holt, Rhinehart & Winston.

Kelvin, P. and Jarrett, J. E. (1985). *Unemployment: Its Social Psychological Effects*. Cambridge, Cambridge University Press.

Laing, R. D. (1971). *Politics and the Family*. London, Tavistock.

Laing, R. D. and Esterson, A. (1970). *Sanity, Madness and the Family*. Harmondsworth, Penguin.

Laite, J. and Halfpenny, P. (1987). 'Employment, unemployment and the domestic division of labour', in D. Fryer and P. Ullah (eds.), *Unemployed People*. Milton Keynes, Open University Press.

Leach, E. (1968). *A Runaway World?* London, Oxford University Press.

Lees, S. (1986). *Losing Out: Sexuality and Adolescent Girls*. London, Hutchinson.

Lein, L. (1984). 'Male participation in home life: impact of social supports and breadwinner responsibility on the allocation of tasks', in P. Voydanoff (ed.), *Work and Family: Changing Roles of Men and Women*. Palo Alto, Mayfield.

Leonard, D. (1980). *Sex and Generation: A Study of Courtship and Weddings*. London, Tavistock.

Liebow, E. (1967). *Tally's Corner*. Boston, Little, Brown.

Linton, R. (1936). *The Study of Man*. New York, Appleton-Century.

Livock, R. (1983). 'Screening in the recruitment of young workers', *Research Paper No. 41*. London, Department of Employment.

Lukes, S. (1973). *Individualism*. Oxford, Basil Blackwell.

MacLeod, J. (1987). *Ain't No Makin' It: Leveled Aspirations in a Low Income Neighbourhood*. London, Tavistock.

Macfarlane, A. (1985). *Marriage and Love in England: Modes of Reproduction 1300-1840*. Oxford, Basil Blackwell.

MacPherson, C. B. (1962). *The Political Theory of Possessive Individualism*. Oxford, Oxford University Press.

Marsden, D. and Duff, E. (1975). *Workless*. Harmondsworth, Pelican.

Marsh, D. C. (1965). *The Changing Social Structure of England and Wales, 1871-1961*. London, Routledge & Kegan Paul.

Marshall, G., Rose, D., Newby, H. and Vogel, C. (1988). 'Political quiescence among the unemployed in modern Britain', in D. Rose (ed.), *Social Stratification and Economic Change*. London, Hutchinson.

Martin, J. and Roberts, C. (1984). *Women and Employment: A Lifetime Perspective*. London, HMSO.

Mauss, M. (1954). *The Gift*. London, Routledge & Kegan Paul.

McKee, L. and Bell, C. (1985). 'Marital and family relations in times of male unemployment', in B. Roberts *et al.* (eds.), *New Approaches to Economic Life*. Manchester, Manchester University Press.

(1986). 'His unemployment, her problem: the domestic and marital consequences of male unemployment', in S. Allen *et al.* (eds.), *The Experience of Unemployment*. London, Macmillan.

McRae, S. (1987a). 'Social and political perspectives found among young unemployed men and women', in M. White (ed.), *The Social World of the Young Unemployed*. London, Policy Studies Institute.

(1987b). *Young and Jobless: The Social and Personal Consequences of Long-term Youth Unemployment*. London, Policy Studies Institute.

McRobbie, A. (1978). 'Working class girls and the culture of femininity', in Women's Study Group, *Women Take Issue*. London, Hutchinson.

McRobbie, A. and Nava, M. (eds.) (1984). *Gender and Generation*. London, Macmillan.

Mead, M. (1942). *Growing Up in New Guinea*. Harmondsworth, Pelican.

(1943). *Coming of Age in Samoa*. Harmondsworth, Pelican.

Meyer, P. (1983). *The Child and the State*. Cambridge, Cambridge University Press.

Morgan, D. H. J. (1975). *Social Theory and the Family*. London, Routledge & Kegan Paul.

Morris, L. D. (1985a). 'Renegotiation of the domestic division of labour in the context of male redundancy', in B. Roberts *et al.* (ed.), *New Approaches to Economic Life*. Manchester, Manchester University Press.

(1985b). 'Local social networks and domestic organisation: a study of redundant steel workers and their wives', *Sociological Review* 33: 327–42.

Musgrove, F. (1964). *Youth and the Social Order*. London, Routledge & Kegan Paul.

Myrdal, A. and Klein, V. (1968). *Women's Two Roles: Home and Work,* 2nd edn. London, Routledge & Kegan Paul.

Nadel, S. F. (1957). *The Theory of Social Structure*. London, Cohen & West.

Nichols, T. and Beynon, H. (1977). *Living with Capitalism*. London, Routledge & Kegan Paul.

Oakley, A. (1972). *Sex, Gender and Society*. London, Temple Smith.

(1974a). *Housewife*. London, Allen Lane.

(1974b). *The Sociology of Housework*. Oxford, Martin Robertson.

(1987). 'Gender and generation: the life and times of Adam and Eve', in P. Allatt *et al.* (eds.), *Women and the Life Cycle*. London, Macmillan.

Owen, D. W., Gillespie, A. E. and Coombes, M. G. (1984). ' "Job shortfalls" in British local labour market areas: a classification of labour supply and demand trends, 1971–1981', *Regional Studies* 18: 469–88.

Pahl, J. (1980). 'Patterns of money management within marriage', *Journal of Social Policy* 9: 313–35.

(1983). 'The allocation of money and the structuring of inequality within marriage', *Sociological Review* 31: 237–62.

Pahl, R. E. (1984). *Divisions of Labour*. Oxford, Basil Blackwell.

Parsons, T. (1954). *Essays in Sociological Theory*. New York, Free Press.

Parsons, T. and Bales, R. F. (1955). *Family, Socialisation and Interaction Process*. New York, Free Press.

Pleck, J. H. (1984). 'Men's family work: three perspectives and some data', in P. Voydanoff (ed.), *Work and Family*. Palo Alto, Mayfield.

Pocock, J. G. A. (1972). *Politics, Language and Time*. London, Methuen.

Popay, J. (1985). 'Women, the family and unemployment', in P. Close and R. Collins (eds.), *Family and Economy in Modern Society*. London, Macmillan.

Rainwater, L. (1971). *Behind Ghetto Walls*. London, Allen Lane.

Rees, T. L. and Atkinson, P. (eds.) (1982). *Youth Unemployment and State Intervention*. London, Routledge & Kegan Paul.

Roberts, K. (1984). *School Leavers and Their Prospects.* Milton Keynes, Open University Press.

Roberts, K., Duggan, J. and Noble, M. (1981). 'Unregistered youth unemployment and outreach careers work ... Non-registration'. *Research Paper No. 31.* London, Department of Employment.

Roberts, K., Dench, S. and Richardson, D. (1987). 'The changing structure of youth labour markets', *Research Paper No. 59.* London, Department of Employment.

Robertson Elliot, F. (1986). *The Family: Change or Continuity.* London, Macmillan.

Roll, J. (1988). *Young People at the Crossroads: Education, Jobs, Social Security and Training.* London, Family Policy Studies Centre.

Romaine, S. (1984). *The Language of Children and Adolescents.* Oxford, Basil Blackwell.

Rosser, C. and Harris, C. (1965). *The Family and Social Change.* London, Routledge & Kegan Paul.

Sarsby, J. (1983). *Romantic Love and Society: It's Place in the Modern World.* Harmondsworth, Penguin.

Sennett, R. and Cobb, J. (1977). *The Hidden Injuries of Class.* Cambridge, Cambridge University Press.

Sewel, J. (1975). *Colliery Closure and Social Change.* Cardiff, University of Wales Press.

Sillitoe, K. and Meltzer, H. (1986). *The West Indian School-Leaver.* 2 vols. London, HMSO.

Simmel, G. (1978). *The Philosophy of Money.* London, Routledge & Kegan Paul.

Smart, C. (1984). *The Ties that Bind.* London, Routledge & Kegan Paul.

Solomos, J. (1985). 'Problems, but whose problems? The social construction of black youth unemployment and state policies', *Journal of Social Policy* 14: 527–54.

Stack, C. B. (1974). *All Our Kin.* New York, Harper & Row.

Stewart, A. and Blackburn, R. M. (1975). 'The stability of structural inequality', *Sociological Review* 23: 481–508.

Stone, L. (1977). *The Family, Sex and Marriage in England, 1500–1800.* London, Weidenfeld & Nicolson.

Study Commission on the Family (1982). *Values and the Changing Family.* London, Study Commission on the Family.

Thorogood, N. (1987). 'Race, class and gender: the politics of housework', in J. Brannen and G. Wilson (eds.), *Give and Take in Families.* London, Allen & Unwin.

Townsend, P. (1979). *Poverty in the United Kingdom.* Harmondsworth, Pelican.

Townsend, P. and Davidson, N. (1982). *Inequalities in Health: The Black Report.* Harmondsworth, Pelican.

Wall, R. (1987). 'Leaving home and living alone: an historical perspective', *Discussion Paper No. 211.* London, Centre for Economic Policy Research.

Wallace, C. (1986). 'From girls and boys to women and men', in S. Walker and L. Barton (eds.), *Youth Unemployment and Schooling.* Milton Keynes, Open University Press.

(1987). *For Richer, For Poorer: Growing up in and out of Work,* London, Tavistock.

Walsgrove, D. (1987). 'Policing yourself: social closure and the internalisation of stigma', in G. Lee and R. Loveridge (eds.), *The Manufacture of Disadvantage.* Milton Keynes, Open University Press.

Watson, I. (1985). *Double Depression: Schooling, Unemployment and Family Life in the Eighties.* Sydney, Allen & Unwin.

Wells, W. (1983). 'The relative pay and employment of young people', *Research Paper No. 42*. London, Department of Employment.

Whitehead, M. (1987). *The Health Divide: Inequalities in Health in the 1980s*. London, Health Education Authority.

Willis, P. (1977). *Learning to Labour*. Farnborough, Saxon House.

— (1984a). 'Youth unemployment: thinking the unthinkable', *Youth and Policy* 2 (4): 17–24, 33–6.

— (1984b). 'Youth unemployment – 1. A New Social State', *New Society* 67 (1114): 475–77.

— (1984c). 'Youth unemployment – 2. Ways of Living', *New Society* 68 (1115): 13–15.

— (1984d). 'The Land of Juventus', *New Society* 68 (1116): 57–9.

Willmott, P. and Young. M. (1960). *Family and Class in a London Suburb*. London, Routledge & Kegan Paul.

Wilson, G. (1987). 'Money: patterns of responsibility and irresponsibility in marriage', in J. Brannen and G. Wilson (eds.), *Give and Take in Families*. London, Allen & Unwin.

Windsor, P. (1984). *Out of Sight: A Study of Young Women's Lives on a Swansea Estate*. Swansea, Youth Enterprise Swansea.

Young, M. and Willmott, P. (1957). *Family and Kinship in East London*. London, Routledge & Kegan Paul.

Youth Review Team (1985). *The Social Conditions of Young People in Wolverhampton in 1984*. Wolverhampton, Wolverhamptom Borough Council.

Zaretsky, E. (1976). *Capitalism, the Family and Personal Life*. London, Pluto.

Zerubavel, E. (1981). *Hidden Rhythms*. Chicago, University of Chicago Press.

INDEX